STOP
PLAYING
SAFE

D0664420

STOP PLAYING SAFE

Rethink Risk.
Unlock the Power of Courage.
Achieve Outstanding Success.

MARGIE WARRELL

WILEY
John Wiley & Sons, Australia, Ltd

First published in 2013 by John Wiley & Sons Australia, Ltd

42 McDougall St, Milton Qld 4064

Office also in Melbourne

Typeset in 12/13.5 pt Bembo Std

© Margie Warrell Global Pty Ltd

The moral rights of the author have been asserted

National Library of Australia Cataloguing-in-Publication data:

Author:	Margie Warrell
Title:	Stop Playing Safe: Rethink risk. Unlock the power of courage. Achieve outstanding success/ Margie Warrell.
ISBN:	9781118505588 (pbk.)
Notes:	Includes index.
Subjects:	Self-actualization (Psychology).
	Risk.
	Self-confidence.
	Success.
Dewey Number:	158.1

All rights reserved. Except as permitted under the *Australian Copyright Act 1968* (for example, a fair dealing for the purposes of study, research, criticism or review), no part of this book may be reproduced, stored in a retrieval system, communicated or transmitted in any form or by any means without prior written permission. All inquiries should be made to the publisher at the address above.

Cover design by Michael Freeland

Cover image © Getty Images/Jupiter Images/Hemera Technologies

Printed in the USA

10 9 8 7 6 5 4 3 2

Disclaimer
The material in this publication is of the nature of general comment only, and does not represent professional advice. It is not intended to provide specific guidance for particular circumstances and it should not be relied on as the basis for any decision to take action or not take action on any matter which it covers. Readers should obtain professional advice where appropriate, before making any such decision. To the maximum extent permitted by law, the author and publisher disclaim all responsibility and liability to any person, arising directly or indirectly from any person taking or not taking action based on the information in this publication.

Contents

About the Author

A *Forbes* columnist, best-selling author and media commentator, Margie Warrell is an internationally recognised thought leader in human potential who is passionate about challenging people to live and lead with greater courage.

Drawing from her background in business, psychology and coaching, along with her diverse personal experiences, Margie supports individuals and organisations globally to expand their vision, engage in bigger conversations and make a more meaningful contribution. Her clients include Hitachi, Accenture, United Healthcare, NASA, Bechtel, British Telecom, ExxonMobil, Best Buy, and Wells Fargo Bank. She has also been a regular guest lecturer at the Georgetown University in Washington DC and Southern Methodist University in Texas.

The best-selling author of *Find Your Courage: 12 Acts for Becoming Fearless in Work and Life*, Margie is a sought-after media commentator who regularly contributes her expertise on leading media outlets including The Today Show, FOX News, CNN and CNBC. Her advice has been featured in *The New York Times, The Week, Washington Post, Sunday Telegraph* and *Cosmopolitan* magazine. Margie has also contributed to two other books with renowned experts Stephen Covey, Ken Blanchard, John Gray and Jack Canfield.

Margie is the founder of Global Courage, an organisation focused on empowering women to become more powerful catalysts for change and leaders within their organisations, community and society.

As a mother of four busy (and noisy) children and an intrepid traveller who grew up on a dairy farm in rural Victoria, Margie walks her talk when it comes to living boldly and challenging what's possible. In 2012 Margie returned to Australia after a decade based in the United States so her children could spend more time on 'Grandpa's farm'. A popular keynote speaker, she travels widely with her work and still enjoys returning to the US regularly where she is getting to know the immigration officials at LA airport on a first-name basis.

Acknowledgements

I've often heard it said that writing a book is a bit like having a baby. While the writing process is a solitary pursuit, it takes a team of people to deliver a book safely into the world. I've been blessed to have worked with some of the finest over the process of researching, writing, editing and publishing the book you now hold in your hands.

Firstly, thank you to all the team at Wiley. Lucy, Elizabeth, Alice, Keira, Gretta, Katie and everyone involved in the many steps along the way. Thank you for working with me as the shape of this book has evolved and my writing has progressed. In particular, thank you to my editor, Sandra Balonyi. You have been an absolute pleasure to work with. I'm so delighted that your enthusiasm for what you were editing inspired your husband to ask for a pay rise!

Thank you also to the league of courageous leaders and entrepreneurial trailblazers who generously gave of their time to share with me their insights on the importance of acting with courage in business and beyond. The opportunity to spend time with so many incredibly smart, brave and thoughtful people was a gift all of its own. While passages in this book share your experiences, your wisdom threads through every page. My thanks also to Nanette and Winston Moulton for all you've done to help me get on my way since arriving in Australia.

Of course, with four children I could never have written this book without the support on the home front (or at least not in the same time frame.) So the person who deserves the greatest debt of gratitude is my incredibly supportive husband, Andrew. Thank you for always providing a listening ear and an encouraging word, for reading over draft chapters at the end of your long work day, and for your constructive yet candid feedback. As we near 20 years of marriage, I feel more blessed than ever to be sharing my days and life with you.

I'd also like to acknowledge my children—Lachlan, Maddy, Ben and Matthew. As the deadline for completing my manuscript drew near, you rallied behind me as I closed my office door and sent you out of earshot when your sibling antics grew too loud (which was often). As I've written in this book, there is nothing more rewarding than working hard at work worth doing. It's my prayer that you will gain the same fulfilment in your work one day as I gain from mine and that you will pursue it with the courage I know you each possess.

I must also include a note of appreciation to Margie Edmonds—my very own Alice from the Brady Bunch! Thank you for the cups of tea that magically appeared on my desk as my energy waned near day's end. You truly dropped straight from heaven into our home on our arrival back in Australia. As my dad likes to say, 'Your blood's worth bottling'.

Finally, heartfelt thanks to my dear family and friends—near and far, new and old—who I can count on for good company, wonderful humour and encouragement when it's needed. There are more names to list than space allows but you know who you are and I hope you know how highly I value your friendship over the many miles and years. Mum and Dad, you top that list—thank you for always telling me how proud you are of me. I'm so proud of you too.

With gratitude to all with whom I have shared my journey so far.

Margie

Introduction

Imagine yourself 20 years from now, looking back on the intervening time. What would you love to have accomplished in your career and life? What impact would you like to have made? What kind of person would you like to have become by making it?

Twenty years from now there will be people no smarter or more capable than you who will have accomplished extraordinary things across all spheres of life. While it's impossible to know who they will be, what is certain is that they will all have made courageous choices, taken bold actions and refused to succumb to the fear that drives so many to think small and play safe.

Life is the lump sum of our choices. Too often though, our choices are driven by fear, self-doubt and insecurity rather than a clear sense of purpose, confidence and courage. Fear drives us to avoid risk, play safe and settle for the status quo, however unrewarding or miserable it is.

Sombre economic forecasts, corporate cutbacks, natural disasters, fundamentalist extremism, international conflict — look at what's making news today and chances are at least one headline is fuelling fear and feeding insecurity. While this may not have you racing to stock up your pantry on canned tomatoes and bottled water, there's no escaping that we live in a culture that breeds fear and drives us to play safe, avoid change and settle for less than we want.

Research shows that our brains are wired to overestimate risk, exaggerate its consequences and underestimate our ability to handle it. Confronted with ongoing economic instability and mounting global competition, fear in the workplace has grown so pervasive that playing safe and avoiding risk has become the norm. Yet history has shown that when fear runs most rampant, courageous action reaps the greatest rewards. And nowhere is courage more needed right now than in the work we do, and the way we do it.

I wrote my first book, *Find Your Courage*, to help people overcome the doubts and fears that were undermining their relationships and wellbeing, and confining them to their lives of quiet desperation, immaculate mediocrity or both. Meanwhile, the world has suffered its worst economic collapse since the Great Depression, and the fear that stifled people's personal lives has infiltrated into the corners of organisations globally. We live in a complex, competitive and fast-changing world. The actions that got you to where you are today will not be sufficient to take you to where you want to be 10 years from now. As the world has changed, so you too must change how you engage in it.

I have written this book because I have a passionate belief in the potential of human beings to create lives rich in meaning and contribution. In my work within organisations around the world, I constantly encounter people trapped inside prisons of their own making, failing to utilise their potential—people whose experience of going to work every day is marred with anxiety, resentment and resignation. Perhaps you relate.

What you do matters. How you do it matters even more. Sadly, global surveys on employee engagement tell us that many people don't believe so. The cost to the bottom line runs into the billions. The cost to the human spirit is immeasurable. Underlying this disengagement is the fundamental fear of failing, of looking foolish, of not having enough and not being enough.

The fact is you have all the resources available to you for creating a life *and* a career that fulfil you so that your work not only enables you to make a good living, but also to enjoy a more rewarding everyday experience of life (rather than just weekends and holidays). Research has confirmed what my experience has shown me: when people connect to a deeper purpose in their work they're not only more engaged and effective in their work, but also more inclined to take the risks essential for success.

There are countless business books filled with strategies for becoming a more proficient networker, strategist, salesperson, negotiator, 'hi-po' employee, manager and leader. There are very few that get to the heart of what holds people back from applying them. The reality is that it's not a lack of knowledge that prevents most people from doing more and being more—it's a lack of clarity about what they truly want, and the courage to go and get it.

While this book is written for the individual, the principles, concepts and strategies it contains can benefit any team, group or organisation. After all, while organisations are living entities in their own right, they comprise individuals. An organisation cannot become more competitive, focused or innovative unless the people who work in it are. Indeed, the greatest competitive advantage available to any organisation is its people. But it's not just their experience, expertise or skills that can give the competitive edge. It's their commitment to the organisation's mission, how openly and effectively they communicate with each other, customers and suppliers, and most of all, their willingness to 'push the envelope' of possibility. All of this entails a degree of risk and demands a measure of courage. If everyone in your organisation practised the principles in this book, it would propel your organisation forward in every way—from customer service to product innovation, from sales to project execution—building bottom-line outcomes as never before.

This book comprises eight chapters, the first seven of which form *The Courage Key* model, which you can view in the appendix. The chapters of *Part I: Core Courage,* form the core foundation of *The Courage Key. Part II: Working Courage* provides you with concepts and practical strategies to be both more courageous and effective in handling the many challenges and seizing the opportunities in your work and life. The theme of each chapter in Part II—Confront, Adapt, Leverage and Lead—create the CALL acronym and are your 'call to action' to stop playing safe. *Part III: Take Courage* is where the rubber hits the road as you step out of your comfort zone and into action in making the changes and taking the chances needed to experience the success and fulfilment that prompted you to pick up this book in the first place. Part III is focused on helping you set yourself up for success over the longer term, creating an environment that supports you in *getting* and *staying* in purposeful and courageous action, no matter what.

Interspersed through all eight chapters are case studies of numerous people—from CEOs of global organisations to trail blazing entrepreneurs—whom I've interviewed while writing this book for their insights and experiences of acting with courage. Finally, I have also included Courage Keys and Courage Challenges to help you apply the concepts I discuss to the challenges and opportunities you face today. I encourage you to invest the time to do the challenges as you go along. Together, the following eight chapters will help you to rethink risk and unlock the power of courage in your life so that you can soar above the fears and beliefs that have kept you from achieving the level of success you want.

While I hope this book will equip you with practical tools for engaging in courageous conversations and taking brave actions that will elevate the trajectory of your career, my greater hope is that it will elevate the trajectory of your life. By unlocking the power of courage in your life, you'll tap into the unbridled potential within you and enjoy the genuine satisfaction that flows from working hard at work worth doing.

I hope you'll return to this book again and again as you navigate your way through the maze of choices, changes and challenges that are certain to unfold before you in the years ahead. May it become a trusted guide for unlocking your courage in a fearful and fast-changing world and for finding the clarity to make smart decision, not just safe ones. I hope also that you'll be able to seize opportunity in your adversity so you can add the full quota of your contribution and enjoy the full quota of rewards and satisfaction you'll earn by doing so.

Icons explained

Courage Key

When you see this box throughout the book, it will highlight a strategy or idea you can use in your daily life to be more effective in what you do, improving your ability to communicate with more confidence, to add more value and to become more valued by others. Each Courage Key will help you to unlock courage, clarity and confidence.

Courage Challenge

Growing self-awareness is crucial to your success in every arena of life. When you see this box throughout the book regard it as an invitation to build your awareness of where your actions may be getting in the way of your success. If you don't have time to do each Courage Challenge right away, make a point to come back to it later as each of these challenges is designed to help you elevate your thinking and respond more constructively and courageously to the people, problems and opportunities in your work and life.

Part I
Core Courage

Build your foundation

*It is when we all play safe that we create
a world of utmost insecurity*
Dag Hammarskjöld

Chapter 1

Know your *why*

*There is no passion to be found playing small— in settling for a
life that is less than the one you are capable of living.*
Nelson Mandela

You may have picked up this book because you're looking for
some quick-fix ideas for reigniting your career, negotiating a
better salary, dealing with a difficult co-worker or simply gaining
more recognition for your work. I trust it will help you with all
of that. But to accomplish all you are capable of, there is nothing
more important than answering the perennial burning question,
'For the sake of what?'

That is, why should you bother to work hard and take on
new challenges that stretch you and put your safety, security and
even your reputation at risk? To answer this question you need
to reflect not just on *what* you want to do in your working life,
but *who* you want to become through the work you do each day.
In an accelerated age of superficiality and distraction, at a time
when so many people are struggling with an uncertain future and
unexpected challenges, finding purpose in work has become the
new 'mission critical'.

Psychiatrist Victor Frankl, who was the only member of his
family to survive the Nazi concentration camps, devoted his
life to understanding the power of purpose. Frankl bore witness
not only to the murder of his extended family, but to the death
of thousands of men who were unable to survive the barbaric
conditions in which they found themselves. However, he also saw
men whose resolve to live enabled them to fight off despair, defy

death and survive long enough to bear witness to the brutality and deprivation forced upon them. His experiences in World War II and thereafter led him to believe that the power of the human spirit can only be fully unleashed when our purpose for living transcends merely surviving.

If you've ever faced a significant crisis in your life you'll have experienced the power of purpose to tap reserves of energy, strength and courage you didn't know you had. Your mission was clear. Your goal was compelling. Your focus was laser. Your potential was tapped.

The power of a focused purpose is similar to the energy of light focused through a magnifying glass. Diffused light has little use, but when its energy is concentrated—as through a magnifying glass—that same light can set fire to paper. Focus its energy even more, as with a laser beam, and it has the power to cut through steel. A clear sense of purpose enables you to focus your efforts away from distracted busyness to what matters most. Nowhere is this more important than in your work and how you employ your skills, talents and time throughout your life.

The search for meaning

You have everything it takes to achieve whole new levels of success in your work and to make a meaningful impact on the lives of everyone it affects, directly and indirectly. But doing so will require your commitment to refuse to give in to the forces of mediocrity that pull so many people into the ranks of disengagement and resignation. It's also conditional on you making a pledge to stop playing safe in what you think, do and say, knowing every worthwhile endeavour demands an element of risk. And finally, it's conditional on you making a stand for greatness, engaging in your work with the bold belief that what you do with your talents and skills over the course of your working life matters, and that how you do it matters even more.

Ever more people today have the means to live
but not the meaning to live for.
Albert Einstein

The search for meaning has been one of the most enduring and compelling themes of humanity since our origins. Where animals are driven by a purpose to simply survive, we want more from life than mere survival. Without an answer to the question, 'Survival for the sake of what?' we can quickly fall into disengagement, disillusionment, distraction and a quiet sense of despair.

Study after study done by organisations around the globe tells us that up to 50 per cent of the workforce don't believe that what they do matters. In fact, it's estimated that only 30 per cent of workers are actually engaged in their job and 50 per cent would leave it if they could afford to. That adds up to millions of people who spend one-third of their adult lives going through the motions of their job without any belief that what they do matters much beyond the fact that they get paid for it. Perhaps you're one of them.

What you do with your time and talents each day matters. How you do it matters even more.

It's not just a lack of meaning in our work, and the rise and rise of employee disengagement that are at issue here. Many people also live with a nagging doubt about the lack of meaning in their lives, reflected in the increased rates of drug and alcohol abuse, depression and suicide, and the increasing reliance on the use of antidepressant medications. The statistics are alarming and point to a crisis of meaning on an unprecedented extraordinary scale. Studies have found that once we earn enough to have our basic needs fulfilled (estimated at about $70 000 per annum), extra money adds only incrementally to our happiness. It's an epic tragedy that so many people spend so much of their lives disengaged, disillusioned and desperate to be doing something other than what they are doing. The stakes could not be higher.

There's a marked difference between being well off and wellbeing. Given we're wealthier today than at any time in history, it seems the answer to a more rewarding life cannot be found by chasing more money, but by finding greater meaning. In an accelerated age of shallow superficiality and distraction, people crave purpose and a meaningful reason for being. I'm not being glib; I just want to be straight with you. You're smart, so you understand that your best thinking got you where you are today. Reading this book and wondering what it may offer you that you haven't already thought of shows that you also appreciate that if you want to get to the next level of success, you have to think differently about *what* you do, *how* you do it and *why* you do it.

Finding meaning and discovering a deeper purpose to life takes deep reflection and serious soul searching—something many people have become very good at avoiding. As John Gardener, President of Carnegie Corporation, wrote in *Self-Renewal: The Individual and the Innovative Society*, 'Human beings have always employed an enormous variety of clever devices for running away from themselves. We can keep ourselves so busy, fill our lives with so many diversions, stuff our heads with so much knowledge, involve ourselves with so many people and cover so much ground that we never have the time to probe the fearful and wonderful world within'. Probing the 'fearful and wonderful world within' is what's required to step out from behind a curtain of comfort and onto centre stage in your own life.

Know your *why* and you can figure any *how*

Having done a lot of international travel over the years, I've passed through customs lines more times than I can count. Like me, you've probably experienced customs officers bombarding you with a blast of questions just when you're weary and in dire need of a strong shot of caffeine.

'So, what brings you here today?'

'What do you do?'

'Where are you planning to travel while you are here?

'Why?'

I always try to answer these questions as quickly and simply as possible so I can get on my way. However, I think everyone can benefit from asking themselves these same questions through the wider context of our lives. Let me reframe them for you in that bigger context:

'So, what brings you here today (to reading this book)?'

'What matters most to you in your work and life?'

'Where would you like to go in the future?'

'Why?'

Why indeed.

Of course, I didn't write this book to convince you to change career, quit your job or start your own business (though perhaps you will). Rather, I wrote it to help you re-evaluate the unique value you have to add to the world and to rethink how you've approached risk so that you can enjoy more success in your work and add more depth to your life. A quick web search will yield many dozens of methods, tips and techniques for discovering your life purpose — some supposedly in as little as 20 minutes (I kid you not). Ahhh — if only life's biggest question could be answered on Wikipedia! While it's unlikely that you'll find a quick-fix way to discover your life purpose, the abundance of search results reflects the struggle so many people have with finding a deeper purpose to their lives, and even more so in their work.

German philosopher Frederick Nietzsche once said, 'He who has a why can endure any how'. Knowing your *why* is the first step towards figuring out your *how*: how you will achieve the success you want. Without a clear *why*, it's hard to figure out your *how*, and harder still to persevere with it when the going gets tough. In John F. Kennedy's words: 'Effort and courage are not enough without purpose and direction'. You must start with a clear sense of purpose and direction.

Too often it's easy to think that if you could just have the success you want, you could be the happy and courageous person you aspire to be. You can mistakenly assume that only then you could afford the luxury of asking yourself the deeper question of life: 'Why does what I do matter?' But it actually works in reverse. As illustrated in figure 1.1, only when you know *why* what you do matters can you be the courageous person *who* you need to be to work out *how* to reach your goals, and *have* the success you want in life.

Figure 1.1: begin with *why*

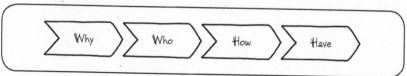

If you were to meet a stranger later today and they asked you why you did the work you do, what would you tell them? Often the first answer is a fairly obvious and superficial one: you need the money. But if they kept asking you, 'why?' eventually they would drill down to the deeper values, motivations and aspirations in your life. In the end the underlying *why* that drives you has a profound impact on your experience in life and your ability to create the success and make the difference you truly want. For this reason, it's important to begin with *why*.

Your *why* will compel you to take on bigger challenges that stretch you; to engage with people around you more meaningfully; and to make an optimal impact on the lives of those you work with, those you serve and the world at large. Yes, I know this sounds very largesse... perhaps a bit pie in the sky. But bear with me here. Put any doubts or cynicism to the side for a moment and give your heart and mind the opportunity to explore the possibility that there are things you—and only you—can do on this earth, and that if you don't do them, no-one else will (or at least not in the same way you would). It's your fears, doubts and cynicism that have confined your actions until now and that, if left in the driver's seat of your life, will steer you towards safety and away from the courageous actions needed to create the changes, opportunities and success you aspire to.

Human beings have extraordinary potential yet, as psychologist William James once wrote, most of us live in a 'very restricted circle of our potential being'. Research in neurophysiology of the brain is beginning to show us just how much. Using conservative estimates, researchers have projected that the human brain has approximately 100 trillion neuron junctions. This means that our possible mental states exceed the total number of atoms in the universe. When you have a big enough *why* to reframe the work you do each day from what you can *get* to what you can *give*, you can tap internal resources like never before. Then—and only then—will you be able to step out of your comfort zone more bravely, engage in bigger conversations and become the full quota of the person you have it within you to be.

Defining what matters most: job, career or calling?

From the events of 11 September 2001 to the more recent global financial crisis (GFC), many people around the globe have found their lives turned upside down in recent years. For the majority, it's been in ways they could never have predicted, much less planned for. The sources of security, safety and comfort that shaped their reality have disappeared without warning or precedent. Yet it's when the world you know falls apart and you're compelled to piece it back together in a whole new way, that you can discover greater meaning in your life and purpose in your work. While you may not be facing a major crisis right now, if you're sitting at a crossroads, then let this be the catalyst for stepping back from the busyness of your work and life and re-evaluating what matters most to you.

So — what does matter most to you?

The answer to that question obviously depends on your current situation and may well change over the years as your values evolve, your responsibilities change, your career develops and your life experiences broaden your perspective.

If you've lost your job and are struggling to make mortgage repayments, what probably matters most to you is money, or any job you can find to earn it. If you're currently working your tail off in a new job to gain your boss's recognition, then your efforts will be motivated by your need to be recognised for the value you bring and the potential you have to add even more value in the future. When you get that recognition, your need will be fulfilled — at least temporarily. This is why, more and more, people want to feel that what they do is more than 'just a job'. While people often struggle to balance the need to make a difference with the need to make an income, the desire to do something that brings meaning to life — not just income — has grown increasingly more important.

In Abraham Maslow's hierarchy of needs pyramid, as explored in his book *Motivation and Personality*, all of our basic needs — 'food, firewood, safety and money' — are called 'deficiency based needs'. Until these basic needs are met, we can't focus on meeting higher level needs.

In figure 1.2 I have translated Maslow's hierarchy of needs pyramid into the three levels at which you can operate in your working life.

Figure 1.2: from survival to significance

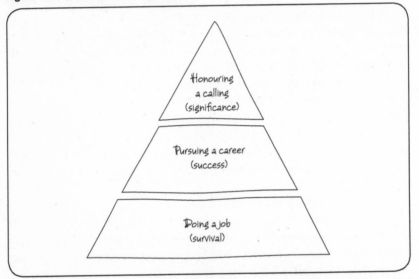

Source: Adapted from Abraham Maslow's hierarchy of needs pyramid in *Motivation and Personality*.

Where you see yourself on this pyramid profoundly impacts your experience of work, as found by Harvard psychologist Amy Wrzesniewski. She spent years researching how the mental conceptions we have of our jobs affect performance. After hundreds of interviews with workers across diverse professions she found that employees have one of three 'work orientations' or mindsets: viewing their work as a job, a career or a calling.

Doing a job

People who view their work as a 'job' see it as an unavoidable chore and their wages as the reward. The focus here is on financial security: a job puts food on the table and a roof over your head and the funds to enjoy your life outside work. By its very nature, a job neither invites risk-taking nor rewards it. While it may use skills that you've developed and call on unique talents, it may not align with any personal ambitions or long-held aspirations. Accordingly, when people see their work as 'just as job' they tend to be reluctant to put in any more effort than is required to stay employed and in good standing.

Pursuing a career

People who view their work as a career are motivated to do well not just for the money, but to enjoy a sense of accomplishment and the fruits of success. A 'career' usually reflects personal interests and ambitions while drawing on skills and talents and so has a longer term focus than a job. It tends to reward risk-taking behaviour, particularly in today's environment. Accordingly, people generally invest more of themselves in their career. Viewing work as a career deepens engagement and elevates the performance outcomes relative to a job.

The most notable part of Wrzesniewski's research was that it wasn't the kind of work people were doing that determined whether they saw it as a calling, but rather the mindset they brought to what they were doing. In one study of 24 administrative assistants, one-third viewed their work as a job, one-third as their career and one-third as their calling. Interestingly, it was those who saw their work as a calling who were the most successful.

Honouring a calling

A calling is about pursuing a purpose larger than yourself that extends beyond fulfilling your personal needs for survival and ambitions for success, to fulfilling a need in the world. People who view their work as a 'calling' view work as an end in itself—not something to be avoided if possible, but something that brings a rewarding dimension to the business of life. Honouring a calling enables people to use their talents and skills in ways that bring their lives greater meaning, transforming their day-to-day experience of 'work' and fulfilling a deep and innately human desire to feel they are truly making a difference.

Pursuing a career and honouring your calling are not mutually exclusive. Your career is something that you can transform into your calling simply by shifting your mindset. Some people choose to change career to pursue their calling so that they have a greater sense of alignment with their talents and passions. A calling also differs from a career in that you'll never grow complacent or stall, as many people do once they've achieved their career goals. Your calling is more than achieving goals and fulfilling ambition. It's about honouring your values, talents, passion and skills to live a more rewarding and meaningful life.

If you feel awkward about elevating your job or career to a calling or vocation (or whatever word you like to use), just keep in mind that your calling can be found in whatever brings a sense of meaning to your life. All that matters is that it honours who you are and enables you to unlock the courage to speak more candidly, engage more authentically, adapt more flexibly, persist more tenaciously and influence more powerfully (all of which are the focus of part II of this book).

> *Dare to work each day as though what you do makes a difference. It does.*

Pursuing a calling may seem risky, but in the context of your life, it's actually the safest bet you can make. While you can fail at getting a job promotion, securing partnership, making it to the executive ranks or building the global empire you want, you can never fail at honouring a calling. The irony is that by reframing what you do as a calling rather than a career, you actually improve your chances of achieving greater success because you become more engaged, willing to take risks and driven to access reserves of resilience and resourcefulness that would otherwise have lain dormant.

Work on purpose

Some people have their purpose presented to them very clearly, often through great adversity or a major life crisis. But the other 99 per cent of people whose lives may not have been marked by tragedy, oppression or injustice, have to make it their personal mission to find purpose in their work and meaning in their lives. It's possible you may have a moment of personal epiphany, but more likely your purpose will gradually, over years and life's tests and trials, reveal itself to you.

As illustrated in figure 1.3, your purpose sits at the intersection of your talents, skills/expertise, passions and deepest values. Just as a boat under power can handle any size wave if perpendicular to it, if you have a purpose you believe in, there is little you *can't* do. Clarifying your purpose will not only infuse greater meaning into your work, it will enable you to find the courage to stop playing safe when risks are necessary for jumping the chasm from where you are to the success you want to achieve.

While there's no one pathway for discovering your life purpose, there are many ways you can gain deeper insight into yourself, and a larger perspective on what it is that you have to offer the world. This can make all the difference as you look ahead at the work you want to do over the rest of your working life.

Figure 1.3: finding purpose in work

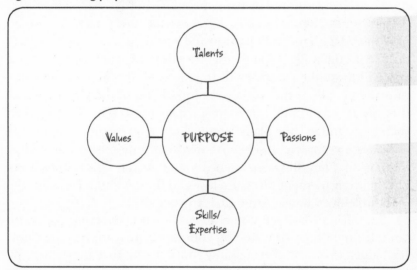

What follows are four questions and two courage challenges to help you find the 'sweet spot' that rests in the intersection between what you care about, what you can contribute and what will be valued most from you:

- *Passion*—What makes you come alive?

- *Talent*—What are your innate strengths?

- *Skills/Expertise*—Where do you add the greatest value?

- *Values*—How will you measure your life?

What makes *you* come alive?

My two youngest sons Matthew and Ben were fortunate enough to have a woman called Emmy Bocek as their kindergarten teacher. When I met Emmy she had been teaching for 30-odd years but she had no shortage of energy and passion for teaching a classroom of busy and noisy little people. Emmy once shared with me that she believed she had the 'best job in the world'. From the enthusiastic and patient way she interacted with her class full of noisy young kids, this was self-evident. Needless to say, Emmy saw her work as far more than 'a job' and I was always grateful for her passion (almost as much as I was that I didn't have a classroom of kids in my charge!).

I have been inspired by many people over the years — from taxi drivers and lobbyists to civil engineers and sheep farmers — who have shared with me their passion and enthusiasm for the work they do. Yet if you walk through the corridors of many organisations you will most likely notice a distinct lack of 'aliveness' on the faces of many people. Some may even remind you of the walking dead: they are there in body but their spirit seems to have long ago left their body. Indeed, the blank, zombie-like expression on their faces indicates a complete absence of anything remotely connected to inspiration. They show up each day and go through the motions, but their engagement levels are low and their willingness to go the extra mile even lower. After all, it's 'just a job'.

So, what makes *you* come alive? I'm not referring to taking your dream holiday or watching your favourite team win the game. It's bigger than that. I'm talking about a *why* that moves up the food chain from being about you to being about something bigger than you. It's about connecting with what you feel passionate about, knowing that when you focus your attention and effort on something that puts a fire in your belly — that draws on your innate talent — you will have an invaluable and unique influence on all those your work impacts.

There's no reason to feel daunted. You don't have to declare at this point that you want to end world hunger, invent the next iPad, solve the world's energy problems or cure cancer. This is about you connecting to a cause that's bigger than you are, but which is also congruent with who you are and ignites something deep within you—something that inspires you. I use the word 'inspire' because to me it resonates with energy, excitement and passion. Of course, you can pick your own word to describe whatever it is that ignites in you a spark of inspiration: that jazzes you, buzzes you, stirs your spirit and awakens a sense of passion. The word 'inspire' comes from the Latin *inspirare*, which means 'to breathe life or spirit into'. So when you think about something that really lights you up, you will feel a sense of 'new life' awakening within you.

Inspired to build local community

An incredibly passionate man who loves people, Kevin Reynolds began his career with a major bank. He worked hard, was good at what he did and soon began moving up his bank's career ladder. His future looked promising. But Kevin wanted more than to be a banking executive: he wanted to be a banker who built and benefited community. Over time he began to realise that he could accomplish this best outside the structure of a large corporation. Kevin had long been inspired by the idea of building a bank that would be an active part of the local community, supporting small business and supporting community-building initiatives. Together with several colleagues he established a small community bank that eventually became Cardinal Bank. Since then Kevin and his team have created an organisation with 27 branches that are a central part of the communities in which they operate.

As it did for Kevin, whatever inspires you will evolve and change as you do. You don't have to be smarter than you already are, or more strategic, or more educated. When you work towards something that inspires you, you're able to simply be more of who you already are. As Laura Berman Fortgang wrote in *Now What?*, 'Your vision has to fuel you. It's your stamp on the world and a stamp only you can make that is unique to you'. Your vision, just like you, is unique and unrepeatable because you are unique and unrepeatable. By pursuing it with purpose and courage, you can make a difference that is equally unique and unrepeatable.

Create your own calling statement

As you think about what inspires you, I encourage you to create your own 'calling statement' that speaks to the difference you would like to make in your working life. A calling statement isn't so much about what you do, but about who you are. It reflects whatever brings you a deeper sense of meaning and purpose. Regardless of how much 'success' you achieve as measured by income, position, or profit it's a powerful way to measure your life. Here are a few calling statements people have shared with me:

- to help clients create smarter strategies for building their dream business

- to improve the world through innovative thinking

- to be someone my organisation can count on to get the job done well, no matter what

- to be a leader who helps people harness the best of themselves and positively impacts all stakeholders

- to help people design and decorate homes that nurture their spirit and express their individuality

- to build a business that will outlive its employees and make a lasting contribution to the communities in which it operates.

What are your innate strengths?

In *The Element*, Sir Ken Robinson writes that our element is the point at which natural talent and skill meets personal passion. People are in their 'element' when they are doing something they are both passionate about and good at. When passion, talent and skill intersect, people are able to add the greatest value, make the biggest difference and enjoy the deepest sense of fulfilment. It's also often where people can be the most successful and maximise their income.

What are the things you've always been good at, sometimes making you wonder why other people find them so hard? Are you a catalyst for change who can take initiative in complex situations? Are you a great listener who is able to take in different perspectives and synthesise a way forward? Are you creative and able to find solutions for issues 'outside the box'? Are you a natural born rebel with an innate ability to identify where the status quo is in need of a makeover? Are you proficient at focusing on detail and ensuring that things are executed with a precision that others find tedious?

Of course, you can also be passionate about things you have no natural talent for, and talented at things for which you hold little passion. I was always good with numbers, but had little interest in pursuing a career that involved maths. I would have enjoyed being gifted with Barbra Streisand's voice because I've always been quite passionate about singing her songs, but a lack of Barbra-like vocal talent (outside the shower) meant that was not to be. Truth be told, doing what I do today makes me come alive more than singing ever could.

In this age of perfectionism, it's all too easy to burden yourself unnecessarily by thinking that you have to be the 'world's best' at a particular field of endeavour: the *best* accountant, the *best* sales rep, the *best* writer. If I thought I had to be the best writer before I set out to write this book you wouldn't be reading it now. I know there are much more gifted writers than me, many of whom actually know where apostrophes go! So don't let your attachment to having to be the 'best' keep you from doing the best you can with your natural talent.

Where do you add the greatest value?

Doing work that you're good at, but which you loathe, is not a pathway to fulfilment. That said, knowing your greatest strengths and where you can add the most value—through the application of your education, skills, knowledge and experience—can help you focus on the opportunities, roles and career paths where you are most likely to succeed and therefore find the greatest sense of accomplishment and contribution.

Know where you add most value

My friend Sue Larkey studied teaching, specialising in children with special needs. More and more Sue found people asking her to help them use better strategies for teaching children with autism. Sue's insight into how children on the autism spectrum best respond enabled her to provide very practical solutions for teachers and parents struggling to help children with autism. Sue began to run workshops and seminars for teachers and carers.

At first Sue wasn't sure which method would work best so she tried different formats. Sue's passion for helping kids with special needs, combined with her expertise in that field, has enabled her to help tens of thousands of people, while simultaneously building a successful business that supports her own family.

Too often we undervalue our strengths, skills and the expertise we naturally acquire over time. If you reframe the concept of adding value through the lens of solving problems, you can ask yourself what you're well placed and equipped to help solve in your workplace, career, organisation or industry. You can also ask yourself what problems you really enjoy solving and what problems you feel passionate about trying to solve.

Aristotle said finding one's purpose is merely a matter of knowing where one's talents and the needs of the world intersect. Finding that intersection should be your utmost priority.

You'll then be more successful at focusing on your natural strengths and those things you're innately good at than trying to bolster or eliminate your weaknesses (although that doesn't mean you shouldn't be mindful of how they may trip you up!).

Think about what the people around you—at work and in your life outside work—often rely on you to help them with. They come to you because they see that you're not only talented but you have the knowledge and skills needed to get things done, solve problems and add value in ways they don't think others can (or at least not as well as you!).

About 15 years ago, while working in corporate consulting, I arrived at a point where I was no longer excited about the direction of my career. A few rather significant life experiences—an armed robbery, a mid-term miscarriage and a series of less-than-inspiring work environments—were catalysts for me to reassess what mattered most to me in life, and the type of work I would find most rewarding.

At about the same time, I increasingly found myself the confidant of friends and acquaintances who were struggling with various aspects of their work and life. I drew a lot of satisfaction from trying to help them—the operative word being 'try' because I had a limited skillset for doing so. So I returned to university to study psychology. Upon finishing my studies four years later, I was introduced by a friend to the new growing field of 'coaching'. I discovered it didn't require any ball-handling skills (phew!), but leveraged something I seemed to be naturally good at: connecting with and empowering people. Along with my business experience and my passion for helping people overcome the (often internal) obstacles to achieving their aspirations, I decided that coaching would suit me well. Running my own business also provided the flexibility to honour my family values as a mother with young children. Back then I had no idea my work would evolve as it has—to speaking, writing and working in the media—but as I have discovered, when you move in a direction that calls to you, often opportunities and possibilities open up that you could never have imagined. As Martin Luther King Jr once said, 'You don't have to see the whole staircase. Just the first step'.

How will you measure your life?

There are many people who milk their talents, expertise and skills for all they're worth but fail to be true to their values. Wealthy executives estranged from their families after years spent focused on building their careers and bolstering their bank accounts have become a cliché. Being true to your values—whether related to your family, health, community, faith or anything else—is vitally important as you plan out the direction in which you want to head in your career and the actions you will need to take to get there. Success takes sacrifice but those sacrifices should not violate the values you hold most dear.

While some people can afford to give up the security of a regular salary to pursue a passion, many simply can't—at least not in the short term. But following the money and following your heart while being true to your values don't have to be mutually exclusive actions. While organisational psychologists call reframing how you see your work as 'job crafting', ultimately it's really about shifting how you view your work, knowing that *all* work holds intrinsic value.

My dad left school at 16 to work on his parents' dairy farm in East Gippsland, south-eastern Victoria. He spent almost his entire life milking cows morning and night to make ends meet and raise his seven children (I was number two—bossy big sister!). As much as my dad enjoyed living on the farm, it was tough getting up before the crack of dawn every day to round up the cows, and tougher still dealing with the many uncertainties and hardships that come with making a living on the land. What inspired my dad were his values to raise his family, be a loving husband and father, an active and generous member of his local community and live out his faith as best he could. It was *how* he did what he did that brought meaning to his life and provided the answer to his *why*. As my dad approaches his eighties, he often shares that his health, children, marriage and life living on the Gippsland lakes where he spent much of his childhood make him feel like the richest man in the world. Needless to say the 'riches' Dad speaks of are not about money—which begs the question: How do you want to measure *your* life? It is the single most important question you can ever ask yourself.

> *The highest reward for a person's toil is not what they get for it,*
> *but who they become by it.*
> **John Ruskin**

Often when we think about linking a sense of purpose to our work, we assume that we have to be engaged in some great and noble endeavour. But in trying to think about how you can make a bigger difference, it's important not to ignore the small daily differences you can make which, over time, add up to big ones. No matter what your job, you can draw meaning from it and find purpose through *how* you do what you do that will one day allow you to measure your life in a positive and peaceful way. The word *charity* means 'love in action', and there's nothing stopping you from starting your own personal unregistered charity by simply doing what you do each day with more love. If you don't like the word love, pick a word that resonates better for you and enables you to engage in what you're doing more meaningfully.

From *What* to *How*: finding meaning through mentoring

Jane was the accounting manager for an international shipping firm. While she didn't have a strong passion for shipping, she found a lot of meaning in her work by mentoring the people who reported to her. Encouraging and developing the talents and skills in those around her enabled Jane to show up at work every day fully engaged and ready to give her best to all of the tasks her job involved. While what Jane does is important, it's how she does it that makes the most meaningful difference for those she works with and those she serves through her role.

What you do matters. How you do it matters even more.

By shifting the frame in which you view your current role, you can profoundly shift your experience of it. Doing so helps you deepen your engagement in the task at hand because you'll be more focused and less distracted, while enjoying yourself more. It also enables you to be the kind of person others — who might feel equally or more disengaged and disillusioned than you — want to work with and gain inspiration from. If you have any doubts you're the kind of person you'd want to work with, then consider that it may not be because of the job you do each day, but the attitude you are bringing to it.

I can't tell you what your purpose should be, but I can tell you that every one of us can find a bigger purpose in the job we have right now. All it takes for you to connect to a bigger *why* in your job is to shift your focus away from *what* it is you do each day to *how* it is you want to do it and *who* you want to become through doing it.

Michelangelo said that the greater danger is not that our goals are too lofty and we fail to achieve them, but that they are too small and we do. Never once have I met a person who regretted thinking too big. However, many times, people have confided to me that if they had their time over, they'd have taken more risks and not spent years treading water in jobs they loathed or that left them lacking fulfilment. They've shared that if they knew then what they do now, they would have settled less and spoken up more, veered off the beaten path more often and trusted themselves more deeply to meet the challenges along the road less travelled. Make the decision that you won't be one of those people.

If you weren't afraid of failure, what would you do?

When my younger sister, Anne was nearing the end of high school, I remember asking her what kind of work she'd like to do. She replied that she thought she'd like to be a nurse, or something like that: 'something that helps people who are sick'.

This was a natural fit for Annie, who had been a mini Florence Nightingale in our family since she was a toddler. So I asked her, 'Why not a doctor?'

'It's really hard to get into medicine. I'm not sure that I could,' she replied, clearly awed by the idea, but lacking confidence in her ability.

'Sure you can,' I replied. 'You will just have to work really hard and there's nothing stopping you doing that.'

And nothing did. Anne became a doctor and by the time she was 29 she was managing a hospital in Darfur with Médecins Sans Frontières, taking care of nearly 30 000 people (with only a temperamental generator for electricity!)

One of the greatest privileges of my work is the opportunity to support and challenge people to expand what they see as possible for themselves. Of all the questions I like to ask people to think about, my all-time favourite is this: 'What would you do if you weren't afraid of failing or looking foolish?'

Fear is the number-one emotion that stops people from being who they were born to be. It keeps them stuck in jobs they despise and relationships that leave them lonely, and trapped in a prison of their own making. In our careers, fear of not having what it takes—of not being 'enough'—keeps us from even stepping out of the starting gates to pursue the career aspirations and honour the callings that inspire us most deeply. Indeed, it's our fear of failing and looking foolish to those we'd like to impress that disconnects us from our purpose and keeps us from living the meaningful (albeit sometimes scarily exciting) life we want. Don't let your fear of not having what it takes keep you from creating a vision that inspires the socks off you, as being a doctor did for my sister Anne.

This begs the question, 'Where is it that you would like to go?' and brings to mind one of my favourite scenes from *Alice's Adventures in Wonderland*:

'Would you tell me, please, which way I ought to go from here?' Alice asked the Cheshire Cat.

'That depends a good deal on where you want to get to,' said the Cat.

'I don't much care where—' said Alice.

'Then it doesn't matter which way you go,' said the Cat.

People who have no sense of where they want to go often end up in places they don't much want to be. Without a vision for what you want to do and who you want to become you may end up at the whim of external forces, living your life by default rather than by design, taking the course of least resistance, and winding up in a place that you would never have consciously chosen.

The same is true for organisations (which are really just collections of people) that don't have a clear sense of purpose and direction for engaging and inspiring those within it. This is true at every level of any organisation. An organisation without a clear and compelling vision for the future—one that provides a sense of purpose and meaning for every person within it—is an organisation that will often end up out of business.

Helen Keller, who was born deaf and blind, once said, 'The only thing worse than being blind is having sight but no vision'. Your vision holds power. It provides a compass to guide you forward. It sets you on a path and helps you make course corrections as you move along. It helps guide your decisions about the opportunities, requests and offers you will say yes to, and, just as importantly, those you will say no to. Just as setting out on an orienteering course without any end point isn't a particularly smart way to use your time efficiently, neither is moving forward in your career without any sense of where you'd like to be, and more importantly, who you'd like to be, five or 25 years from now. That's not to say you mightn't adjust your end point as you move along, but if you don't have one starting out, you run the risk of spending time and effort moving in a direction that will leave you dissatisfied, frustrated and resentful down the road.

It's always difficult to know how big is too big when it comes to crafting a compelling and fearless vision. We can't all be Bill Gates, Richard Branson or Mark Zuckerberg, can we? No. But the reality is that we don't *all* want to be!

Whatever you're thinking, think bigger.
Tony Hsieh

If your vision doesn't cost you something it's merely a daydream. For a vision to hold power it must not only inspire, it must demand a level of effort, sacrifice and boldness to bring it into reality. Lowering your sights and downgrading your vision to one you know you can achieve dilutes its potency.

Does the idea of being half successful inspire you? I hope not. You can't put the full weight of your talent and energy into a vision that doesn't really excite you just because it's 'more realistic'. Take my vision, for instance. I'd love this book to be read by millions. Sure the royalty cheques would be nice, but what I would enjoy infintely more would be the sense of fulfilment I'd get from living out my purpose to empower people globally to work, live and lead more courageously. I don't like failing or looking foolish any more than you do, but I know there are unavoidable risks required for every meaningful endeavour.

So, back to the question: what vision inspires you?

What you focus on is what you attract into your life. Focus on a future that inspires you. Your vision has to honour what matters most to you, reflect what you care about deeply and align with the amazing person you aspire to be in the world—for those you love most, those you work with, those you serve through your work and, most importantly, for yourself. The only way your vision can possibly do that is if you have the courage to put what's 'realistic' to the side and let your imagination off the leash. After all, every great feat begins in the imagination.

Pursuing a bigger purpose in your life will demand fearing regret more than failure. Courage is the price that life exacts for living a life that inspires you.

When Paul Allen and Bill Gates started Microsoft they had big dreams for the software they were developing and the impact it could have. They would often talk about their dream to have a computer on every desk and in every home. It was an audaciously bold dream at the time but they believed it would revolutionise the world and level the playing field for private citizens to have access to machines that had previously only been accessible to people working in large companies. Their ability to get their employees to engage in that vision, to believe in that *why*, was instrumental in growing their company from a small, 30-person operation based in Albuquerque into the multinational behemoth it is today.

Of course, creating a fearless vision for yourself (or your team or organisation) isn't a one-off affair. What you wanted to do when you were 18 and fresh out of high school and what you might want to accomplish at 48 as your kids head out into the world are likely to be two different things. Your values and priorities change over your lifetime in response to the changing social, political and economic landscape. The only important thing about creating a vision is that it should provide you with a clear sense of purpose and direction.

While this book is focused on being courageous in the realm of your working life, a vision should never be limited just to work. Even though you may wear separate hats for the different roles you have, who you are isn't divided up into lots of separate parts. There's not a 'work' you, a 'play' you and a 'family' you. There's just *you*! Your life is one indivisible whole. And given that you spend many hours every week doing what most of us would call work, creating a vision for what you want to do and who you want to be must transcend the boundaries of your office, the title on your business card or whatever you write in your tax form when it asks for your occupation.

If you're passionate about building a business that provides excellence in producing widget x or service y or trading commodity z, then that passion will infuse everything you do. A vision that gives you a sense of purpose in the professional arena of your life will permeate through every other area of your life.

Courageous action can reshape your life, but unless it's guided by a clear sense of purpose it can steer your life in a direction that leaves you wanting for something more. Much more. Simply committing yourself to contemplating the question, 'For the sake of what?' and daring to believe that you can make a truly meaningful impact in the world will set the stage for you to embrace the challenges you're facing today and to rise above those that will come your way in the future.

> *Twenty years from now you will regret far more those things that you did not do than those you did.*
> **Mark Twain**

Successful people do things that others don't. Sometimes they take action others haven't thought to take, but most of the time it's action others aren't willing to take. Too much risk. Too much work. Too little immediate reward. So, whether you're the CEO or a new intern, when you clarify your *why* you'll be able to pave your way forward purposefully to accomplish the goals or aspirations that inspire you and that serve the world in a unique and valuable way.

Decide how you'll measure your next 20 years

Cast your mind back to when you were about 20 and recall what you were doing. If you could transport yourself back to those days right now and whisper in the ear of the younger you what would you like to tell the handsome/gorgeous (take your pick) younger version of yourself? Where would you encourage making a stronger stand for yourself, taking bolder risks or trusting your intuition better? No doubt there are many things you'd like to share with that less-lived you. But alas, you can't. You can't re-live the past, but you can extract lessons from it to transform your future.

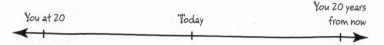

You at 20   Today   You 20 years from now

Now project your mind ahead 20 years from today. What age will you be? (Don't shudder—there was a time you thought your current age was old!). What advice would that wiser person give you? Where would they encourage you to make a change or take a chance in your work and life? What might they advise you to stop doing and what would they urge you to start? Listen carefully.

With that advice foremost in mind, imagine the life you would like to have created for yourself 20 years from now. What work would you be doing? What life would you have created outside work with your family and in your community? How would you be adding value? What kind of people would you be working with? What would they value about you? How would your work reflect your deeper sense of purpose and reflect the calling statement you created for yourself?

You don't have to be specific about the exact job, company or industry (although you can if you want), but be as specific as you can about the nature of the value you will be adding and the type of person you will have become. Make your vision one that really calls to you, that honours the best of who you are and the value you have to give. Most of all, get really clear about the type of person you aspire to be 20 years from now—regardless of what you will or won't have accomplished—so that you can measure the intervening years in a positive and self-affirming way.

Have the courage to follow your heart and intuition.
They somehow already know what you truly want to become.
Everything else is secondary.
Steve Jobs

Right now, you have the opportunity to make a conscious decision about how you'll spend the rest of your life. Don't underestimate the power of that decision to change your life.

Your purpose will continue to evolve and unfold as you move forward in your life, as new opportunities arise and as new possibilities emerge that you're yet to imagine. But unless you're already moving in a direction that calls to you, you'll risk missing those opportunities because your focus will be elsewhere. So, invest some time doing the challenges in this chapter and then take a moment to tune into the quiet voice of your intuition. It's far wiser than you may think.

Key points

> 'Know your why' is about connecting to a bigger purpose that gives your work and life meaning. Given the level of disengagement in today's workforce, finding purpose at work has become 'mission critical'.

> Answering the question, 'For the sake of what?' helps you decide how you will measure your life and focus your time and talents on what truly matters most.

> When you *know your why* you can access potential that otherwise lies dormant, accomplishing far more than you otherwise would.

> Whether you view your work as a job, career or calling impacts your engagement, fulfilment and long-term success. While honouring your calling may lead you along a new path, you can create meaning from any type of work simply by how you approach what you do now.

> Finding purpose lies at the intersection of passion, talent, skills/expertise and values. To discover a purpose that is truly meaningful to you, ask yourself:

>   – What makes me come alive?

>   – What are my innate strengths?

>   – Where do I add the greatest value?

>   – How will I measure my life?

> Fear of failure is the greatest obstacle to taking on challenges that stretch and inspire you. Yet in the big game of life, there is little security in playing safe.

Chapter 2

Rethink risk, commit to courage

We have not journeyed all this way across the centuries, across the oceans, across the mountains, across the prairies, because we are made of sugar candy.
Winston Churchill

Every day you're bombarded with reasons why you should feel afraid. Fear of another dive into economic recession. Fear of job loss. Fear of losing your retirement savings. Fear of personal safety. Fear of radicalism, fundamentalism, government, racialism, terrorism, isolation, mutant viruses, random violence, identity theft, global warming...the list is long.

Marketers prey on your fears. The media preys on your fears. Politicians play on your fears. Fear sells products. Fear sells papers. Fear wins votes. Fear makes profit. Fear grows power.

And fear fuels fear.

In a world that's so filled with fear, refusing to become its pawn—to not playing safe or thinking safe—becomes an ever more courageous act. Nowhere is this more needed than in the workplace. Nowhere will it be more rewarded.

Fear is a primal emotion wired into your psychological DNA to protect you from harm and to alert you to danger. Its sole purpose is to steer you away from situations that could cause harm or pain and endanger your physical, mental or emotional wellbeing. Fear can be traced back to the Neanderthal cave-dwelling days when recognising a potential threat to a person's safety was the difference between life and death. Today the risks you're confronted with on a daily basis are far less about the loss of life or physical injury and more about emotional injury, whether it be social embarrassment or professional humiliation.

Left unchecked, fear keeps people from taking action to generate opportunity, forge relationships, innovate and build a successful career. Fear limits people's careers, relationships and lives far more than any external obstacle ever can. If you're wondering where it might be limiting yours, take a moment to answer these questions.

- Do you get uncomfortable when faced with an uncertain future?

- Do you worry about people realising you're not as clever as they think you are?

- Do you often try to avoid conflict or confrontation?

- Do you doubt whether you have what it takes to really succeed, and sometimes fear that you will be uncovered as a fraud?

- Do you loathe the idea of taking on a goal and failing miserably?

- Do you sometimes 'catastrophise' about worst-case scenarios, particularly when you're contemplating making a change or taking a chance on something new?

No-one relishes the prospect of being rejected or criticised, or having their intelligence questioned. No-one savours giving feedback that others may find upsetting, or having to retrench staff. No-one likes to raise issues that could raise the ire of managers above, much less jeopardise their job. But unless you're willing to take risks such as these right throughout your life you'll never be able to achieve the bigger — and yes, more risk-laden — goals that really light you up and align with your bigger *why*. You have to be willing to risk the familiarity and safety of where you are now to create a more rewarding future.

Lean towards risk

Lean towards risk. This was one of the core lessons *New York Times* columnist David Brooks extracted from the hundreds of essays he received after inviting readers aged over 70 to submit their 'life reports'. He noted that the happiest respondents were those who had taken risks in life rather than avoiding them. *Lean towards risk*: it's a lesson you don't have to wait until you're 70-something to learn.

> *The desire for safety stands against every great and noble enterprise.*
> **Tacitus**

The word 'risk' often conjures up images of people engaged in activities that involve physical risk, such as mountain climbing, race-car driving and free-fall skydiving. Or of corporate mavericks and entrepreneurs—such as Richard Branson—ready to put everything on the line for a high-risk venture. But risk is not only the domain of speed demons, mavericks and trailblazers. Risk is relevant to us all. Every day. Sometimes you have to assess risk in the big decisions in life, but most of the time the risks you're confronted with are more mundane: whether to push back on the consensus thinking in a weekly team meeting, raise your hand to lead an important client presentation or project, or set a boundary with a colleague who has overstepped it. So, if avoiding risk has been your success strategy until now, I encourage you to rethink the nature of risk and how not taking risks may have kept you from achieving more of the success you want.

Courage is not the absence of fear or doubt or misgivings, but action in their presence.

Let me be clear though: being willing to take risks isn't about being reckless or foolhardy. Neither is it about denying or discounting the real risks—political, financial, strategic, operational or otherwise. Rather, it's about being willing to stick your neck out when the situation calls for it and exposing yourself to becoming vulnerable to the things that scare you. As Nelson Mandela once said, 'The brave man is not he who does not feel afraid, but he who conquers that fear'.

This chapter is focused on helping build and bolster your Courage Mindset. The term 'mindset' refers to the overarching approach you bring to your life. It includes your commitment to developing new skills and cultivating a certain type of attitude. The idea that you have a mindset, whether you know it or not, was made popular by Carol Dweck, a professor from Stanford University, whose book *Mindset* explored the concept in depth. Dweck's research led her to believe that it is essential to have a 'growth mindset' if you want to be successful in sports, business and life, and that its opposite, a 'fixed mindset', stifles your ability to adapt, to grow and to learn the skills necessary to get and stay ahead in all arenas of life. But having a growth mindset takes courage because it hinges on your willingness to try new things and be open to learning, unlearning and relearning as you move through life. (We'll explore this further later in the book.)

When it comes to fulfilling your potential at work and throughout your career and life — making the full contribution you're capable of and being valued and rewarded for it accordingly — there are two fundamental mindsets that separate those who experience deep career fulfilment and success from those who don't. The first mindset is based on the premise that risk is to be avoided; the other that risk is to be embraced as a crucial element of success. I call these mindsets the Risk–Averse Mindset and the Risk–Ready Mindset. One is driven by fear; the other by courage.

Don't let fear run your life

At the age of 15, Ita Buttrose left school to pursue her ambition to be a journalist. By the time she was 23 she had asked Sir Frank Packer, then head of Australian Consolidated Press, to appoint her as Women's Editor at the *Daily Telegraph* and *Sunday Telegraph*. Her boldness paid off, as it has many times throughout her trailblazing career.

When it comes to asking for what you want, Ita believes it's vital to put yourself 'out there'. 'You have to let people know you have ambition. You have to flag it with them. They can't guess by looking at you.'

Her willingness to take risks led to her launching the ground-breaking *Cleo* magazine. Highly risqué at the time when its first edition was released in 1972—complete with sealed section—*Cleo* was an immediate hit, selling out its first print run in two days.

'You have to risk your reputation or you will never know what you can do. The world would be a very dull place if no-one rocked the boat.'

Ita went on to become editor of *The Australian Women's Weekly*, Australia's leading magazine, and later made the bold move of launching her own *ITA* magazine. While the magazine eventually folded, Ita has no regrets. 'I don't believe in them,' she told me. 'Life is full of challenges and setbacks. What's important is that you are there participating.'

Ita confided that she has had some agonising moments throughout the years. While she worked hard to make smart decisions, she believes that mistakes aren't to be avoided but to be accepted if you're going to achieve the success you want. 'Every experience shapes you, gives depth, builds resilience and helps you decide which step you are going to take next.'

Many times over the years Ita has refused to play safe or conform to expectations. Working right through her second pregnancy, and never pausing in her career to raise her two children at a time when most women left the workforce to raise their family, is just one example. But Ita has never let concerns of what people think hold her back.

'You can't spend your life worrying about others' opinions, disappointing people, getting approval and making others happy. If you do that you will make yourself miserable. Your life is your business—no-one else's. You have to forge a path that's true for you.'

Of course, veering off the beaten path isn't always the smoothest path, but Ita believes what matters most when the chips are down is to stay focused on the future and never succumb to self-doubt.

'You have just got to pick yourself up and never give up. Never. Some of the best opportunities can emerge out of failure, but you have to be willing to look for them and then be brave enough to take them. What's important is not to dwell on where you are now, but to focus on where you'd like to go from here.'

Of course, not all risks are created equal and not all risk should be leaned towards. This book is focused primarily on the social–emotional risks that get in the way of personal effectiveness, success and fulfilment. If my child needed surgery, I'd want my surgeon to avoid risk wherever possible. Likewise, if you're running a manufacturing operation where people's lives are at stake, it's your moral and ethical obligation to mitigate all risk. Taking risk without doing a thorough risk assessment in any situation is not brave; it's foolish. What I want you to focus on though is emotional risk, because when you've learned how to manage social–emotional risk you'll become far more effective in managing all the other types of risk.

How your brain assesses risk

While your natural temperament and outlook incline you towards or away from risk, there are also complex neurobiological factors at play in how you approach decisions and process the risks involved. As brain imaging technology has advanced, so too has our understanding of how our brain processes information, assesses potential risks and makes decisions. Your brain is wired to avoid risk. Not only does it naturally exaggerate the potential consequences of failure, but it underestimates your ability to handle them.

Your brain is wired to avoid risk and play safe

Research has found that most people are about twice as sensitive to potential losses as to potential gains, which leads to risk aversion. Using Magnetic Resonance Imaging (MRI) technology, a team of psychologists from UCLA presented the first neuroscientific research in the January 2007 issue of *Science*, comparing how our brains evaluate the possibility of gaining versus losing when making risky decisions.

Participants in the study were given $30 and then asked whether they would agree to each of more than 250 gambles in which they had a 50-50 chance of winning an amount of money or losing another amount of money. Would they, for example, agree to a coin toss in which they could win $30 but lose $20?

What the researchers were interested in wasn't the subject's reaction to winning or losing, but the neural activity in different regions of the brain during the decision-making process. By studying which parts of the brain became more active or less active as the amount of money participants could win or lose increased, the researchers could predict how risk-averse people were.

Regions of the brain that become more active as the amount increases are considered 'reward centres'. Those who show much more neural sensitivity to losses relative to gains are the same people who are very reluctant to gamble unless they are offered extremely favourable odds. Conversely, those who are neurologically about as sensitive to losses as gains are the ones who are more willing to take a risk.

The researchers also found that the brain is more sensitive to possible losses than to possible gains, which confirmed previous research showing that most people are more turned off by potential losses than they are turned on by potential gains. This research provides a neurological explanation for why so many people opt to stay in situations they dislike with rather than risk the possibility of finding themselves in a worse situation.

Research shows that many people will avoid taking a risk that involves losing something unless the potential gain is really exceptional. This explains why so many people linger in jobs they really don't enjoy, year after year, for the sense of security it provides, rather than taking the inevitable risks involved in finding a new one. The problem is that too often people aren't really honest with themselves about the price they pay for not taking a risk. They delude themselves into thinking that avoiding risk, and sticking with the status quo—however miserable—is the smartest and safest course of action. In the process, they surrender any possibility of creating a future that's infinitely more rewarding. By talking up the risk of taking action, and discounting or denying the very real price of playing safe, they become complicit in their own misery.

Which hemisphere of the brain you rely on the most also impacts on how you assess risk. The left side of your brain is the logical, 'play it safe' side. Being more focused on probabilities than possibilities, it's the side that's most risk-averse. The right side of your brain is the 'experimental' side. It's more likely to pay attention to your feelings, engage in creative problem solving, think outside the box and consider big-picture possibilities rather than statistical probabilities.

Neither side is superior to the other. We need both sides of our brain, engaging in 'whole brain' thinking when assessing risk and making decisions. People who operate more out of the left side of their brain are more analytical when it comes to measuring and weighing up risks. They need to see the facts or run the numbers. They may well create a spreadsheet with weightings against the various component factors for the options being assessed. Whereas people who operate more from the right-side cerebral hemisphere (where I mostly like to hang out!) are more likely to visualise a possibility and lean on their intuition to help them decide which option is best. Of course, as brilliant a guide as our intuition can be, sometimes we can confuse an intuitive feeling with wishful thinking. Operating only from the right side of the brain can lead to poor, irrational and often rash decisions. We need to do our homework. Run the numbers. Read the contract. Assess possible risks. We just have to be careful not to end up with a severe case of 'paralysis by analysis'—something that's far more likely to afflict someone who doesn't spend much time in the right frontal lobe.

The more we think a certain way, the more habitual we become. So when you're approaching decisions, be careful not to rely on one approach to the detriment of the other. Yes, ask yourself, 'What do the numbers say? What's probable?' but balance it out with 'What feels right? What's possible?'

Courage is a muscle: use it or lose it!

Last year I found myself standing seven metres above the ground on a trapeze platform—in a harness, attached to safety ropes from every direction, with a safety net below me and a muscle-bound bloke standing right behind me—after signing up for a girls' day out at a trapeze school. As I peered down at the net, I became overwhelmed with fear. Of course intellectually I knew I couldn't hurt myself, that I should trust muscle-man holding my harness and that I could do exactly what I'd been instructed to do. Yet emotionally, I found myself paralysed by all-consuming fear.

The experience was a distinct reminder that unless we manage our fears they will manage us. Brain research has found that perceptions go straight to the emotional brain (the amygdala), by-passing the thinking part of the brain (the cortex). Cortisol floods our neural pathways, mobilising us to act: to move away from danger, protect or defend. The amygdala triggers a fear-reflexive fear response before our cortex has the chance to evaluate the situation. As I will discuss further in chapter 6, a 'neural hijack' ensues. Certainly my experience on the high-trapeze platform was a potent reminder of just how powerful and physical the fear reaction can be. This is why one of the most powerful questions you can ever ask yourself is: *What would I do if I didn't fear failure?*

It's possible that what keeps you really pondering this question, much less acting on your answer to it, is also fear. Fear of all the risks involved. Fear of messing up or losing your job. Fear that you don't have what it takes to succeed. Fear that others will think you were foolish for trying. Fear that you will fall short of the mark. Fear of losing face in front of your peers, or losing the respect of those whose opinions you value. Fear that you will leave those you care about behind. Fear that you will be alone. Fear of your ability to handle the as-yet unknown challenges, changes and chances you will have to face...

Fear. Fear. *Fear.*

Embracing risk is key to succeeding in the bigger game of life. Those who lose aren't those who have dared greatly and fallen short of the mark. They are those who played so safe that they never lived at all.

But what if you dared to believe that what you really want is truly possible for you: what then? What if, instead of trying to avoid the emotional pain that could follow failure, you were willing to risk your comfort for the sake of something far bigger and better—for the prize of a life that was richer, fuller and more meaningful than the life you've led up until now? What if, instead of living with a Risk-Averse Fear Mindset, you committed to living with one that embraced risk as essential to success: a Risk-Ready Courage Mindset?

Committing to live your life with a Courage Mindset requires adopting an approach that accepts that all life is risky.

Did you catch that?

All life is risky.

When you can embrace the essential truth that all of your life is risky—from your job, to your relationships, to the sport you play, to the car you drive—you are then free to stop worrying about what 'bad things' you don't want to happen, and to take the risks you need to take to experience more of the 'good things'.

While it's convenient to believe that courage is a personal attribute some people are endowed with at birth, ultimately courage is a mindset that every single person—including those who are naturally timid and cautious—can choose to adopt. And while some people are naturally more comfortable taking risks than others, science has proven that courage is a skill and, like all skills, it can be learned and developed to a level of mastery with consistent effort and commitment. When you choose to develop a Courage Mindset, your psychological courage muscles are strengthened every time you use them. You sharpen and shape your courage skills every time you intentionally choose to step beyond what's comfortable, put yourself at risk and bravely render yourself vulnerable to something you fear.

When you focus on what you don't want to happen, you psychologically enlarge the holes in your safety net, amplifying any trepidation into full-blown terror. As I stood on that trapeze platform looking down, the holes in the safety net beneath me seemed to grow larger by the second until my imagination had me falling right through them.

Somehow I convinced myself to focus instead on taking flight. I remember taking a few very long, deep and deliberate breaths to get the oxygen flowing back into my brain. Then I leaned out from that platform, trusting myself and the muscle-man behind me to keep me safe as I reached out into the open space far above the net to grasp the trapeze bar … and off I flew as I let out one almighty scream. There's a fine line between exhilaration and terror.

Choosing to adopt a Courage Mindset is not a one-off decision. You don't just choose to be courageous and then never have another moment of cowardice or even hesitation. No, becoming more courageous is more about moving in the direction from which courage calls.

Moving from a Fear to a Courage Mindset

Courage is ultimately a mindset. So is fear.

This table lists the 10 core attributes of a Courage Mindset along with the corresponding attitudes of a Fear Mindset, phrased as both words and questions.

Think of a current challenge or opportunity you're facing. As you read through the list below consider how you would approach your situation differently if you were to embrace a Courage Mindset. Write your answers on the margins of the page or in a notepad. These will be good to reflect back on when you create your action plan in chapter 8.

Risk-Averse Fear Mindset	Move towards	Risk-Ready Courage Mindset
1 Resist change	⟶	Embrace change
2 Narrow-minded	⟶	Open-minded
3 Critical	⟶	Curious
4 Pessimistic	⟶	Optimistic
5 Rigid	⟶	Flexible
6 Self-doubt	⟶	Self-confidence
7 What's probable	⟶	What's possible
8 Left brain analysis	⟶	Logic and intuition
9 What people think	⟶	What do you think
10 What you give up	⟶	What you gain

Some days you'll feel like you've just hit the ball out of the park. You've been bold and assertive, spoken up to your boss about the new role you'd like to take on, volunteered to lead the next sales meeting, signed up for a marathon... you're on a (courage) roll, moving in the direction of courage.

Then, on other days you're not. You keep your mouth closed during meetings even though you really don't agree with what's being said. You shy away from rocking the boat. You're operating from fear, moving away from courage. It's what you *do* when you realise you're moving away from courage and towards fear that makes the difference.

> *Courage is a muscle that grows stronger with use. Every time you step out of your comfort zone you build your tolerance for risk, and your confidence to handle more of it.*

Cultivate your Courage Mindset

Often when people don't like the circumstances they find themselves in, they look to their external environment to explain their situation: why their career has plateaued, why their business has failed to grow, why their customers have gone elsewhere, and so on. Instead, they should be looking at the mindset they have brought to the challenges and opportunities they have.

The mindset you bring to your decisions at work every day, and throughout the course of your life, impacts in subtle and profound ways on the results you produce. Cultivating a Courage Mindset is important if you want to rise above the instinctive drive to seek pleasure and avoid the pain that fuels your aversion to fear.

You can see in figure 2.1 that there are four steps for overcoming the fears keeping you from living with a Risk-Ready Courage Mindset.

Figure 2.1: overcoming fear, cultivating courage

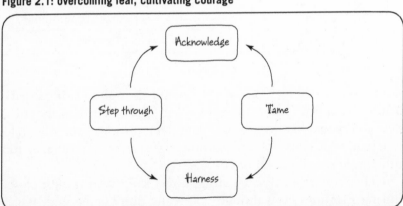

So, let's have a look at each of the four steps for overcoming fear that could be preventing you from cultivating a Risk-Ready Courage Mindset:

- acknowledge what you're afraid of

- tame catastrophism

- harness fear in your favour

- step through it: feel your fear and act anyway!

Acknowledge what you're afraid of

Turn on the TV, read the paper or scan the headlines on your PDA and you won't see statistics on how many people slept comfortably in their beds last night, landed their dream job, travelled safely on a plane or built million-dollar businesses in the past 12 months. You're much more likely to read news and statistics on unemployment, bankruptcies, mortgage defaults and freak accidents.

Good (fear-easing) news doesn't sell. Bad (fear-breeding) news does—which wouldn't be a problem if fear weren't such a domineering emotion that can over-run your live and sabotage your success. Too often your fear of what you can't do and don't want keeps you from doing what you can do and do want...if you let it.

Cultural anthropologist Ernest Becker wrote that people's fears are fashioned out of the ways in which they perceive the world around them. We all know there are valid reasons to feel afraid from time to time. But always keep in mind that what you fear is rarely what you *think* you fear. Rather, it's what you *link to* fear. It's the associations you make in your mind about what 'might' happen that cause you to feel afraid. It reminds me of the popular acronym for fear: *False Evidence Appearing Real.*

Fear serves many constructive and life-giving purposes. It originates in the amygdala, the primitive 'fight or flight' area of the brain. Like all emotions, it has an adaptive role: to protect you from pain and prolong your life. However, left unchecked it can overwhelm rational thought, overlook reality, hijack the brain and be anything but life giving. Rather, it can keep you trapped and settling for circumstances that suck the joy from your life and the life from your years. It drives you to surrender to the status quo—however uninspiring—and sell out on what you really want to become. You become a passive spectator watching life pass you by rather than the central character in the script that is your life.

As you approach a challenge or situation that requires you to take action and that involves some level of risk, it's your fear that lies behind those voices in your head warning you of danger ahead. It's easy to think you're the only person who has a little gremlin inside your head that says, 'What the hell are you thinking, you idiot? You're going to make a total fool of yourself!' or 'You can't do that. I mean, you're not smart/talented/skilled (fill in the blank) enough to do that!'

Of course those voices aren't who you are. But, left unchecked, they have the power to define who you will be for yourself and for those around you. So next time you hear them warning you to play safe, avoid risk and side-step any possibility of ruffling feathers, failing or looking foolish, acknowledge and confront them head on.

Some people call their fears their 'gremlin'. Others call them their 'inner critic'. I've dubbed mine my 'Small Poppy Committee', in reference to Australia's indomitable Tall Poppy Syndrome, the cultural affliction that subtly, yet profoundly, drives so many bright, talented Australians to think smaller and play safer than serves them or anyone else (or to move overseas!). While it has abated somewhat in recent decades, the small-thinking psyche of the Tall Poppy Syndrome still drives too many to tone down their ambitions, or at least not declare them too loudly, lest they be cut back down to earth for being 'up themselves'.

Your Small Poppy Committee represents that legion of doomsayers, nay-sayers and nervous Nellies in your head that is forever urging you to think small, play safe and keep your sights focused on more 'realistic', less lofty goals. Its focus is to keep you out of trouble and as far from the limelight of centre stage as possible. It also cares little about whether your life excites or inspires you. Of course, what name you give to those voices of self-doubt and fear that urge you to think small and play safe doesn't overly matter. All that matters is your ability to identify fear before it takes a grip on you so you can see it for what it is. Naming your fear creates a distance and enables you to be more objective, and helps to separate the voices of fear in your head from who you actually are. Just because your fears say you're going to make a fool of yourself doesn't mean you actually will.

Self-awareness is the first essential step to changing behaviour. If you don't own your fears, they will own you. Take a moment to acknowledge that your fear is trying to keep you safe and spare you the humiliation and emotional bruising that you're putting yourself at risk of experiencing. Doing so will enable you to unlock its grip and move forward.

Know what to fear

Embracing a spirit of adventure, I recently travelled with my husband and four children to Nepal, where I embarked upon my first whitewater rafting adventure. While I was a little apprehensive at first, once we were kitted out in all our safety gear I figured there was nothing to be anxious about.

After the first set of rapids my children at the front of the raft excitedly announced that we had an unpaid traveller in our midst, in the form of a snake. I may have grown up on a farm where snakes weren't uncommon, but I am far from a fan. So discovering there was a snake slithering around the bottom of our raft was not exactly my idea of a fun excursion.

Since I was sitting in the back of the raft, I couldn't see how big it was so my imagination quickly went into overdrive, blowing it up into king cobra–sized dimensions. After manoeuvring myself safely into the middle of the raft, I looked ahead down river to see we were quickly approaching a set of rather intimidating rapids that required my full engagement beside the oars and closer to the snake. I had to make a choice: was this snake a greater threat or the swirling rapids and rocks? The rapids won.

On beaching our raft downriver the guides managed to throw our freeloading passenger (which measured no longer than a ruler and no thicker than my index finger) into the river. As it quickly disappeared downstream it brought home how often we can focus our fear on the wrong things. Of course there is no escaping that there are valid things to be afraid of. But whatever challenges and choices you are facing, be mindful of where you might be magnifying your fears, coming up with all sorts of worst case scenarios that are irrational or unrealistic, and underestimating your ability to handle the consequences of them. As Plato said over two millennia ago, 'Courage is knowing what not to fear'.

Fear is both a potent and indispensable emotion. It can save your life but it can also stifle it. Profoundly. In an increasingly fearful world, we have to become ever more discerning about what fears we pay heed to, and vigilant of where our fear of the wrong things is harming us, rather than protecting us from harm.

In *The Gift of Fear*, personal security expert Gavin De Becker writes, 'Far too many people are walking around in a constant state of vigilance, their intuition misinformed about what really poses danger'. Genuine fear is a signal intended to be very brief. It's a servant of your intuition. But too often fear about what you don't want to happen gets in the way of pursuing and accomplishing what you do.

Not only that, but if you're feeling fearful all the time, there's little or no capacity left for those times when fear is genuinely needed. As De Becker writes, 'Precautions are constructive, whereas remaining in a state of fear is destructive'. Rock climbers will tell you it isn't the mountain that kills, it's the panic.

Like every emotion, fear is contagious. The more often you feel fear, the more pervasive it becomes in your life. Left unbridled it can colour every perception and undermine every experience. Therefore, the more you succumb to your fears—rational or not, perceived or real—the more they set up residence in your psyche and dominate your emotional landscape. From your career and business to your relationships and family life, fear can subtly sabotage you having what you want.

While many of our fears are valid, many of them actually stifle our happiness and success. In an increasingly fearful world, knowing what to fear (and what not to fear) is increasingly important.

Tame catastrophism

When it comes to fear, at times we've all felt a bit like the lion tamer who put an advertisement in the local paper: 'Lion tamer wants tamer lion'. Of course you can never completely 'tame' your fears. Nor would you want to. But you can learn how to manage them rather than have them manage you. Important in taming fear is to notice when you're letting your imagination get the better of you (literally and figuratively). As stated earlier, your brain is wired to overestimate the negative consequences of risk and to underestimate your ability to handle it. That can drive you to conjure up all sorts of catastrophic scenarios in your head just as I did with that little snake. Just as my fear enlarged the holes in the safety net at the trapeze school, sometimes your fear has you picturing yourself living out of a shopping cart on welfare as you contemplate changing jobs. Or perhaps your imagination has you being marched out of the building for daring to speak up and challenge your boss on an issue. Taming fear isn't just about growing your competence at whatever challenge you'd like to take on. It's also about increasing your competence for reeling in the horror movie images that can get your palms sweating and terrorise you into playing it safe.

If you don't own your fear, it will own you

Courtney Banks, Founder and CEO of National Security Associates Worldwide, shared with me that this was how she overcame her phobia of flying: by continually refusing to give in to what she acknowledged as an irrational fear of flying, over time she became more comfortable with it. While she has never become entirely at ease flying around the world as head of an organisation that provides top-level security advice, she has refused to let her fear of flying have the power to limit her success. By reminding herself that she'll be okay she has become more confident in her ability to work through her anxiety as it arises. This has helped her overcome a phobia that confines so many people to life on the ground—as far from airports as possible.

Courtney's courage in this area of her life has emboldened her in her career as one of the few women who have created successful businesses in a very male-dominated industry. As Courtney said to me, 'If you're not willing to take risks you shouldn't be in business. Too many people play safe through complicity, fail to speak up when it matters and take the bold actions needed to get ahead'. By regularly pushing the boundaries of what's comfortable, Courtney has become someone people in her industry know never takes the soft option.

Fear has a wonderful way of hijacking our imagination. Images of the worst possible outcomes often splash across the movie screen inside our heads. The only way to end the movie is to focus on the movie you want it to be; that is, visualising yourself successfully doing whatever it is that's causing your angst, and enjoying the outcome of your courageous actions. If you have a particular image that keeps cropping up whenever you think about doing something bold — whether speaking up to your boss and asking for a pay rise or starting your own business — observe the link between the image and what you fear. Only when you start to 'unlink' those associations — often reinforced by the sensationalised headlines blaring around you — will you loosen the grip your fear has on you and tame it back into submission ... until next time.

> *I am an old man and have known a great many troubles in my life.*
> *Most of them never happened.*
> **Mark Twain**

Harness fear in your favour

I returned home from my day at the trapeze school totally wiped. That's because far from being inert, fear holds tremendous energy. Given the amount of energy that fear holds, it can also be a tremendous force for action when channelled in the right way. So the question is, how can you harness the power of fear to your advantage?

The trick is to overturn what you're afraid may happen if you take action into what you're afraid may happen if you *don't* take action. By doing this, you harness the power of fear to your benefit. The Hebrew word *yirah* means both 'to fear' and 'to see'. *Yirah* teaches that the essential choice of life is to open your eyes to available opportunities, and to fear the consequences of avoiding that reality. So when you become fully present to the often profound cost of not taking action, you harness the energy of fear to motivate you away from unwanted consequences or situations and towards the outcome or goal you do want, as illustrated in figure 2.2.

Figure 2.2: harness the fear of inaction

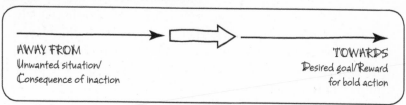

AWAY FROM
Unwanted situation/
Consequence of inaction

TOWARDS
Desired goal/Reward
for bold action

Too often we disregard or downplay the impact that fears can have on the decisions we make. It can keep you from taking the bold actions required to build your career brand, catalyse change when needed and create value that didn't previously exist. When your actions are confined to the limits of your comfort zone, your results will also be limited.

Don't let self-doubt run your life

When she was 24, Leslie Sarasin, CEO of the Food Marketing Institute, quit her secure job working at a seafood company in San Diego to move across the United States to the nation's capital in the hope of pursuing a more exciting and rewarding career.

'There's a fine line between stupidity and bravery,' she said, 'but there are times you have to be willing to walk it if you want to create a rewarding career'. While she knew it was risky, she knew that staying where she was offered little opportunity to make the broader impact that inspired her. She recalled that her father didn't speak to her for months afterwards but she was determined that she wouldn't look back with regret.

Since that courageous career move many years ago, Leslie has continued to take on numerous challenging roles, many of which have been out of her comfort zone, but which have given her a great sense of accomplishment. Today, in her role as CEO of the FMI, which represents about 1500 companies in 50 countries worldwide, Leslie has learned to trust her instincts: 'Sometimes you have to do what's right for you, even if it's not popular or offers no guarantee of success'. While Leslie still has moments of doubt, she believes you shouldn't give your self-doubts the power to make you settle for less from yourself, from others or from a life than you really want.

Making choices requires wrestling with trade-offs: trade-offs between the pros and cons of one course of action (which is often doing nothing) against another. Too often, though, when we compare our list of pros against cons for each option, we make invalid comparisons based on the false assumption that the present situation will remain the same.

There are risks and costs to a program of action. But they are far less than the long-range risks and costs of comfortable inaction.
John F. Kennedy

Professor Philip Bobbit from the University of Texas called this human tendency the 'Parmenides fallacy'. It is named after the Greek philosopher who argued that the world was static and that all change was an illusion. Of course in reality nothing remains static; the present state is an ongoing process of evolution and change. When you try to justify to yourself that not taking an action because it may result in failure is riskier than doing nothing, you need to keep in mind the risks associated with doing nothing. Usually things that aren't working well only get worse. Doing nothing doesn't mean that nothing will change about the present situation, because it will continue to evolve. Or—perhaps more likely—devolve. So, when assessing risk, you have to ask yourself what will happen if you don't take the risk: if you do nothing and continue on with the status quo.

It's a general rule of life that the biggest risk we can take is avoiding risk. Unless you're willing to make yourself vulnerable to losing what you value, you will never gain what you want. When you're unwilling to take risks and experience potential loss of security, status or esteem, you prevent yourself from making greater gains.

In an effort to take the safest path possible, many people end up living a life they would never consciously have chosen. Just look around you at people who have avoided risk all their lives and observe the shape of their lives.

Nothing worthwhile has ever been achieved with a guarantee of success. Nothing ever will be.

Since fear is wired into your DNA, you can't choose whether or not you'll sometimes feel afraid or experience self-doubt. You can, however, choose whether or not you'll allow these fears, and the self-doubts they give rise to, to run your life. Recognise that there is always—I repeat, *always*—a choice. You might not feel the alternative is very palatable. You may think that the cost you have to pay, or the pay-off, just isn't worth it. But never kid yourself that you don't have a choice. That's simply untrue and it's a cop-out.

Decide the kind of person you want to be

Fashion designer Diane von Furstenberg once said, 'I didn't know what I wanted to do, but I knew the person I wanted to be'. It echoes the words of comedian Lily Tomlin, who said, 'I always wanted to be "somebody"; I should have been more specific'.

Who do you need to be in order to stop playing safe and achieve outstanding success in your career? Select two or three adjectives that resonate with you and write them down somewhere you will see them often. When I do this exercise with groups, I get everyone to write down their words on the back of their business card and then, time and group size permitting, to stand up and declare to their table or the entire group who they're committed to being, phrased in the present tense. For instance, 'I am focused, courageous and tenacious' or 'I am resilient, confident and bold'. If they don't say it in a way that oozes with conviction, I ask them to repeat it until they do. It may sound a bit cheesy to you, but this simple exercise has proven to be deceptively powerful, even if it initially feels a bit awkward for some people.

So right now I invite you to choose three words to define the person that you're committed to being—words that reflect your commitment to embracing your career with a Courage Mindset and making a more meaningful impact in what you do at work each day.

(continued)

Decide the kind of person you want to be (cont'd)

You can draw from the list below if any of these words resonate with you, or you can come up with your own words.

courageous	reliable	encouraging	genuine
authentic	forthright	optimistic	unyielding
tenacious	candid	fair	adventurous
resilient	unrelenting	approachable	daring
focused	consistent	accessible	discerning
confident	persistent	thoughtful	passionate
assertive	firm	compassionate	purposeful
bold	resolute	audacious	tolerant
disciplined	determined	self-expressed	involved
organised	open-minded	brave	engaged

Of course, who you are is bigger than any three words can ever encapsulate. Over time you may change them and choose other words that may be better suited to the new challenges you face. However, for now I encourage you to choose only three so that you can commit them firmly to memory and call on them whenever you find yourself wrestling with indecision, doubt or despair. At that moment, ask yourself this question: 'What would I do right now if I were being [insert your word]?'

For example:

- What would I do right now if I were being focused?

- What would I do right now if I were being tenacious?

- What would I do right now if I were being self-assured?

Whatever your answer is to that question will be a solid indicator of the action you need to take to move towards whatever it is that inspires you most.

You can make any change you want. You just have to choose to step up from your fear into courageous action.

Step through fear: feel your fear and act anyway!

Action is the most potent antidote to fear. By doing the things you think you can't do, you realise how much more you *can* do.

The only way out is through.

Courage is far less about heroism on the battlefield or in the midst of a natural disaster and far more about the seemingly ordinary everyday choices you make as you navigate your way through life. It's not the absence of fear (or doubt or misgivings) about your ability to see your endeavour through to a successful completion. It's action in the *presence* of fear. True courage is really about connecting with what you fear and stepping forward bravely despite it, however nervous you may feel. Or, in the words of John Wayne, 'It's being scared to death but saddling up anyway'.

As you can see in figure 2.3, your mindset feeds your actions, which in turn create the results you experience in your life. When you approach your career and the world with a Risk-Averse Mindset, your decisions are guided more by fear and a desire to avoid risk, which in turn limits your actions and deprives you of the opportunities, connections and results that bolder action would produce. But when you approach life with a Risk-Ready Mindset, it breeds confidence and compels you to step outside your comfort zone and embrace the risks you must take to get ahead. In turn, you generate new opportunities and outcomes that set you up for greater success down the track.

Figure 2.3: why mindset matters

You will grow more courageous when you start acting more courageously. Neuroscientists have found that cells that fire together, wire together. The more often you engage in activities that are courageous (and beyond your comfort zone), the more adept you'll become at them. You don't have to start with the most courageous action in the world. You can think big and aim high, but you should start by focusing on the choices right in front of you and the challenges in your day-to-day ordinary life. Don't try to take on some enormous feat from the get-go. If you want to make a big change, start with a series of smaller ones. Had I started on the trapeze at one-and-a-half metres up, and then gradually worked my way up to the full height of the trapeze platform, I would most likely not have been so terrified when I tried my first jump. Likewise, if you want to step into a management role (or any role with greater responsibility), start by putting your hand up for opportunities that will build your skillset and confidence at management tasks.

Behave as the person you aspire to become

Fear is very physical. If you've ever felt truly afraid you know that it wasn't just a feeling in your head; it was in your body, in the tightness of your throat, the sick feeling in your stomach, or sweat on your brow and the palms of your hands. I recall my first interview with the *Today* show at NBC's studios overlooking New York's iconic Rockerfeller Plaza. I was so nervous that my teeth were chattering and my legs trembling as I sat down on the stool beside Kathie Lee Gifford. No-one seemed to notice how nervous I was but I vividly recall pursing my lips together in the seconds prior to the interview going live to avoid looking like an idiot in front of *Today's* few million-odd viewers. Fortunately, as so often happens, when the cameras started rolling, my focus on saying what it was that I wanted to convey to viewers distracted me from my anxiety and off I went. I've had similar experiences many times either doing live TV or speaking to audiences from a stage.

What I've learned, besides the value of long deep breaths, is that the most powerful way to overcome the physical manifestations of fear is to focus attention on the thoughts you want to feel in that moment, and then to move your posture, expression and body into alignment with those thoughts of confidence, courage, self-assurance and capability. Then direct your attention to the impact you want to have on the people around you—what do you want them to know, learn or feel?

The great surrealist artist Salvador Dali was described by his fellow students at the Madrid Art Academy as 'morbidly' shy according to his biographer, Ian Gibson. He had a great fear of blushing and his shame about being ashamed drove him into solitude. It was his uncle who gave him the sage advice to become an actor in his relations with the people around him. He instructed him to pretend he was an extrovert and to act like an extrovert with everyone, including his closest companions. Dali did just that to disguise his mortification. Every day he went through the motions of being an extrovert and, eventually, he became celebrated as the most extrovert, fearless, uninhibited and gregarious personality of his time. He became what he pretended to be. Likewise, when you behave as the person you aspire to become, you will eventually become that person.

Find your 'power pose'

When you shift how you hold yourself physically, it shifts how you feel mentally and emotionally. Research at Harvard University by Associate Professor Amy Cuddy has now proven what many have long intuitively known: that your physical state has a direct and immediate impact on your emotional and mental state. Cuddy's research has proven that moving into what she coined a 'power pose' releases hormones in your body that generate feelings of greater strength, confidence and power. She found that brief nonverbal displays of power stimulate the release of testosterone (the hormone that links to power and dominance in animals and human beings alike), which lowers the levels of cortisol, the 'stress' hormone that can undermine your ability to think, speak and act in a calm, clear-headed and confident way.

Step forward confidently, hold yourself powerfully. When you shift how you hold yourself physically, it shifts how you feel mentally and emotionally.

Cuddy's research found that you express power through open, expansive postures, and express powerlessness through closed, contractive postures. In short, putting yourself into a 'power pose' not only makes you think and feel more powerful (and courageous!) but changes your actual physiology and, subsequently, your behavioural choices. Even just changing the expression on your face can alter your mental and emotional state. Indeed, studies have found that by simulating facial expressions we take on the emotions those facial expressions portray. That is, even if you don't feel like smiling, when you smile, you ultimately feel happier and friendlier. It's not just psychological, it's physiological. Likewise, if you furrow your eyebrows and frown, you will eventually feel more angry, forlorn and depressed. In another study researchers asked participants to make different facial expressions while being asked a question. Those who were asked to smile were more likely to agree to the request being made than those who were asked to keep a serious facial expression. Such is the power of a smile!

Embody the boldness you aspire to feel

If you want to feel more courageous and self-assured, hold yourself in the way that a courageous and self-assured person would. Often the easiest way to do this is to bring to mind someone you know (or know of) who comes across as very confident, brave and sure of themselves. Visualise how they would hold themselves if they were facing the same challenge, situation or decision that you are. Imitate their posture, stance and even their expression. By shifting how you hold yourself physically, you shift how you feel emotionally.

Shifting your body and expression into a 'power pose' can shift the level of power (as measured by courage and confidence) you feel in any situation. It can also help you to communicate more confidently and influence people more powerfully. So whether you're feeling very angry or anxious, take a minute to pay attention to your body and how you're holding yourself physically.

If you're feeling nervous or anxious about a situation, and are a long way from feeling as brave, confident or assertive as you'd like to, hold yourself as though you are confident. Back straight. Chin up. Firm handshake. Solid eye contact. Warm and friendly, but firm and assertive with a confident expression. Strike your power post before you enter into a situation that will trigger fear, self-doubt or anxiety. If you need to, mimic someone you look up to for their confidence and courage. It's not unauthentic to start acting like the person you want to be. Start where you are, however timid or nervous you may feel, but stay focused on where you want to go, knowing that the more confidently and powerfully you hold yourself, the more confident, powerful and courageous you'll feel.

So lift your chin up, put a confident yet determined look on your face, look people directly in the eye with your shoulders back, feel the ground firmly beneath your feet and then step forward with a confident and purposeful stride. Practise it. Sometimes you have to 'fake it 'til you make it'. By shifting how you hold yourself physically, you shift how you feel emotionally.

It's also important to dress like the successful and self-assured person you aspire to be. While it may sound superficial to some, the clothes you wear and how you wear them (which includes personal grooming!), impacts not just how others perceive you, but on your actual performance. In a study at Northwestern University, researchers had subjects wear white coats while performing a test that measured attention. One group was told they had on doctors' coats; the other, painters' coats. Subjects in the first group outperformed those in the second by nearly 30 percent, suggesting that the effect our clothes have on us may be even more powerful than we thought. That is, people who dress for success not only leave a positive impression, but have greater confidence to take the actions needed to create more success.

The actual decision you're facing is never as significant to your future as the mindset with which you face it. Sometimes decisions are small, and you know that in the big scheme of life they're not the be-all and end-all. But whether the decision you need to make is about something huge or something fairly mundane, it doesn't make your fear any less consuming.

It's the reasons behind why we do what we do that matter more than what we do. Too often though we make choices in life — sometimes really big ones — for reasons we're not even conscious of — to keep our parents happy, to prove ourselves, to avoid confrontation, to avoid friends thinking we're getting big-headed.

Research has found that the worries and fears that occupy most of your thinking are about relatively insignificant things; such as how to ask your boss for a day off during the busy season; how to tell your co-worker they need to pull more weight; in which school to enrol your child; or how to tell your girlfriend you don't want to join her on the annual family camping trip. Mundane stuff like this tends to consume a lot of our waking (and sleeping) energy.

Committing to a Courage Mindset requires having faith in yourself that whatever happens, you can handle it. After all, isn't that the ultimate security in life: knowing that within you reside all the resources you need to handle whatever challenges, hardships or hurdles might come along as you live the richly rewarding life you aspire to?

The reality is that there's no security in life except what lies inside us. No job, career, business, investment or material balance is ever 100 per cent secure. It can all be lost or taken away. The only things that can't be taken away are your ability to choose how you'll approach life, your sense of pride in how you've lived it and the deep peace that comes from knowing you did so with character and courage.

> *If you want to conquer fear, do not sit at home and think about it.*
> *Go out and get busy.*
> **Dale Carnegie**

So trust yourself. You're capable of far more than you think — courageous action being at the top of the list.

Key points

> Fear is a primal and instinctive emotion that has evolved to protect us from harm.

> If left unchecked fear runs our lives and keep us from taking the actions needed to effectively address our challenges and enjoy the success we want.

> We live in a culture that breeds fear, driving people to settle for unfulfilling lives for fear of trying to change the status quo.

> Fear is contagious. The more often we experience the emotion of fear, the more fearful we become. Many people today live in a constant state of fear and anxiety.

> Neuroscience has proven that our brains are wired to overestimate risk and underestimate our ability to handle its consequences.

> People are about twice as sensitive to potential loss as potential gain, which helps explain our natural risk aversion.

> Courage is like a muscle that strengthens with use. Every time you step out of your comfort zone you build your tolerance for risk, and your confidence to be bolder in the future.

> Studies have found most people regret not taking more risks when they look back on their lives.

> Courage is a mindset that embraces risk as a prerequisite for success. It counters the Risk-Averse Fear Mindset that undermines the success and happiness of many people in their careers and lives.

> There are four steps to cultivating a Courage Mindset:

>> – acknowledge fear

>> – tame fear

>> – harness fear

>> – step through fear.

Chapter 3

Align bold action with right action

Always do right. This will gratify some people and astonish the rest.
Mark Twain

For years, Lance Armstrong dominated the world of professional cycling, building a multimillion dollar business around his seven consecutive Tour de France wins. Armstrong was the poster child of courage. Yet as the world discovered in 2012, the courage and determination Armstrong had demonstrated was built on deceitfulness. To the shock, disappointment and outrage of millions, we learned of the elaborate and devious measures Armstrong had gone to in order to evade being uncovered as the drug cheat he was.

Armstrong's fall was sudden, steep and dramatic. Few could have imagined what Armstrong, hailed as a hero by so many, had been willing to do to win such glory, status and success on the world stage. As news of him being stripped of his titles and erased from the record books made the airways, I couldn't help thinking what an immense shame it was that his boldness and courage was not matched by his integrity and character. His lack of it wounded us all.

Deciding to think bigger, stop playing safe and engage more courageously in what you do can transform your day-to-day experience of life and alter the trajectory of your career. But if your big goals and bold actions fail to honour your own core values, earn trust and show character, your efforts will unravel and your hard work come undone.

Alignment of bold action with right action is the foundation of everything successful.

Of course, it's easy to do the right thing when the right thing doesn't cost or inconvenience you in any significant way. It's not as easy when it requires giving up something that you value: time, recognition, money, power, information, opportunity or some other material or psychological pay-off.

Your commitment to playing a bigger game in your career must place doing what's right ahead of doing what's convenient, clever or courageous. No amount of bravery or brilliance will compensate for a lack of character or integrity.

Never surrender self-respect to self-interest

William Edwards Deming—the guru of process integrity who revolutionised manufacturing processes in the Japanese automobile industry in the 1950s—taught that it's no good doing all of the right things some of the time or some of the right things all of the time. Excellence in process integrity means doing *all* of the right things *all* of the time. It was Deming's belief that if the resulting output from a process wasn't at the desired standard, the problem might not be in the execution, but in any of the preceding steps.

When you don't like the 'output' in any aspect of your career or business, it will pay you to look back and identify which decisions and actions you took along the way that may have contributed to the less-than-satisfactory result. While you may not have done anything blatantly dishonest, it's possible that you acted in ways that lacked strength of character or which simply failed to build and maintain the trust of your important stakeholders.

You don't have to look too far to find examples of other people whose failure to act with character caused enormous harm to them and others, particularly those they care about most. The news is too often littered with tales of politicians corrupted by power, unscrupulous business people and unprincipled corporate leaders once hailed as trailblazers, whose reputations and careers blazed out quickly as their unethical behaviour was uncovered.

Were these people always lacking in character or did they gradually forfeit self-respect for self-interest? In my experience it is the latter. I'm sure Lance Armstrong never set out to cheat his way into the record books. No-one sets out to become corrupt and deceitful. Rather, they do so with a thousand surrenders of self-respect for self-interest. Eventually every choice they're confronted with becomes so muddied by all that has preceded they lose all sense of right and wrong, moral and immoral. Ultimately a person without character belongs to whatever can make a captive of them, often through the false sense of security gained by acquiring more money, status or power.

Johann Wolfgang von Goethe said, 'Character develops in the stream of life'. It can also be lost in the pursuit of status, wealth and power. As you climb up the company ladder and progress in your career, the pressure to perform becomes greater, the line between black and white grows blurrier, opportunities to deceive more numerous and the temptation to cover up more alluring. As this happens, the stakes grow larger and the fall harder. Power can put even the most ardent truth-teller to the test. But character is much easier kept than recovered; good reputation lost is often lost forever. Which is why it's so important to commit to doing the daily work of ensuring that you never compromise yours. As Theodore Roosevelt once said, 'Character in the long run is the decisive factor in the life of an individual and nation alike'.

While you may think of yourself as a person of good character who lives honestly and speaks truthfully, I want to challenge you in this chapter to think more deeply about how you go about your work and your life. Character isn't just about being honest. It involves having integrity in everything you do — from following through on your seemingly unimportant promise, to following up on something, to going out of your way to let someone know you appreciate the effort they're putting into something. Living with integrity and character is akin to weeding a garden. You know that weeding is good for it, but you don't always see the results of your effort. It's only when you fail to dig out the weeds that they eventually take over. Eventually your garden will become so overgrown with weeds that no flowers will be able to blossom.

Your career, business and life are no different. You have to take time to tend to those patterns of thought and behaviour that can, left unchecked, cause you to act in ways that may lack integrity—however seemingly insignificant—and slowly, gradually, disconnect you from some of the core principles that, if you stopped still long enough to think about them, you want to build your life on.

In your busy life, as you work to fulfil expectations, juggle conflicting commitments and deliver the results expected of you, it's all too easy to justify a little shortcut here and a little white lie there. 'No big deal,' you tell yourself, but over time those shortcuts and little white lies can become your default.

You can only blossom in life when you're planted firmly in integrity and committed to making time to weed out those behaviours and beliefs that can compromise it.

The cost of mistrust

Jack Welch, former CEO of General Electric, once described trust as 'you know it when you feel it'. I would add that, more importantly, you know when you don't feel it. Nothing in the workplace is as precarious as trust. It can take years to build and only moments to destroy. And yet, without trust it's impossible to build the influence, make the difference or achieve the success you aspire to. At the heart of trust is the confidence—or lack thereof—we have in ourselves and in our own integrity, and in others and their commitment to doing what's right even when it costs them.

> *Throughout all my life and with all my heart*
> *I shall strive to be worthy of your trust.*
> **Queen Elizabeth II**

In any relationship, team or organisation, mistrust acts like a 'hidden tax' on every interaction that hampers progress, stifles collaboration, and slows productivity and undermines bottom-line performance. A lack of trust acts like sand in the elaborate network of interactions and relationships that makes up the fabric of every working group of any size. When mistrust runs rampant within a team or organisation, it also impedes the flow of vital information, undermines customer focus and obstructs a group, team or company from delivering the quality of service and products required to keep clients and stakeholders satisfied and loyal. As Professor John Whitney from Columbia Business School observed, 'Mistrust doubles the cost of doing business'. The long-term impact can be lethal.

Hillary Clinton once said that when someone breaches trust we're all worse off. Indeed, the absence of trust doesn't only exact a steep price at the organisational level, it can be profoundly harmful at the interpersonal level. When others don't trust you, they don't extend you invitations and opportunities that would enable you to acquire valuable new knowledge, skills and connections. Likewise, when you don't trust others, you withhold information that could be valuable to them. Distrust can kill relationships before they ever get off the ground. Failing to make a firm commitment to living with integrity, doing what's right and being a person truly worthy of other people's trust doesn't just limit your success, it undermines your health and sabotages your happiness.

Your integrity is worth more than your position.
Your reputation is worth more than your pay cheque.

If you're managing a team or organisation, you want to ensure that integrity is the cornerstone of all the actions of those you work with. There are three steps that make up a simple and yet powerful framework which will minimise opportunities for breeding mistrust:

- Determine what's right and wrong in a business situation. This requires knowing the rules and getting the facts straight.

- Act with the intention of doing what you believe to be right for the team or organisation.

- Disclose what you're doing and that you're acting on your understanding of what's right. Open disclosure is the easiest way to avoid a hidden conflict of interest.

The four domains of trust

While you may feel that you're a person of character—worthy of trust and deserving of influence—if others have any doubts about your trustworthiness, they will impede your efforts to get ahead in ways you may never be able to identify. Countless times people have shared with me their doubts about their ability to trust a person they work with—concerns which the person in question is totally unaware of. Building your awareness around the four core domains of trust—competence, sincerity, reliability and compassion—will help you win and maintain trust more effectively in all your working relationships.

Awareness of these four domains of trust will also help you become more discerning when you find yourself hesitating to trust others. All four domains of trust, as illustrated in figure 3.1, are built on the common foundation of integrity.

Figure 3.1: the four domains of trust

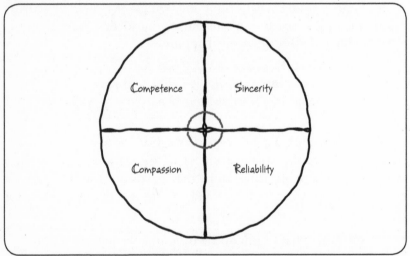

The four domains of trust work together, each supporting the other, each reinforcing the other and each magnifying the perception of the other, for better or worse. When any of them becomes weakened or cracked, they are all compromised. Staying focused on acting with integrity within each domain will enable you to build the trust you need to add the level of value you have within yourself to bring.

Audit your trustworthiness

In *The 7 Habits of Highly Effective People*, Stephen Covey wrote, 'Until a person can say deeply and honestly, "I am what I am today because of the choices I made yesterday", that person cannot say, "I choose otherwise"'.

This challenge consists of a series of statements that reflect on behaviour and assess the level of integrity in each of the four domains of trust: competence, sincerity, reliability and compassion.

Give yourself a rating between 0 and 4, where 0 = never, 1 = not very often, 2 = often, 3 = most of the time and 4 = absolutely always. Add up your score for each domain out of a total possible 20. Any area in which you score below 15 needs attention. Any area where you score below 10 needs it urgently!

In the spirit of not playing safe, ask people you work with to rate you on each domain. Invite them to be totally honest and to expand verbally on any domain where they can't rate you highly. That's where the value lies!

Competence

☐ I have all the skills and knowledge needed to do my job and when I don't I get the help I need.

☐ I don't overestimate my ability to do my work as needed; I'm confident but not cocky.

☐ I do the research and preparation I need to ensure that I have the knowledge and skills required to succeed.

☐ I only take risks when I've done my homework and gained the knowledge I need to optimise success.

☐ I don't underestimate my ability to achieve a new goal, and trust that I have what it takes to learn what's required.

Score out of 20: ___

(continued)

Audit your trustworthiness (*cont'd*)

Sincerity

☐ I don't pretend things are okay when they're not.

☐ I don't cut corners or tell half-truths or harmless 'white lies' even when it's difficult not to.

☐ I'm honest in all my dealings, transactions and record keeping.

☐ People know they can always count on me to tell the truth, even when that puts me at risk.

☐ I always maintain confidentiality. People know they can trust me not to share anything.

Score out of 20: ___

Reliability

☐ I do what I say I'll do on time and to the standard others expect.

☐ I'm consistently punctual and arrive at meetings ready and prepared to start on time.

☐ People can count on me as dependable and when I can't get something done, they know I'll inform them as soon as possible.

☐ I get back to people when I say I will.

☐ I don't say 'yes' to someone unless I know I can keep my commitment.

Score out of 20: ___

Compassion

☐ I take an active interest in the people around me.

☐ I take time when I communicate to make sure people know I understand their perspective.

☐ People know I have a genuine interest and concern for their wellbeing.

☐ I think about how my actions will impact those around me.

☐ I temper my truthfulness with what I know will be helpful, not just what will be hurtful.

Score out of 20: ___

Competence

Competence is the one element of trust that has firm parameters: it is task-specific. That is, you can be competent at one particular skill or area of expertise and not others. For instance, I trust my husband implicitly as a man of immense integrity. Yet I wouldn't trust him to bake a soufflé if we had guests for dinner. It's not that he isn't capable of learning how to make a soufflé, or that I wouldn't trust his very best intentions to do the job well; it's just that with his current skill level, I wouldn't trust him to do it. I also wouldn't trust him to give me root-canal treatment. Not in a million years!

If you're putting yourself out there, taking on bigger challenges at work and laying more on the line, you have to be careful to ensure that you have the competence needed to deliver results. Too often, promising careers take a steep nosedive when people are assigned to positions they simply don't have the competence to do well. It's not that they don't have the capability to learn, but they're not given, or they don't proactively get, the skills, training, knowledge and support needed to win and maintain the trust of key stakeholders.

In most career paths it's technical competence that tends to kick-start success. Whether you're a nurse, analyst, engineer, accountant, attorney or architect, being technically competent (i.e. really good at your job!) is a prerequisite to advancement. Those around you trust your ability to execute a particular set of tasks with a high level of proficiency. Often as you advance in your career, the hard 'technical' skills become less important and the softer human skills become more so. This is why so often 'rising stars' with technical brilliance find themselves in a jam when they're placed in a management role for which they have never had any training and may not have any natural affinity.

And it's why, should you find yourself in a role where you don't have the competence needed to do it well, you need to take proactive and assertive action to get the support and training, backup and resources needed to ensure you don't damage the trust others have put in you.

Now this may all seem pretty logical and simple. So, what's the big deal? The big deal is that it can sometimes take courage and humility to admit to yourself, much less to others, that you don't have the competence you'd like to have or that you sense others may assume you have (or expect you to have). Asking for help is something most people try to avoid. It's why people put into new roles, or assigned new responsibilities, don't ask for help or enlist support from those with the necessary knowledge and skills, but instead try to bluff their way through. Of course, if you think you'll be able to pick up the knowhow you need pretty quickly, that strategy may work just fine. But 'winging it'—or bluffing your way into or through a job you don't have the competence to do, or can't learn quickly—can end badly, as in David's case.

When you need help, ask for it!

David worked for a large consulting firm. He had been one of the firm's brightest young 'up and comers' and had been given new and bigger assignments every 18 months since joining the firm six years earlier. He had become quite attached to the idea that no matter what challenges were presented to him, he could 'fake it 'til he made it'. This strategy worked fine until he was put in charge of a large project on a client site that was implementing a total business re-engineering program and using a software package with which he was unfamiliar. It was a disaster. Not only did they run over time and over budget, but the mistakes cost the client, and David's firm, millions. It also lost his firm other spin-off business. The ultimate cause of the problem was that David wasn't willing to acknowledge his own limitations or ask for help when things started to veer off course.

David's pride and reluctance to ask for help ended up costing his firm and his reputation dearly. It took several roles after this one to restore the trust others had placed in him, a situation that could have been avoided if David had been willing to ask for help when he needed it.

So while competence may be a given for you *most* of the time, it may not be a given *all* of the time. And when it's not, it's crucial to be honest with yourself about it, and to ask for the extra support, training or information you need before committing yourself to accomplishing anything that will require it.

Likewise, if you want to take a bold plunge into a new role, job, industry or career, be willing to get the training and support needed to do it well. Statistics tell us that 50 per cent of businesses fail in the first five years. Often their failure boils down to the fact that the business owner didn't know what they were doing, and lacked the breadth of skills and knowledge needed to build a profitable business.

On the flip side of the coin, don't underestimate your ability to learn the skills and knowledge needed to become competent in a job. Ladies, this applies particularly to you since it's my experience that women are more inclined to underestimate themselves when it comes to rising to the challenges a new role will involve than their more risk-ready male counterparts. While many men will look at the requirements of a role and jump right in if they think they can fulfil most of them—confident that they can learn the rest—women want to meet all of the requirements before (and then some) they put their hand up or even accept an offer. (But don't get me started on this—that's my next book!)

Sincerity

I bet you've met plenty of people who are full of 'BS': whose language is so pockmarked with half-truths and exaggerations, spin and hyperbole that it seems they're forever running their own infomercial. We've become so used to a diet rich in empty jargon, false flattery and hollow commitments it's easy to think that dishonesty, deceitfulness and disingenuousness are normal—acceptable even. But in an era where so many people seem to prefer saying whatever they think others want to hear, those who are genuine, authentic and sincere make so much more impact on the people around them.

Playing a bigger game in your career doesn't require stretching the truth or appeasing those more senior than you. Rather, it means having the courage to express yourself sincerely, say what you mean and mean what you say, balancing candour with kindness. Doing so will positively affect the trust you earn and the influence you ultimately wield over the course of your career.

If you're like most people you probably relish working with 'what-you-see-is-what-you-get' people. You know that they mean what they say and say what they mean—even if people don't like to hear it. They're people of their word: sincere, honest, authentic, without pretension and willing to speak the truth even when it costs them. Beyond what's obvious, you intuitively sense that there's no gap between what they really think and what they say. That said, they're not unkind or uncaring. Sincerity without caring (another pillar of character) can be cruel, so they don't say what's on their mind unless they truly believe it will serve the person they're saying it to.

To know what is right and not to do it is the worst cowardice.
Confucius

When you're consistently sincere, you win the trust of your leaders, your team, your colleagues and your clients. Sincerity is a characteristic we look for in leaders and if it's lacking it undermines our trust in them more profoundly than a lack of competence, care or reliability combined. It's for this reason that I believe when recruiting people into your organisation you need to focus first on character and sincerity, and then on skills and talent. There are too many highly skilled, talented and charming people who, when push comes to shove, can't be trusted to do what's right, speak the truth and make the hard decisions that may well not be popular ones.

Reliability

Debbie Kissire, vice-chairman of Ernst & Young, shared with me that one of the things she sees which holds capable people back in their careers is a lack of follow-through, whether on key responsibilities or the seemingly insignificant commitments made in a passing conversation. Responsible for 2500 people, Debbie said that being able to rely on someone as a 'go to' person — that is, someone who manages their time well and consistently demonstrates the tenacity, resourcefulness and reliability to get the job done — is valuable to any person in a senior role who needs to achieve their performance goals via those around them. Likewise, your ability to deliver on your commitments and become someone others can depend on to get the job done can open up opportunities for you that you may not even know exist.

Follow-through is really about how reliable you are. Reliability can be divided into two core components, each of which can impact on your reputation and undermine your credibility. It's about doing *what* you say you will do *when* you say you will do it, in the way you committed to doing it.

When you fail to do what you say you will do, it damages trust and has lasting effects on how others perceive you. And while it should go without saying, it's important never to make promises you can't keep or try to cover up for failing to keep them.

Of course, most people like to think of themselves as reliable and able to keep their word. Yet, how often have you had to wait for the same people, time and time again, before starting your meeting? And how often have you kept others waiting on you? The fact is that when you fail to keep your promises (which includes being punctual), you undermine the trust others can place in you and damage your reputation in the process. Perhaps not in a huge way. But every broken promise, even the small ones, builds on the previous one and reinforces your identity (aka brand) as someone who can't be counted on. Not fully.

Build trust through reliability

Suzanne prided herself on her professionalism. I know this because she would regularly tell me as much during our coaching conversations. Yet time and time again, even after specific requests that she be punctual, she would be late calling in to our coaching sessions. She always had some pressing reason for her tardiness and for the first few sessions I gave her the benefit of the doubt.

By our fourth session I decided it was time to address the issue with her. Experience had taught me that how we do anything is how we do everything. If she was always running late for our appointments, she was most likely also not reliable for others, and that was very likely damaging to the perceptions other people had of her. It wasn't that Suzanne wasn't smart or capable. She was both in abundance. But she had fallen into a habit of overcommitting herself and treating everyone else's time as less important than her own. Mine included. I was pretty sure that if it was offensive and annoying to me, it was probably even more so to those she was managing and working with.

(continued)

Build trust through reliability (*cont'd*)

When I raised the issue with Suzanne she became defensive at first, interpreting it as an attack on her professionalism. Of course, what I wanted to do was get to the core of what a lack of reliability is ultimately all about—a crack in her integrity. What Suzanne came to realise was that she was trying to fit more into every hour than she could reasonably do. The cost of doing this was that she was constantly acting in ways that undermined her trustworthiness. Sure, she was all about integrity and professionalism and working smarter not harder, and yet every time she arrived at a meeting late, or failed to keep a promise, the message she was sending was that she was unable to manage her own commitments in a way that respected those of others.

The natural desire to keep others happy and be agreeable makes saying no very difficult for many people. However, failing to say no when we need to can lead to over-commitment, overload and damaged relationships as we fail to fulfil promises and expectations. So I suggested to Suzanne that before making any commitments she should ask herself these questions:

- Is this aligned with my top priorities, goals and values?
- If I say yes to this, what will it mean (by default) saying no to?
- Do I realistically have time to fulfil this commitment properly?

If she couldn't tick all three boxes, then she needed to say no with grace and confidence, and without any guilt. Suzanne's ability to manage her commitments well required her to get super clear about what her top priorities were and to reassess how much she could get done in any given day.

And so, if saying yes to something or taking on one more responsibility is going to jeopardise your ability to fulfil other commitments or keep your promises, then it's a matter of integrity that you say no. Offer people an alternative if you can. Refer them on to someone else. Negotiate a lesser commitment. But don't say yes to something unless you know you can do it. Sometimes you have to say no to the good to make room for the great.

I've yet to meet a person who would rather someone say yes and not follow through, than say no because they simply can't honour their promise.

Compassion

In a Gallup Poll, 10 million employees around the world were asked how strongly they agreed or disagreed with the statement, 'My supervisor or someone I work with cares about me as a person'. Those who agreed were found to be more productive, to contribute more to the bottom-line profitability of their team or organisation and were more likely to stay with that organisation for a longer time.

> *I try to treat people as human beings. If they know you care,*
> *it brings out the best in them.*
> **Sir Richard Branson**

Showing genuine care and concern for the needs of others doesn't require donating a liver. Nor does it require foregoing your ambitions because they may upset or adversely impact other people in the short-to-medium term. It does mean taking time to think about how you can take care of people as you go about playing a bigger game, whether it be taking extra time to listen to their concerns, showing interest in something they care about or following up with a note of thanks.

Text or talk: building trust in the digital age

Email (and technology in general) has revolutionised the way we communicate. It's a brilliant tool for communicating efficiently, but can be a very blunt one when used inappropriately. The pressure to keep up with an ever-burgeoning inbox—combined with the convenience of digital communication tools and our natural aversion to confrontation—drives people to shoot off a short, sharp and poorly worded email when taking the time to talk would be much more fruitful. Far too often we take the easy, and often cowardly, option of using email or text messaging to avoid the work and emotional discomfort of a real-time conversation.

(*continued*)

Text or talk: building trust in the digital age (*cont'd*)

When it comes to communicating issues that can be awkward or emotionally sensitive, nothing can ever replace a good, old-fashioned face-to-face conversation. Hiding behind your computer screen not only lacks courage and courtesy, but can be very costly and damaging to the trust you need to succeed in work and in life. The lack of consideration combined with misinterpretation can risk permanent damage to your relationships and all of your efforts to be productive and efficient can unravel, as time spent on damage control quickly overtakes any time saved by belting out a quick written message.

Hiding behind email spares us the discomfort of dealing with other people's reactions. It can also give a false sense of bravado as we type things we would never have the courage to deliver in person. Email desensitises us to the emotions of others. Unable to see their expressions, we become disconnected from the impact our communication can have.

I've heard numerous stories of people being made redundant by email. As insensitive and lacking in basic courtesy and respect as it is, it reflects the wider trend towards sacrificing caring, quality communication on the altar of efficiency. The cost to interpersonal trust, team productivity and organisational culture shouldn't be underestimated.

Emotions can all too easily get 'lost in translation'. As soon as you start using text phrases to characterise emotions that would normally be delivered with vocal intonation, subtle nuances, facial expressions and body language, your intended message can be completely misinterpreted. If you've ever had a sarcastic remark via email backfire badly, you'll have discovered this already.

To mangle a cliché from Hallmark, 'When you care enough ... try talking!' Novel idea, I know. When it comes to sensitive issues, nothing will ever trump a good, old-fashioned, albeit occasionally awkward, face-to-face conversation. If it's not practical, at least pick up the phone to talk instead of texting. You never know, you might actually find it's not as scary as you think and the trust you build by making the extra effort to talk can lead to a far better outcome than you might have imagined. As you move up in any organisation, how much people sense that you care about them—and by default, what they care about—impacts the depth of trust they place in you. The terms 'having compassion' and 'co-suffering' come from the Latin word *compatior*. Genuine compassion often gives rise to a strong desire to alleviate someone else's suffering, to take care of their concerns or to help improve their situation. The so-called Golden Rule—'Do to others what you would have them do to you'—embodies compassion. Compassion can drive you to being more generous towards people and to engage in acts of service, philanthropy and altruism.

Of course, you may not feel deeply compassionate towards the people who'll be impacted by your actions, but you should always be considerate of them and weigh into your decisions how your actions will impact those who will be affected by them. Robin Lineberger's story is a good case in point.

Principle over power or profit

The son of an airman who was shot down and killed in combat over Vietnam when he was a child, Robin grew up with a strong sense of duty and belief in the importance of working hard. He was recruited out of the US Air Force into BearingPoint's federal consulting business. He rose up through the 'ranks' and was ultimately appointed as executive vice president of BearingPoint.

(continued)

Principle over power or profit (*cont'd*)

While the business was highly successful, for myriad reasons the firm he worked for found itself unravelling financially. A new management team was brought in to fix the problem, but Robin felt they were being short-sighted and not doing the right thing by their clients, his team of consultants or the federal business itself. So he decided to hunker down and lead his team through the turmoil, all the while seeing a large amount of his personal wealth diminish. Other industry leaders saw the writing on the wall and tried to recruit him into other executive leadership roles. Again and again Robin had opportunities to take up roles with other organisations—to save his own skin—and again and again he turned them down. He refused to abandon his team of people or just walk away from the business they had built up together over more than 20 years.

As it became clear to Robin that venture-capital firms wanted to piece apart the business, he realised his 4000-plus employees would likely find themselves out of work. So he steered the negotiations to firms that valued the people and what they had built. In the end, in the worse economy in history at that point in time and in the throws of bankruptcy, he managed to get all of the 4000 employees positions at Deloitte, including transferring partnership positions for many of those who had been partners already. Robin had demonstrated leadership, calm and grace under pressure and solid decision-making capability in a very challenging business environment marked with mass layoffs and high unemployment. Ultimately he was appointed CEO of Deloitte's federal business.

A very humble man, Robin doesn't see himself as having done anything courageous. He shared with me that he just did what he felt was right, 'what any person of character would have done in the same situation'. By having character, and aligning bold action with right action, Robin won the life–long respect and loyalty of many people. (Having met a few of them, I can say that's actually an understatement.) One actually said he would have followed Robin off a cliff. When people know that you have a genuine concern for them that extends beyond how their success impacts your own, it builds trust and wins loyalty in ways that nothing else can.

When people know that you have a genuine concern for them that extends beyond how their success impacts your own, it builds trust in ways that nothing else can. Likewise, when they assess that you aren't interested in or concerned about what's going on in their world, it limits trust. I recall my client Sophie telling me how little compassion her boss showed when her mother had been undergoing treatment for cancer. Every week for six months Sophie was flying interstate to be with her mother, yet not once did her boss ever ask how her mother was doing. Sophie said it didn't stop her working hard, or giving her best, but it did impact her sense of loyalty to her manager and her company. She has since left the company to work with a competitor. Had Sophie felt greater concern from her manager, perhaps that company may have retained her talent and dedication.

When it comes to creating the impact that you want to make in your career, job or business, always keep in mind that how much you care for those around you will filter into every conversation, interaction and business deal. As it does, it will influence — in both subtle and profound ways — your ability to achieve maximum success and influence.

Your actions will always speak far more loudly than your words. People won't always notice what you say, but they will always notice what you do. Live the values you espouse, practise what you preach and consistently act with integrity in what you say and do — day to day, from person to person, from situation to situation. When you align bold action with right action, you forge a path in your career and life on which you can never get lost.

Key points

> Bold action aligned with right action is the foundation of everything successful.

> No amount of bravery or brilliance will compensate for a lack of character and integrity.

> Trust is the cornerstone of influence. Being a trustworthy person takes character and a solid commitment to doing what's right above what's easy or expedient.

> The four core domains of trust are:

  - Competence: Do you have the skill, knowledge and resources to do the job?

  - Reliability: Do you manage your commitments well, doing what you say when you say you'll do it? (This includes being punctual!)

  - Sincerity: Do you mean what you say, and say what you mean – both genuine and kind?

  - Compassion: Do you care about what others care about?

> When people don't consider you to be trustworthy in any of these domains it undermines your relationships, limiting your ability to work with and through others to achieve what you want.

Part II

Working Courage

The CALL of courage

*Life shrinks or expands in proportion
to one's courage.*
Anaïs Nin

Chapter 4

Speak candidly, listen bravely

*While no one conversation is guaranteed to change the trajectory
of your career, any single conversation can.*
Susan Scott

In the late 1980s, as Nelson Mandela neared the end of 27 years
in the infamous Robben Island prison, then-President of South
Africa F.W. de Klerk met with him privately several times. Their
conversations were respectful, candid and courageous. They didn't
meet only to negotiate the contentious issues embedded in the
apartheid system, but to discuss how to pave a way for South Africa.
Both men held power—one through the office of President; the
other through the respect he had won from the 84 per cent of
South Africa's population whose dark skin matched his own, and
the millions around the world who condemned the apartheid
regime as immoral and unjust.

After Mandela was released in 1990, their conversations
continued (albeit, I assume, in more comfortable surrounds). While
their opinions differed, they were united in their commitment to
a better, more just and equitable future for their country. Their
mutual concern for the welfare of the people of their country and
the generations to follow transcended their differences, enabling
them to come together in dialogue to navigate a path forward in
a deeply divided country. By speaking candidly, listening bravely
and staying focused on a mutual aspiration, their conversations set
the stage for the profound, dramatic and unprecedented change

that was to come. As I write this I can't help but think what a shame it is that some of those leading South Africa today lack the courage and character that we admired so much in both Mandela and de Klerk.

Your conversations are powerful

That words you speak create the reality you inhabit. Your conversations hold power. Immense power. Power to open up possibilities. Power to close them down. Power to forge relationships that last a lifetime. Power to end them in seconds. Power to build trust. Power to erode it. Power to incite violent rage. Power to inspire peaceful revolution.

Often we don't give the conversations we engage in each day the credit they're due or respect they warrant. It wasn't through war that the apartheid regime was dismantled, but through a series of what I call 'courageous conversations' by brave people who refused to side with the status quo.

If conversations have the power to alter the trajectory of a nation, they certainly have no less power to alter the trajectory of your career, or for that matter, any of your relationships, or any area of your life.

Before we go any further, take a moment to complete this courageous conversations quiz. It may help you to identify where you may have been playing too safe in your conversations and failing to harness the power they contain.

 Courageous conversations quiz

Read through each of the statements and take note of how many of them apply to you at least some of the time.

- At times I avoid situations that might bring me into contact with people I'm having problems with.

- Often when people bring up a touchy or awkward issue I try to change the subject.

- Sometimes I hide behind email rather than have a face-to-face conversation that could be awkward.

- I'm uncomfortable with confrontation and often hold back or step around it.

- I have a really hard time saying no to people and often end up overcommitted.

- When people don't do their job properly I often just do it myself rather than hold them accountable.

- I often feel undervalued but am loathe to 'toot my horn' lest people think I'm showboating.

- Often when I'm listening I'm really just 'reloading', waiting for my turn to fire back my opinion.

- There are times when I tell people what I know they want to hear rather than the truth.

- I often resort to sarcasm to convey what's really on my mind.

- I often don't ask for what I really want because I'm afraid I won't get it and don't want to seem overly demanding or high maintenance.

- I sometimes hold back from offering a conflicting opinion, afraid that others mightn't see its merit or that I might ruffle feathers.

How did you fare? If you found yourself relating to the majority of these statements, or even just a solid number of them, then it's likely you've been playing too safe in your conversations while also failing to listen as openly and bravely as would serve you, those you work with, your organisation and your life over all.

Conversations that require you to come out from the shelter of silence and speak candidly take many forms. Some set (or reset!) boundaries. Some involve a bold request or a brave invitation. Others address sensitive issues where emotions can run high and opinions vary widely. Others again may involve advocating for yourself to ensure people know not just who you are, but what you have done and what you want to do in the future.

While no two courageous conversations are ever the same, they all involve an element of risk (that's why they're courageous) and demand a degree of vulnerability. They are often scary and rarely easy, but they are always valuable.

Safe conversations can be expensive

If there's something you genuinely want to say, chances are there's someone who genuinely needs to hear it. Unfortunately though, your innate instinct to avoid pain and discomfort, combined with the pressures of your job (to have all the answers, get things right the first time, execute decrees from above), sets the stage for playing it safe when having conversations with those around you. The path of least resistance is always easier, at least in the short-term — which is where people are so often focused.

But every choice you make has a consequence, and the price you pay for staying silent and engaging only in 'safe conversations' that fail to address important issues can be profound. Over time, issues that are left unaddressed can drive a wedge into your relationships, damage trust, grow resentment, undermine engagement and sour all your interactions. Likewise, withholding your opinion for fear that it mightn't be valued undermines the contribution you make, deprives others from knowing the full value you have to bring, and caps the value other people place on you. All the while your unwillingness to share how you feel and say what you think chips away at your self-confidence and cuts off opportunities that you may have created by speaking more candidly and engaging more openly and authentically.

Playing safe in your conversations is not just cowardly, it's costly. If there is something you genuinely want to say, chances are someone genuinely needs to hear it.

As illustrated in figure 4.1, your relationships are built through conversations. The quality of those conversations determines the quality of your relationships. It's through your relationships that you're able to grow influence and coordinate action. In other words, it's through your relationships that you're able to get your job done and deliver results, from customer satisfaction to bottom-line profitability. Failing to speak candidly and engage authentically with others, therefore, isn't just a nice thing to do that fosters friendship and makes work more enjoyable and less stressful; it actually impacts the bottom line of the organisation you work in.

Figure 4.1: conversations count

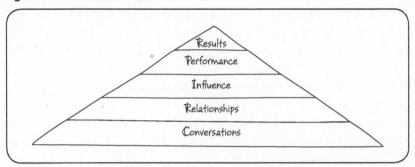

The words you speak, and the way you speak them, wield immense power. Regardless of how cowardly or courageous you've been in your conversations until now, you have the ability to become someone capable of creating profound and positive change — in your organisation, your career, your life and in the lives of others — one well-intentioned, candid and courageous conversation at a time.

The conversations that take the most courage, demand the greatest vulnerability and involve the most risk are those that hold the most importance and potential. Courageous conversations create a clear pathway to building the relationships, growing the influence and improving the outcomes you want in your work, team, business and in every area of your life. While they may sometimes be uncomfortable, the cost of not engaging in difficult conversations far outweighs the discomfort you feel having them.

So no matter how much you've shied away from giving voice to your thoughts and feelings for fear of rocking the boat or looking foolish, you have within you the ability to learn how to speak up about *any* issue with *any* person at *any* time throughout your life. Let me repeat that, because it's crucial to your success:

You have within you the ability to learn how to speak up about any issue with any person at any time throughout your life.

You may not think you do. You may not think it's worth the effort. You may not have had much success in the past. Your throat might constrict at the thought of putting yourself in a situation where you're vulnerable to rejection, criticism, side-lining or humiliation. But that doesn't mean you can't. It just means that you've probably never realised how much playing safe is costing you and have discounted, denied or ignored the cost of safety. Getting real about how profoundly you're limiting yourself when you stay in your conversational comfort zone is paramount. Only when you have the courage to speak up can you make the impact you want, build the influence you'd like and earn the recognition you deserve in whatever career field you choose to plant yourself.

Issues that aren't talked out are acted out, exacting a steep price on your relationships, your success and your life.

Playing safe and staying silent—or burying your head in the sand in the vain hope that an issue will 'go away' on its own—is not only cowardly, it's costly. Pretending otherwise (as many people do) does you and others a huge disservice.

When issues that cause upset aren't talked out, they're acted out. They're acted out in sarcastic remarks and subtle (or not so subtle) innuendos. They're acted out through back-stabbing and gossip mongering or through passive aggression such as 'the silent treatment'. They're acted out through progressive disengagement: arriving late, leaving early and taking phony 'sick days'. They're acted out through taking longer and longer to perform everyday tasks and cutting corners to get things done. More drastic is if they're left to fester long enough and are acted out in emotional outbursts to rival Mt Vesuvius—or quitting your job. They can also impact people's lives in far more tragic ways. The people I met and worked with at NASA know just how much.

Never discount the cost of silence

In January 1986, NASA's Space Shuttle *Challenger* broke apart 73 seconds into its flight, claiming the lives of all seven astronauts onboard. In the wake of the *Challenger* disaster, the Rogers Commission was appointed by President Ronald Reagan to investigate what had gone wrong. It found that NASA's organisational culture and decision-making processes had been key contributing factors to the accident.

Warnings from ground engineers to managers at NASA's Marshall Space Flight Center about a potentially catastrophic flaw in the O-rings if launching in low temperatures were disregarded. On the night before the launch, the engineers maintained their objections but the managers took off their 'engineering hats' and put on their 'management hats'. The stakes were high and the cost of aborting the mission at this late stage was immense. As a result, it was decided not to pass this vital information on to NASA superiors. The mission proceeded and within minutes the seven crew onboard the *Challenger* were dead. The O-rings were unable to withstand the extreme low temperatures, as the ground engineers had predicted. The *Challenger* disaster has become a case study in workplace ethics, risk management and engineering safety.

Of course this is the simplified tale of a terrible tragedy. There were many complex variables at play. But the Commission's findings were clear: the flow of information had been thwarted; communication had been neither transparent nor candid. Indeed, the unwillingness of those with the power to abort the mission and speak candidly exacted a steep human price.

NASA has worked hard to address this issue in recent years. I met with Lori Garver, deputy director of NASA, as I researched this book to get her perspective on the importance of being courageous in our work and career. She shared her belief that communicating directly is essential to the success of not just the individual in an organisation but to the organisation itself. She shared, 'Sometimes I over-communicate. But people have grown to appreciate that they know exactly where they stand with me. They don't have to wonder what I think about an issue. I share candidly and while sometimes my candour is difficult for people to hear, they have come to respect that I'm open, upfront and transparent. When people can trust that you're not going to say one thing and then do another, it sets the stage for greater collaboration and better bottom-line results for the organisation'.

Courageous conversations

If you're unsure how you should go about discussing a potentially sensitive issue, the following keys will help guide you to achieving the optimal result.

- *Start with heart.* There's a distinct difference between speaking up and talking down to someone. Take time upfront to clarify your highest intention and the outcome that will ultimately best serve everyone. If you march into a conversation to 'win' you're guaranteed to damage trust.

- *Mean what you say, but respect dignity.* Issues that aren't talked out get acted out. If there's something you genuinely want to say, chances are someone genuinely needs to hear it. Don't sugar coat it with disingenuous flattery. People can intuitively sense when you're being sincere. They can also sense when you're not.

- *Set the emotional tone.* Emotions are contagious. Be the change you'd like to see in others. If emotions get heated, respond calmly, kindly and with curiosity. Set clear boundaries, stand your ground and when others act small, act big. Don't let other people's poor behaviour be an excuse for yours.

- *Listen for unspoken concerns.* These lie at the heart of the issue. What's left unsaid in a conversation is often more important than what's spoken. Be willing to 'discuss the undiscussable'; doing so can breathe new life into your relationships, team and organisation.

- *Distinguish your story from the facts.* Your story about a situation can roadblock fruitful communication before it even begins. Start with the facts; then express your opinion in a way that respects alternative views. Address the problem, not the person. When you present your opinion as fact, you're guaranteed to get people off-side.

- *Prepare in advance.* The more sensitive the conversation, the more vital it is to invest time preparing what you want to say and how you want to say it. Write down key points. Practise through role-play. If it's a sensitive issue, request a time to discuss it. By framing the conversation upfront you'll take some charge out of it.

- *Be bold in your requests and clear in your commitments.* Don't assume others know what you want them to do. Make clear requests and set clear expectations. Likewise, only agree to things you know you can do. Keep your word and hold others accountable to theirs.

- *Stay future focused.* Laying blame, throwing stones and criticising the mistakes of others is easy. Staying focused on what needs to change so that the same problem doesn't arise again takes courage and discipline. If you can't yet commit to the next steps, at least agree to stay in the conversation.

- *Speak powerfully.* Your way of being speaks more loudly than your words. You have something important to say that needs to be heard. If you don't yet feel as brave and confident as you'd like, act as though you do. Start where you are but stay focused on where you want to go.

To have effective action conversations you have to have the courage to ask for what you want: say no to what you don't want and negotiate to get the best outcome you can; and be willing to hold people accountable when they fail to follow through on their commitments.

The Here-to-How (H2H) Model: advance your cause through conversation

If you think of the people in your life with whom you have the best relationships, they're most likely the people who are as open to hearing what you have to say as they are to sharing what's on their mind. Sometimes they will say things that you don't like to hear. On occasion you'll disagree, sometimes fiercely. But even when you can't see eye to eye and fail to agree with them, you always respect their dignity and their right to hold their opinions. Accordingly, you'll always feel a strong sense of mutual respect, a commitment to the relationship and a willingness to be vulnerable. As a result, the relationship is able to weather the inevitable challenges that arise in all relationships and, over time, grow stronger, more valued and more rewarding.

The Here-to-How (H2H) Conversational Model in figure 4.2 breaks down the kinds of conversations in which you need to engage into three core domains. Each stands alone, yet each overlaps and leads into another. They all move towards change, expand possibility, challenge assumptions, and focus on creating a better future rather than getting stuck dissecting and complaining about the past.

Figure 4.2: the Here-to-How (H2H) Conversational Model

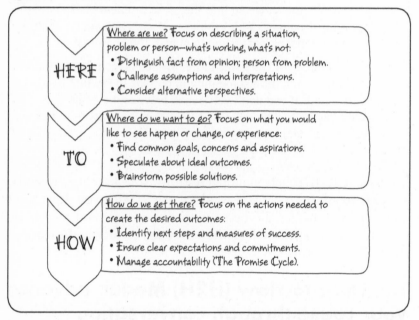

HERE — Where are we? Focus on describing a situation, problem or person—what's working, what's not:
- Distinguish fact from opinion; person from problem.
- Challenge assumptions and interpretations.
- Consider alternative perspectives.

TO — Where do we want to go? Focus on what you would like to see happen or change, or experience:
- Find common goals, concerns and aspirations.
- Speculate about ideal outcomes.
- Brainstorm possible solutions.

HOW — How do we get there? Focus on the actions needed to create the desired outcomes:
- Identify next steps and measures of success.
- Ensure clear expectations and commitments.
- Manage accountability (The Promise Cycle).

The H2H Conversational Model for engaging in fruitful, frank and effective dialogue has its origins in the work of the ontological approach to coaching developed by Chris Chittenden, a thought leader in the world of ontological coaching and a student of the work of Fernando Flores and Rafael Echeverria. The beauty of this process is in its intrinsic simplicity: it takes a conversation from where things are right now in a forward direction towards a desired outcome or state. If you think about a situation you're in right now that you feel less than happy about, applying this process will help you be more effective in resolving it, so long as you give up the need to prove yourself right and make others wrong, and you're open to finding a path forward that respect the needs, values and concerns of all involved.

Here conversations: how did we get here?

Where am I (are we)? How did I (we) get here? What's working? What's not working?

Here conversations are descriptive by nature because they describe the current situation or problem as you and others see it. Because people automatically bring their own assumptions, biases and beliefs into a conversation, it's important from the outset to distinguish between the facts of a situation (for example, 'Sales are down 20 per cent') and your opinion about them (for example, 'Marketing has not been doing a good job'). You don't own the truth, just your version of it. Someone else's version may differ dramatically. Keeping this foremost in your mind is vital if you want to avoid getting caught up in 'he said, she said' stone-throwing matches.

To create bigger results you must engage in bigger conversations.

When you express your opinion as 'the truth' you're guaranteed to put others offside and trigger defensiveness. For instance, perhaps you're unhappy about how something is working, but someone else thinks it's absolutely fine. That's okay. They're entitled to their opinion just as you are yours. Stepping into a conversation to address an issue isn't about telling other people they're wrong. Rather, it's about getting an issue on the table so you can share your concerns, find common ground and engage the person you're speaking to in helping find a solution.

In any work environment or relationship, issues will inevitably arise with the potential to cause conflict and tension. The content of those issues is not the problem. It's how you handle them that is. So if you have to discuss a difficult issue, remember that your opinion is just that: *your* opinion. Be open to adjusting it as you listen openly to others (remember, conversation is about 'changing together'). Having a different opinion doesn't mean it's not valid. It just means you need to explain to others why it is you see something the way you do. And that requires speaking up with the intention of improving the situation — being part of the solution rather than the problem. You'll quickly hit a brick wall if others perceive that you're trying to lay blame at their feet, or just complaining for the sake of it, without a clear and actionable plan for improving the situation.

Speaking your mind is not fruitful unless it's done thoughtfully and with a clearly defined rationale for why your view would ultimately be of service to all parties. So be sincere, but don't be righteous. In business as in life, a message that comes from the heart, lands on the heart.

Speaking candidly should be balanced with listening bravely and openly. You have to be willing to step into the other person's shoes, and be open to viewing things in ways that may well conflict with how you see things. This takes courage. You have to listen at a deeper level — from a place of vulnerability and compassion — to get past *what* the other person thinks to *why* they think it. Just as your view feels totally valid to you, so too does their perspective feel totally reasonable, logical and valid to them.

> *Courage is what it takes to stand up and speak;*
> *courage is also what it takes to sit down and listen.*
> **Winston Churchill**

When you genuinely try to put yourself into someone else's shoes and look at the world through their eyes, it means also feeling the fear, anxiety, sadness, resentment or hurt they may be feeling. But when you understand what has led them to think, feel and act as they have, you can impact how they think, feel and act more in the future. You do this by being able to 'speak to their listening' and communicate your thoughts so that they'll interpret them as you want them to. After all, the meaning of conversation is not defined by what's being said, but by what's being heard.

Be mindful that if you're addressing a contentious or very personal issue, emotions are likely to run high. If the issue you're addressing is likely to push emotional buttons, be extra careful to ensure you step into it calmly, with a clear idea of what you want to say. It may be worth rehearsing the conversation ahead of time, writing down the key points you want to convey (in case emotions start to hijack your brain) and how you'll respond constructively to whatever accusations, grievances or upsets may arise. You have to manage your own emotions before you can respond well to someone else's and influence how they think, feel and act. So if you start feeling upset, suggest continuing the conversation later when you've had the chance to collect your thoughts (and emotions). You'll be far more effective in generating the changes you want once you've done so.

The more sensitive an issue, the more rapidly emotions can escalate and hijack the conversation.

Here conversations can trigger emotional responses people aren't expecting. If so, take time to ask questions. Be genuine, be curious and be willing to step into their shoes and view the situation through their eyes. In *The 7 Habits of Highly Effective People,* Stephen Covey writes that we must 'seek first to understand before being understood'. So put your beliefs to the side as you genuinely try to gain a better understanding of not just *what* others think, but *why* they came to think that way.

Often disagreements can be resolved at this level when you discover facts about a situation that you were previously unaware of. At this point in a conversation your aim is to ensure that everyone feels safe in sharing their perspective and not worried about being made to feel foolish because they see things differently. As you and others share, be careful to distinguish the facts of the situation from the various opinions and interpretations of those facts. If there's any disagreement about what the facts are, attempt to clear it up. The more facts you have on the table, the better placed you'll be to come up with a workable plan or solution.

While not every conversation you have will flow smoothly and result in the outcome you want, by stepping into it ready to explore alternative explanations, perspectives and solutions, you set it up to progress in a positive way.

Take criticism on the chin

It's par for the course that sometimes you'll be the recipient of criticism. Even more so if you've been pushing the envelope, challenging the status quo, or saying or doing things that could be threatening to people (and the reality is, some people feel easily threatened!). Human beings are wired to respond defensively to criticism because it threatens the image they have of themselves, so when criticism is directed your way, be mindful that to respond well you'll have to overcome your own sensitivity. You are human, after all.

Rather than reacting from defensiveness, you can choose to respond with curiosity. If you're feeling too upset in the moment to do so, ask if you can meet to discuss the issue later (after you've had time to cool down and collect yourself). Then, when you do have the conversation, embrace a spirit of curiosity as you try to uncover exactly why the other person criticised you or your actions. It may be that they don't see the whole picture or have different expectations. But be open to the possibility that their criticism could actually be fair and reasonable. By demonstrating that you're mature enough to accept the criticism as valid, you build trust. By expressing an earnest desire to work on whatever they've brought to your attention, you're not only showing yourself to be someone who can take a candid critique but someone who has enough confidence in yourself that you don't take it too personally (as personal as it may be!).

Pushing back without being pushy

'Whatever your career, you have to be willing to take risks, to speak up and to push back when you don't agree with what others are thinking.' This was the advice Kathy Calvin, CEO of the United Nations Foundation, gave me as we discussed the importance of courage in any organisation and throughout her career.

Named by *Newsweek* as one of the 150 Women Who Rock the World, Kathy's leadership at the UN Foundation has brought together the largest network of corporate, civic and media partners to support UN initiatives globally. A passionate advocate for multi-sector problem solving, Kathy has been instrumental in ensuring that the $1 billion Ted Turner donated to start the UN Foundation in 1997 has been leveraged to double its impact, taking on the world's biggest challenges in bold and innovative ways. I asked Kathy about the most difficult challenge she faced, she replied, 'The hardest thing I ever have to do is to give people performance feedback that they don't want to hear. Sometimes that has involved letting people go. However, I've learned over the years that it's better to be truthful and honest upfront, than to avoid difficult conversations in the hope that the issue will just go away. People don't always like it when others are upfront and honest, but they come to respect you for being that way'.

People who play safe rarely push back. But when you 'go along to get along' you deprive others of the value your perspective holds. Everyone is worse off. It's important to acknowledge that when you disagree with someone, you trigger a natural tension since the very nature of disagreement implies that one way of seeing something is better, and more correct, than another. It's therefore important to know how to push back without being pushy—to disagree without being disagreeable.

Disagreeing can activate people's defences as you challenge their view of reality. It's therefore important to learn how to disagree in a way that others don't feel is arrogant or righteous, but that respects how they came to see things as they do while offering an alternative perspective. So while no-one likes someone who's overly 'pushy' and forces their opinion down the throats of others, sometimes it's important to challenge the status quo and question consensus thinking lest groupthink prevail. As General Patton once said, 'If everybody is thinking alike, then somebody isn't thinking'.

Push back without being pushy

You can push back on what someone else is saying without being 'pushy' in the traditional sense of the word. What's important is that people understand that you're not pushing them back, but rather their position. Obviously every issue is unique and the way you push back needs to fit the situation. Here are a few key things to consider.

- Come armed with a recommended alternative solution. It's easy to say, 'I disagree,' but it's not so easy to develop, present and sell a different solution. If appropriate, consider enlisting a 'co-conspirator' who is trusted by the person you're pushing back against.

(continued)

Push back without being pushy (*cont'd*)

- Prepare ahead with good examples that support your case. Since most people tend towards risk-averseness, demonstrating what others have done in similar situations may lessen their fear.

- Ground your push-back or disagreement in a business-related reason (a mutual concern). Opinion is important, but if people see that it's a legitimate business reason that's driving your concern or disagreement, then it takes personal judgement and personality out of the equation and keeps the conversation focused on the content.

- If there's something you disagree with say, 'I think I understand what you're trying to say but help me with this aspect: I'm having trouble seeing how to get from here to there'. This moves you from advocating for your opinion to inquiring. By inquiring you're better placed to turn the conversation back to your winning points.

- Instead of saying 'yes, but' say 'yes, and'. The former negates anything that came before it and seems combative. The latter creates an extended conversation that builds on ideas already expressed and invites further conversation to expand perspectives.

- If you're not going to win, be sensitive to when it's time to give up the fight and accept defeat graciously without alienating yourself or damaging trust in your relationships. You're then more likely to earn respect as someone with the courage to speak candidly yet respectfully.

In environments where 'yes men' are plentiful, people who are willing to stick their necks out and question consensus thinking are far more valuable than those who forever go with what's safe in the majority opinion. Good managers and leaders value those who are willing to push back on the consensus opinion and respectfully put forward an opinion that may conflict with the status quo. Of course, if you're challenging the consensus opinion, your boss may not always agree with you. Be okay with that—you may not have all the facts or information about a situation. However, my experience is that they will respect your courage to speak up and will know that in future they can rely on you for a candid, even if not politically correct, opinion. When you fail to push back on something you don't agree with for fear of rocking the boat, you do everyone a disservice.

> *You don't get paid for the hour. You get paid for the value you bring to the hour.*
> **Jim Rohn**

To conversations: where to from here?

To conversations are 'conversations for possibilities'. They tap into the power of creativity, unleashing imagination, innovation and ingenuity. It may well sound like a grand claim, but conversations about what is possible hold magic within them and, if given free reign, plant the seeds for new realities to emerge.

Consider the magic word itself: 'abracadabra'. Abracadabra was the incantation used to remind the Kabbalists—those who believe in a form of Jewish mysticism—of the power of their speech. *Bra*—meaning 'to create'—comes from the ancient language of Aramaic; *ca* translates to 'as'; and *dabra* is the first-person for the verb *daber*, 'to speak'. In other words, 'abracadabra' literally means 'I create as I speak'. See—magic!

If anything was possible, where would you love to get to? If you could wave a magic wand, what would you wish for? What is your ideal outcome?

To conversations are about creating a new vision for the future. In the context of relationships within your team and organisation, 'conversations for possibilities' are about creating a shared vision with outcomes that reflect the concerns and aspirations you share. They involve brainstorming new possibilities for action and new solutions to the challenges you collectively face.

If you have a clear idea about what you would like to see happen or change, or a solution to a problem, make sure you can articulate it clearly. Plan the key points you want to make and be sure whatever changes you think should be made are logical and have a clear benefit. If you're presenting to an executive, remember that you need to be able to present what you want to say succinctly, confidently, professionally and powerfully. They want to know what value you have to bring to their problems and opportunities. With many demands on their time, they don't want to wait all day for you to get to the point. Studies have found that executives turn off and tune out those who can't quickly bring value to the table. So plan ahead and practise what you want to say in the confident way you want to say it.

If, on the other hand, you're not quite sure of what you think needs to happen, be open about it and enlist help in exploring possible solutions and steps forward. Sometimes there is no clear answer or path forward, in which case you need to take time to speculate about what may be possible.

When all the possibilities are put on the table, and everyone is committed to finding a solution, the forces of creativity can be unleashed and the results can be powerful. Whether it's finding a way for someone to cut back their working hours while still contributing to a team's outcome, or working out how best to respond to a new threat or opportunity, when all the cards are on the table, and no possibility is out of reach, the solutions that can be uncovered can seem truly miraculous!

How conversations: how do we get from here to there?

How conversations focus on the actions needed to create the desired changes identified through *here* and *to* conversations and get you (and your team or organisation) from where you are now to where you'd like to be. They set out a plan of action, with specific action items and a system of accountability and clear measures of success; that is, 'Who needs to do what?', 'By when?', 'How will we know when it's done?' In short, *how* conversations work out how to close the gap from 'current point A' to 'ideal point B'.

Ask for what you want (and don't take 'no' personally)

To help you become more courageous in each of the types of conversations and more effective in how you have them, I want to introduce you to the concept of The Promise Cycle (see figure 4.3). This can help you see where the various linguistic acts fit together in the big picture of the many commitments and responsibilities you have in your life. The Promise Cycle stems from the work of Fernando Flores and Rafael Echeverria in linguistics. It was later disseminated more widely via various thought leaders (including Julio Olalla of Newfield Coaching) in the field of ontology.

Figure 4.3: The Promise Cycle

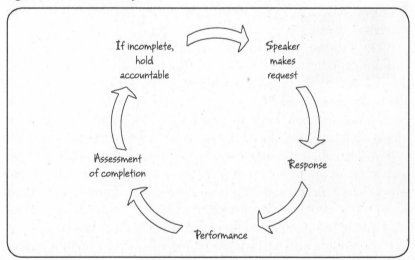

Life tends to pay you only as much as you're willing to ask. The reality is that in your career you will rarely, if ever, be given more than you have the courage to ask for. Too often, though, we temper our requests in order to minimise the possibility of being turned down.

It's important to consider the wider context when making a request. Is this a reasonable request? Is there anything I need to do first to lay the groundwork for this request? If you want a promotion, for instance, it's important to have demonstrated that you're someone who deserves a promotion. So your first courageous request may be to ask for feedback and suggestions on what you need to demonstrate to show that you're someone who could take on a more senior role.

Failing to make requests of people to take new or different actions when you know those actions will ultimately benefit you and them does everyone a disservice. It's playing safe and thinking small. So if you want to play a bigger game, you're going to have to get used to making bigger, better and bolder requests of those around you. As well as people may know you, it's both unreasonable and unrealistic to think they will know what it is that you *really* want. Of course, while you may not always get all that you ask for (whether it be a pay rise or the corner office) at least you have more of a chance of getting something than you otherwise would.

The Promise Cycle can be a useful tool for helping you work out not only how to go about making requests and getting those around you to do what you'd like, but also for how you manage the commitments (aka promises) you make to others. If you think of any organisation, large or small, like an elaborate network of clogs, each enabling the other to move, or impeding movement if one stops, then the effectiveness of any group depends on how well each of its members engage in The Promise Cycle. When one person fails to keep their commitments, and mismanages their time, it has a roll-on effect undermining the entire organisation's performance and ability to meet stakeholder expectations.

You enter into The Promise Cycle whenever someone makes a request of you or issues you an offer or invitation. For the sake of keeping it simple, let's say it's you who wants someone else to do something. For your request to hold water you have to be clear in letting them know exactly what you want and when you want it. That is, you need to have clearly understood the 'conditions of satisfaction' attached to your request. Asking someone to do something for you 'soon' or 'when they get the chance' is a sure-fire recipe for unmet expectation and frustration. For example, if you'd like to be considered for a promotion at work to a role with greater responsibility, not only do you need to ask for it, but you also need to be sure that the person you're asking knows exactly what you want and the timeline you're thinking about. So you could phrase your request, 'I'd like to be considered for a more senior supervisory role. I'm hoping this can happen within the next nine to 12 months. Is that possible?'

Okay, so maybe it is possible, and maybe it isn't. But you won't know unless you ask. And if your request is declined at least you now know where you stand and can make plans accordingly. Isn't that better than to be left wondering? Whatever you do, don't make a 'no' mean more than it does. If they said no, get over it. Don't take it as a personal affront. Whether you agree with them or not, they have their reasons. Who knows, down the track, their thinking may change. By responding well, you leave the door open to ask again in the future.

Self-promotion is not conceited, it's crucial

The old saying, 'It's not what you know, but who you know' simply isn't true. It's not *what* you know, and it's not *who* you know; it's who knows what you know (which includes what you can do and what you want to do!).

Many people struggle with the idea that they should have to 'toot their own horn' in order to be recognised and rewarded for the value they contribute. After all, surely if you work hard, do a good job and continually deliver solid results, you'll be rewarded for it, right? But just because you believe your boss should be thinking about you—noticing the long hours you put in and the stellar work you do—doesn't mean they will. Likewise, just because you think a co-worker, supervisor or even your beloved life-long partner should know what you want, it doesn't mean they will. People are not mind-readers. Not your boss. Not your best friend. Not anyone. Assuming other people know what you want, need or aspire to achieve in your career can set you up for resentment and frustration. It also reduces the likelihood that you'll get it. The reality is that most people are too caught up with what they're doing, and what they want, to focus much on you. It's not personal; it's just human nature.

(*continued*)

Self-promotion is not conceited, it's crucial (*cont'd*)

Of course, no-one enjoys the company of someone who is forever blowing their own horn, hungry for accolades or demanding recognition. But by refusing to advocate for yourself—to toot your own horn—when the right opportunity or need arises, you can do yourself a big disservice, depriving yourself of the support of people who are well positioned to help you. Indeed, numerous studies have found that self-promotion is an indispensible key to getting ahead in an organisation.

Often our reticence to let others know our value is based on a misguided belief that they should simply be aware of it already. Other times it's simply because we're afraid of coming across as too full of ourselves and loathe the idea that someone will think we're self-important with an over-inflated sense of our own worth. But letting others know the value you've added, and the value you'd like to add going forward, isn't about trying to impress people for the sake of stroking your ego. It's about making sure people who need to know what you've done (and what you can do) are aware of it. After all, the more people who know what it is you want, the more who can help you achieve it.

Does that mean occasionally risking rubbing people the wrong way? Perhaps. But the bigger risk is missing out on opportunities simply because you sat back passively and waited for the opportunity or promotion you wanted to be placed at your feet.

Letting others know the value you can—and want—to bring isn't a boastful or conceited action. Rather, it's a bold and courageous action that will enable you to honour your potential more fully and amplify your ability to make the difference you want. So get over yourself. Toot, toot.

Saying 'yes' is easier than saying 'no'. It's easier because most of the time, it's what people want to hear. But when you say 'yes' for the wrong reasons—to keep people happy and to avoid causing offence or the momentary discomfort of disappointing someone—you can quickly wind up overcommitted, overwhelmed and unable to meet the expectations you've created for yourself. In other words, don't say 'yes' to something if you don't have the time and resources available to do it. Saying 'yes' may give you an immediate hit of 'people pleasing gratification', but the damage to trust when you fail to honour your commitment always outweighs any temporary gratification.

Throughout your life you will continually need to say 'no' to the good to make room for the great. It will always take courage.

If you're not sure whether you have the capacity to take on a commitment, you can always respond with a 'counter offer' of what you're willing and able to do. Or offer to give an answer later, giving yourself time to assess whether you can realistically take on this commitment and still honour the other priorities and responsibilities in your life.

How well you engage in The Promise Cycle directly impacts on the trust people place in you as a reliable person who can be counted on to get things done well and on time (as discussed in chapter 2). Making promises you can't keep sets expectations you won't fulfil and damages your reputation in ways you may never be able to repair. People who manage their commitments with integrity don't commit to things they can't do. They fulfil their commitments as agreed and when something comes up that prevents them from fulfilling a commitment, they let the person they made it to know as soon as possible and then negotiate from there.

Often people enter into commitments (aka promises) without first being really clear about what they're committing to. While it's the role of the person making a request to be clear in what they're asking, sometimes they're not. So if you're on the receiving end of a request and you're not sure exactly what's being asked of you, make sure you clear up any ambiguity — you'll be doing yourself a huge favour!

Clarify your commitments

Jon, a management consultant, had been given the task of implementing a software project for his company. His manager, Sol, had tasked him with the role and he'd enthusiastically taken on the project, despite never having worked with the software program before. While Sol hadn't taken a lot of time to explain exactly what he was expecting, Jon felt empowered to execute the role in a way he saw fit.

Jon worked seven days a week for three months to ensure that the task was done by the deadline he'd been given. When D-day arrived there were numerous hitches with the program and the way it was interfacing with the mainframe back at headquarters.

Sol sent me an email asking if we could speak. When I got on the phone to him he was clearly very frustrated with Jon. He listed several things he'd expected Jon to have taken care of that had been completely overlooked and said he was now questioning Jon's competence. When I asked Sol if he felt he had explained the project clearly enough, he replied that if Jon had had any questions he should simply have asked. As Jon never had asked any questions, Sol assumed he knew what needed to be done.

When I spoke to Jon he was equally exasperated after having received an earful from Sol about the project's issues. I asked him how clear Sol had been about what needed to be done and he said, 'Not very. But Sol obviously felt I needed to figure it out myself so that's what I did. I got the clear sense from him that he was too busy with bigger things to go into what he wanted in more detail so I didn't want to bother him. I assumed he just wanted me to figure it out for myself'.

And therein lay the problem. Sol assumed Jon would ask if he needed any clarification. Jon assumed Sol didn't want to be bothered with explaining details and that he trusted Jon's judgement to figure them out himself. While Jon's career managed to survive this incident, many careers have been derailed from unmet expectations built upon false assumptions.

Even if you don't think you should have to ask for clarification, or feel you may be judged harshly for doing so, you need to take ownership of the commitment you've entered into so you're clear about what others are expecting of you.

Hold people accountable

Perhaps you've been in a situation where someone didn't do what they said they would, or didn't do it properly or soon enough (failing to fulfil one or both 'conditions of satisfaction') and you wound up doing it yourself. Of course, when faced with a pressing deadline, sometimes you have little choice but to do it yourself. But time and time again I've heard people complain about continually having to re-do or improve on someone else's work because it wasn't done to their satisfaction. When I ask them if they've addressed the issue with the person concerned, they usually reply no. Sometimes they share that they didn't see any point in raising the issue. Most of the time they simply didn't want to go through the discomfort that such a conversation would entail. It was easier and less of a hassle to just do it themselves. But on nearly every occasion people's reasons for not holding someone accountable boiled down to fear of causing upset, ruffling feathers or getting into an awkward conversation. It was just easier to ignore it. Easier, yes — courageous, no.

Keep your word and hold others accountable to theirs. When you let people get away with behaviour that lacks integrity, it undermines your own. Everyone is worse off.

It's a general rule of thumb in life that you get what you tolerate. If you tolerate behaviour from people that's unsatisfactory in some way, you become complicit in your own misery. You teach people how to treat you, and teaching people that you're someone who expects commitments and responsibilities to be honoured will make a huge impact on your ability to achieve to the level you're capable of—and get those around you to do the same.

If you're going to enter into a conversation to address an issue of accountability, the following steps will help you achieve the best outcome, both for you and for the other person.

- *Restate the commitment.* What did you expect them to do? What did they agree to? It may be that there was a misunderstanding about what the commitment was. If so, then re-clarify what it is so expectations are clear going forward.

- *Share the impact.* Share with them the impact their failure to fulfil the commitment properly had on you. Perhaps you had to work late to get it done yourself. Perhaps you had to go into a meeting without the information you needed. Perhaps you had to get someone else to do it, which wasn't fair on them. Perhaps it simply undermined your ability to trust them in the future.

- *Restate your expectations around commitments.* Share that you take your commitments very seriously and want to rely on others to keep their word.

- *Renegotiate.* Assuming that this wasn't a one-off commitment, be sure you're both on the same page about what has to be done and when in future.

Power up your language

Before Helen Keller discovered language, she said that her world was empty. She didn't say it was boring, lonely or dull. She said it was a void. Nothing. Her observation echoes the truth that it is through language that we bring our reality into being.

Hopefully I have successfully established with you my case that your conversations are powerful. But the specific words you use, and how you use them, is no less important. Psychological research has found that your subconscious interprets what it hears very literally. That is, it interprets the words that come out of your mouth as being the truth, regardless of how closely they resemble the actual truth. This in turn affects how you react to your circumstances, how you react and engage with others and how you feel about yourself.

It also impacts on how others respond to you: whether they perceive you as a 'powerful person' who can be counted on to steer change, get the job done and take challenges in your stride, or someone who needs constant reinforcement, guidance and support. Needless to say, the people who stand out and get ahead in any field of endeavour aren't those perceived as needing extra support, but those perceived as power brokers in their own right, change catalysts and solid bets for handling difficult situations in effective ways.

It may sound clichéd, but the world mirrors you back to yourself. If you use positive language about yourself and your ability to accomplish what you want, then that's what tends to show up for you externally. Likewise, if you often make negative declarations about yourself or see a situation as being hopeless or terrible, then that is the disempowering reality you will live.

I often hear people talking about themselves in ways that limit what they can do and who they can be. Whether it's in how you describe your job, career prospects, boss, 'management', industry, colleagues, clients or any aspect of your job, when you use language in a powerless way, it leaves you disempowered. It can't do anything else. This isn't just relevant to your success at work. It applies to every aspect of your life—from relationships and parenting, to managing your finances and exercising. You name it; for better or worse, your words create your reality.

Likewise, the labels you put on yourself can also limit what you do. If you're always telling yourself and others that you're 'disorganised', 'a technology dinosaur' or even a 'terrible negotiator' then you're setting yourself up to be exactly that. Neuroscience has proven that shifting the language you use to being more positive improves your health at a cellular level. It also has a profound impact on your ability to take the actions needed to achieve the goals that inspire you (or to adopt goals in the first place), and to respond to the many challenges you'll face throughout life. Over time, it will also shift how others perceive you, treat you and value you.

That said, as you think more about the words you use, don't forget that how you say them matters too. As Professor Amy Cuddy—who I mentioned in chapter 2 for her work on 'power poses'—said, 'People often are more influenced by how they feel about you than by what you're saying'. In the end, while the content of your message is important, your ability to communicate it powerfully matters far more. What you have to say is important. Don't let your non-verbal way of being undermine your message.

Speak powerfully, not passively

Successful people don't speak in timid, powerless or pathetic ways. Their language is positive and powerful. Language and words that are qualifying, passive and imprecise lack power and limit action. You can 'power up' how you communicate by using more power-filled language that is positive, specific and declarative. Here are examples of things we say that lack power, and the more powerful alternatives. The first phrase limits your power and what's possible; the second phrase puts you firmly in command.

I think I can do that	⟶	I can do that
I should do that	⟶	I could do that if I wanted to
I'm hopeless at	⟶	I'm learning how to
I will try	⟶	I will do
I'm nervous	⟶	I'm excited
I hope I can	⟶	I'm confident I will *or* I know I will
It's really hard	⟶	It's a great challenge
Might you be able to do this for me?	⟶	Can you do this for me?
I'm no good at...	⟶	I haven't yet learned how to

If you're not sure how powerfully you use language, then observe your language over the next 24 hours and note where you're using disempowering language. Better and braver still, ask a family member, friend or even a co-worker to monitor you. They may well catch you saying things that you can't hear yourself. When you become aware that you've used power-taking language, write down what you said. At the end of the 24 hours ask yourself:

- Where am I most critical, pessimistic, complaining or negative?

- What do I say about myself to others that leaves little or no possibility for me to be any other way?

- From what other perspectives could I look at this person or circumstances?

- How could I describe this situation in a more empowering and positive way?

Paying attention to your language and the words you use will provide an insight into the power of your subconscious and as you begin to shift your language, it will not only be an indicator of how powerful you feel, but it will become a source of power.

Ladies: own your power!

Research has found that when more women sit at decision-making tables, the better the decisions that are made and the more profitable organisations become. This isn't just good for women, it's good for everyone. However, for women to make the full contribution they're capable of making they need to own the difference their decision makes, not continually second-guess themselves and undervalue their experience and ability.

In her book *The Language of Female Leadership*, Dr Judith Baxter writes about her study of how language is used in senior executive and boardroom meetings, to understand power patterns. The study focused on the differences between how women and men use language. It identified a specific type of 'out-of-power' language that women were more prone to use. This involved 'double-voice discourse', which is used by leaders of both genders, but more frequently by women leaders.

Double-voice discourse occurs when the speaker prejudges the audience's response (to be a negative one) and qualifies their initial statement accordingly. For instance, 'Correct me if I'm wrong...' or 'I know I'm not the ultimate expert on this...' In her study, which included a four-million-word sample, Dr Baxter found that women were four times more likely to use double-voice discourse than their male counterparts. Certainly, in my own experience I've noticed that women are far more likely to apologise if their opinion happens to contradict or conflict with someone else's. While many women are naturally compassionate and sensitive of other people's feelings, they do themselves a disservice when they apologise for sharing an opinion that may ruffle feathers or contradict one that someone else has already put forward.

When I asked Debbie Kissire, one of Ernst & Young's most senior women, what she felt was important for women to do to achieve greater success, she replied, 'Women mustn't allow themselves to be intimidated'. Don't undermine yourself by prefacing anything you say that may cause upset, or by apologising when your opinion differs from that of others. While changing your language may not increase your power to four times its current level, it certainly does highlight that how you speak can undermine it. Sure, unconscious bias and overt sexism can work against women in the workforce, but the way women express themselves can undermine how they're perceived in terms of their ability to effect change and influence outcomes.

As someone whose boldness and determination led to her becoming one of Australia's most influential woman, Ita Buttrose believes more women need to stop questioning whether they have what it takes to succeed in a demanding career while juggling the often conflicting demands of raising children. 'Too often women think they can't do it; that it's too hard. But they can. They just have to decide what to let go of, what's really important, and just as importantly, what's not!'

It's not about being more like men, but leveraging what makes women different. Women have a naturally collaborative style, strong at building bridges and fostering engagement. This should be leveraged but it needs to be balanced with speaking up assertively when the need arises, pushing back more courageously and refusing to buy into any doubts they may have about achieving as much success as any man can. There's no better place to start that than by working on the way you engage in conversation on a daily basis and ditching self-defeating habits of speech that undermine your influence before you even share what you have to say! In short, as more women stop playing safe and start owning their power, more organisations will benefit from the unique value, perspective and leadership style that women bring to the table. Organisations, communities and society at large will be better for it.

You teach people how to treat you

Lori Garver, deputy director of NASA, is a woman who has refused to be intimidated by preconceived gender or age stereotypes, who doesn't mince words and who shows what women who own their power and refuse to play safe can do. Lori grew up in rural Michigan but after graduating with a political science degree she headed straight to Washington D.C. She wasn't sure what she would do with her degree but liked the idea of the careers it might lead into. All she knew for sure was that she wanted to pursue a career in public service. 'I felt strongly that I wanted to make a difference,' she shared. She had never stepped foot in Washington DC until the week after she graduated from college and turned up with no more than the phone number of someone she thought might be able to help her get a job, or even just a lead for a job.

She started by working on the short-lived presidential campaign of astronaut John Glenn. While working on that campaign she not only met her husband but also met the man who later gave her the opportunity to work at the National Space Institute. She came in as a receptionist-cum-secretary. Not one for inefficiency, she promptly set about systemising the administration work she had to do, which left her with extra time to initiate new programs and initiatives. She also went back to study at night to get her masters in Science Technology and Public Policy. Her initiative and 'can do' attitude caught the attention of the board and, at age 27, after working at NSI for five years, she was asked to apply for the position of executive director. The man she'd been working under, who was in his 40s and with whom she'd shared an office, was actually in line for the role, but she was encouraged to go ahead and apply all the same. She got the job.

The morning she started in her new role as executive director her previous supervisor left a note on her chair in their office saying that he would never work under her and expected equal pay. She asked him to come into her office and proceeded to fire him. He had been insubordinate and she felt it was the only option if she was to perform well in her new job. He was stunned, as he never expected a 27-year-old 'girl' would fire him—particularly not on

(continued)

You teach people
how to treat you (*cont'd*)

her first day on the job. Lori didn't do it to send a message but it certainly let people know that she would not be a pushover. She was aware that we teach people how to treat us and was not willing to tolerate being treated with anything but the respect she deserved. It's a principle that has served her well.

In the male-dominated field of aerospace, Lori has been a trailblazer in her own right, combining motherhood and career as she paved new ground for other women in her field to eventually become the president of Women in Aerospace. Her willingness to stand her ground, challenge the status quo and trust in her ability ultimately led to her appointment by President Barack Obama as deputy director of NASA, where she continues to push new boundaries, on Earth and in the galaxy far beyond!

Whatever your position, profession or personality type, it's inevitable that people will sometimes do and say things that undermine, frustrate or upset you. There will often be occasions you will not see eye-to-eye with those around you. Sometimes tensions will arise. Other times you will need to say things that may not be welcomed by others. While these scenarios all differ, the common thread that binds them is the need for courageous conversation—for you to to speak up and express how you think or feel about an issue, to set a boundary, make a request or challenge the perspective of others. As you weigh up the possible risks of doing so, always keep in mind what's at stake if you stay silent or tiptoe around the issue.

Your ability to speak up about issues that weigh you down is crucial to your success at work and in life. Don't choose the path of safety and give up the possibility of addressing issues that injure relationships, chip away self-confidence, encumber opportunity and fail to serve you and everyone else. Your conversations are powerful. You build influence and 'make your luck' one conversation at a time. So speak candidly and listen bravely—doing so will enable you to create the relationships, influence and outcomes you want in every area of your life.

Key points

> Never underestimate the power of a courageous conversation to change the trajectory of your relationships, career or life.

> Issues that aren't talked out are acted out. Failing to speak up, say what you think and ask for what you want can be very costly to your relationships and career.

> Communication is not defined by what's said but by what's heard. Be mindful of how others will interpret what you have to say.

> The more emotional or sensitive an issue, the greater the need for you to set your intention ahead of time, prepare in advance what you want to say and be sure not to let other people's emotions hijack your own.

> You don't see things as they are, but as you are. The stories you bring to your conversations can derail them from the outset. Be careful to distinguish what you think about a problem or person from the actual facts.

> The Here-to-How (H2H) Process helps keep conversations focused on resolving issues and producing stronger results.

> Don't let the words you use undermine your influence and the message you want to convey. Use positive and powerful language.

> Women must be extra careful not to use language in ways that undermine their ability to influence change.

> If you aren't feeling as confident, assertive and self-assured as you'd like to be, act as if you are. Your way of being speaks more loudly than your words.

> Committing to learning how to speak candidly and listen bravely will enable you to build more rewarding, trust-filled relationships, expand your influence and generate better outcomes.

Chapter 5

Learn, unlearn and relearn

It is not the strongest of the species that survives, nor the most intelligent. It is the one that is the most adaptable to change.
Charles Darwin

In 1993 about 1600 people belonged to the International Flat Earth Research Society of America. I kid you not.

Their president, Charles K. Johnson, stated publicly that he had been a proud 'Flat Earther' all his life: 'When I saw the globe in grade school I didn't accept it then and I don't accept it now'.

Needless to say, there are people you might call 'late adapters'!

Of course, when it comes to adapting to changes in the world around us, whether they be changes in the prevailing beliefs or changes in the actual environment in which we live, learning how to adapt to change can be difficult. For some, such as Charles K. Johnson, who died in 2001 still adamant that the moon landings had been staged, it can be more difficult than others.

While it's easy to mock someone who maintains the world is flat hundreds of years after it's been proven otherwise, there are many respected people who have made similar statements that, with hindsight, now seem equally short-sighted. For example, this comment made by Darryl F. Zanuck, head of 20th Century Fox, in 1946: 'Television won't be able to hold onto any market it captures after the first six months. People will soon get tired of staring at a plywood box every night.'

Change before you have to

To succeed in today's world, it's vital for you to remain open-minded about what's changing around you and how those changes, including the almost imperceptible ones, will reshape the world we live in five or 25 years from now. Don't walk into the future blindfolded. The more attention you pay to what's changing around you today, the better you'll adapt to the challenges of tomorrow, find opportunities within them and capitalise on them.

My kids can't comprehend how I ever organised a social life back in the ancient pre-Facebook era. Their digital brains boggle even further trying to imagine how anyone ever did their job without computers, email or mobile phones.

'We used to send smoke signals,' I chide them.

In their world, as they sit on the couch with their iPads skyping their friends on the far side of the globe, that may as well have been how we communicated. What they don't realise is that by the time they become parents, their children will think the technology they use today is as antiquated as the pagers so many relied on to do their job just 20 years ago.

Adult education experts estimate that up to 40 per cent of what tertiary students are learning will be obsolete a decade from now when they will be working in jobs that have yet to be created. Indeed, the top 10 most in-demand jobs today didn't even exist 10 years ago. To say that we live in a changing world understates its pace and its vast scope.

Of course it's not just technology that's changing the world. Profound changes in demography and longevity have experts predicting that by 2020 there will be more people aged over 65 than under 15 in the world's developed countries. Add to this the social changes in family structure, the globalisation of talent and continued innovation in technology, and it's hard to imagine just what the world and its increasingly mobile workforce will look like 20 years from now. You can't do either by playing safe and avoiding change. As *New York Times* columnist Thomas Friedman wrote, 'Standing still is deadly'.

Yes, the world is changing fast, and there is no sign of it slowing anytime soon. For the three-plus billion people in the workforce it's not just about keeping up with the rate of change and the nature of the work we do, but how we do it and where.

When anyone can work from anywhere, it changes the nature of work everywhere. Traditional boundaries disappearing and the global talent pool becoming more skilled and mobile presents challenges for people in developed countries to adapt faster in order to simply stay competitive. There's no two ways about it: your ability to adapt to change and proactively make changes in your career is what will make a crucial difference to where you find yourself even just five years from now.

Catalysts for career change

There are many reasons why people choose to change their jobs and careers. Being able to predict the changes you'll make one or five years from now can help you prepare for them. Look at these key reasons for considering a job or career change and think about how relevant they are to you, or how they may become more relevant in the future.

- *Life changes.* Your life has changed and the career you started out on isn't compatible with your life today. This is something I've seen happen to people whose jobs require a lot of travel, or who are on call 24/7 or working family-unfriendly shifts. They usually end up in careers that offer greater flexibility, enabling them to honour the commitments and values in other areas of their life outside the workplace.

- *Maturing preferences.* We're often expected to make career choices in our late teens and early 20s, even though it's often not until we reach our 30s that our preferences really solidify. By then many people feel so invested in a particular career path that changing it seems too costly. But it's important to be honest with yourself about the cost of not changing too, and why. While you once loved going to work and enjoyed the challenges and responsibilities of your job, you no longer do. Perhaps your work no longer challenges you as it once did, taking the reward out of it. Or perhaps it simply doesn't interest or energise you any more. As we age and evolve so too do our preferences.

- *Money.* It's no surprise that money is usually not the reason why people change careers. However, sometimes low-paying work can be the catalyst for people to make a career change, particularly as they have children and financial pressures mount. If you chose a career that's traditionally low paying to begin with, it's likely because you felt it would be rewarding. So be careful when making a decision to change career for money alone. Working in a high paying job that isn't fulfilling is not a recipe for success at work or in life. Hopefully the career you change to will be one that leverages your unique talents and expertise and is meaningful to you beyond improving your bank balance.

- *Stress.* Some jobs are naturally more stressful than others. While the pressure of some roles can be exciting and adrenaline-pumping in the beginning, after a time the stress can take a toll and people can suffer an adrenaline burnout. To preserve mental and physical health it can be worth looking for a less stressful job or career.

- *Market/industry changes.* The outlook in your field was optimistic when you started out, but due to changes in technology, the economy or the industry, job and advancement opportunities are shrinking. You want to work in a field or industry that provides greater opportunities for growth, development and experience in a variety of interesting yet challenging roles.

Whatever reasons drive your decision to make a change, it doesn't change the fact that change—even change for the better—can be difficult. While my first 18 years of life involved relatively little change, ever since then it's been constant. Some of it I've eagerly pursued, albeit with moments of nervous apprehension. Some of it I've tripped through, awkwardly yet openly. And some of it I've really struggled with, often overwhelmed and sometimes resentful. All of it I've grown from. Whether spending a year backpacking around the world with no more than a few nights in the same bed, having four children in five years across three countries in seven homes, or starting down a new and unknown career path in the middle of all those moves and babies, change is something I've become intimately acquainted with. Needless to say, when it comes to adapting—to learning, unlearning and relearning—I've learned plenty by trial and error. As my husband and I support each other in pursuing our respective callings, and our children venture out into the world to explore and pursue theirs, I'm confident plenty more learning awaits.

You cannot become who you aspire to be by staying who you are.

We all want certainty and predictability, because our brains look for patterns. However, because life is the way it is, it can never stay the way it is. Whether in the form of a change of plans or a change of heart, change can be very unsettling and uncomfortable. Just because you've chosen to leave a job, relocate for a new job, taken on a bigger role or transitioned into an entirely new career, doesn't mean it will, by default, be easy. If change were easy, everyone would be doing it.

But here's the deal: you can't become who you want to become by staying who you are. Which is what this chapter is about: helping you become more comfortable with the inherent discomfort of change so you can find hidden opportunities in the changes that are out of your control, and be more proactive in initiating the changes that you can control.

The more adept you are at initiating, navigating and managing change, the more successful you'll be in your job today and in the future. As social psychologist Daniel Spurk found in his research on adaptability in the workplace, employees who are more adaptable are far more likely to leapfrog over those who aren't. The cost of rigidity and resistance grows steeper by the day. Sociologist Benjamin Barber wrote, 'I don't divide the world into the weak and the strong, or the successes and the failures...I divide the world into the learners and non-learners'.

Why we resist change

How often have you heard people make reference to 'the good old days?' It's generally not because life was any better 10 or 30 years ago than it is now but it reflects the affection most of us have for the past, and our innate aversion to what's new, untested, unfamiliar and unpredictable. When casting your mind back to days gone by, your selective recall filters out the anxiety and stress you felt in 'the good old days' and focuses instead on the happier memories, the irony being that you will one day look back on today as 'the good old days'. Why wait?

As difficult as change can sometimes be, we don't always fear it. Most people I know enjoy variety. Many actively seek it. Even the most timid, change-averse people enjoy some semblance of it. We wear different clothes every day. Even men who wear dark suits and white shirts to work each day still change their tie just to mix things up a bit. I've been known to rearrange the furniture in my living room for no other reason than I grew tired of its configuration. After all, 'change is as good as holiday', and often far cheaper. Likewise, there are many people who never go to the same holiday destination twice because they want to explore new places and experience different cultures and climates: mountains one year; beaches the next.

> *Bold action in the face of uncertainty is not only terrifying,*
> *but necessary in the pursuit of great work.*
> **Jonathan Fields**

The reason why so many people enjoy variety in their personal lives yet struggle with change in the workplace largely boils down to control. We like to feel that we have some control over our circumstances and yet in our jobs we often feel anything but. It's our lack of control over the variables, and our uncertainty about what lies ahead, that can overwhelm us and trigger fear and anxiety. We like to make plans based on a future we can predict. When the terrain grows unfamiliar, undermining our ability to plan and predict, it gives rise to stress, chips away at our confidence and fuels our fear. Intellectualising why any change is good is not sufficient to arrest our fear. Emotions will trump logic every time. Unless you confront them, they will continue to fuel any residual resistance and rigidity. So as you read through the four main fears—fear of the unknown, failure, success and loss—consider which ones are at play as you look towards making the changes needed to create the career you truly want, and get off the default path that's taking you somewhere you don't want to be.

Fear of the unknown

'Better the devil you know than the devil you don't.' It's a common adage I've heard people say when considering changing something about their lives they're unhappy with, the logic being that it is better to stick with the status quo—however miserable it happens to be—than to risk it for something that may be worse. The unknown makes us feel vulnerable because, quite simply, we don't know what it holds. We're not sure what threats it may have in store nor how it will shake up our safe, secure and familiar world. It's why people hold firm to beliefs long after they've been proven wrong. It's why people stay in marriages long after they've grown devoid of any joy or intimacy. It's why people stay in jobs they hate:

- *What if* my job is outsourced?

- *What if* I'm not employable elsewhere?

- *What if* my company restructures and there isn't a role for me in the new organisation?

- *What if* the market keeps shrinking and we lose market share? What then?

'What if?' indeed! This question quickly follows any time we contemplate making a change—from our hairstyle to our address. But when it comes to changing careers, our fear of the 'What if?' increases exponentially. It's what stops so many people from moving from a job they find miserable and starting over in a new field, no matter how right it may be. Fear can be paralysing. Learning how to sit with ambiguity and accept the discomfort of uncertainty takes practice. What's important when you're looking at making a job or career change is to acknowledge your fears as valid and normal, but not to let them run the show.

In reality, when it comes to making a big change you should expect a file drawer bulging with fears listed under most categories. Sometimes we're afraid of making career changes even when we know it's time for a change. It should be exciting to do something you've always wanted to do or you're passionate about but even if the changes we seek are ones we want, we still feel anxious because, in the end, change holds uncertainty and involves loss in some way.

Fear of failure

Fear of failure (and losing face) is one of the most fundamental fears we face in life. It keeps us in our comfort zone, where it's a pretty sure bet we won't mess up or fall short. Adapting to change requires being willing to let go of your hold on guaranteed success and trying something you may never have done before. It means stepping out of your comfort zone and into the possibility that you may not have what it takes, that you may make a mistake, or worse, that you may fall flat on your face in front of the people you most want to impress. As Seth Godin wrote in his book *Tribes*, often fear of failure isn't actually a fear of failure at all, but rather a fear of criticism or looking foolish and losing face in front of those whose approval and admiration we value. That is, we're more afraid of being judged for our failure than of the failure itself.

Allowing what other people may think, or say—or what you *think* they may think or say—to run your life is a powerless way to live. In other words, letting your fear of criticism keep you from proactively making changes that you believe would be in your best interest is essentially handing over the reins for running your life to other people.

Fear of success

The concept of being afraid of success will seem like an anathema to some people, and odd to most. I recall the first time I read about 'fear of success': I thought it was a typo. I mean, who could be afraid of succeeding? However, over the years I've realised that fear of success isn't really that we're afraid of success, but that we're afraid of how that success will impact our life.

We have assumptions (often wrong) about what successful people are like. We fear that we may become like them: materialistic, workaholic, egotistical, shallow and lonely. We fear our ability to maintain the routines we enjoy. We fear the pressures and expectations of success. That people will want something different, or more from us than what we're able to deliver. That we won't be able to live up to their expectations. That we'll be uncovered as a fraud. We fear that we'll feel stressed all the time with the extra demands and responsibilities we'll have to manage, and that we may crumble under their weight. So, in a sense, fear of success is really fear of failure in disguise. Just as it's much more painful to fall from the roof off your house than to trip from your front doorstep, so too we fear that a fall from the lofty heights of success will be socially humiliating and professionally embarrassing.

Fear of loss

As noted in chapter 2, research has proven that human beings are biologically wired to overestimate potential loss and potential gain, and underestimate their ability to handle the consequences if things don't work out. That is, for most people the fear of losing $100 is more intense than the hope of gaining $150. The observation that losses loom larger than gains tends to run true: we're naturally averse to loss, and all change involves loss in some way.

In reality, we can't adapt to new situations without being willing to give up something of our current way of doing and being. Sometimes change means we lose colleagues, our salary or even our parking space. Sometimes change means losing our sense of place in a team, group or organisation. Less evident but equally devastating can be the loss of known routines or the things that define who we are (such as a job title or a position). But instead of asking yourself, 'What will I lose?', ask 'What can I gain?' Where we put our focus is the major difference between those who change well and those who don't. Those who embrace change discover opportunities within it that those who are busy resisting it and whining about it miss out on.

Most people who have made a significant change in their career say their only regret is that they didn't make it sooner. Many have shared with me that they held off making a change until they were either so miserable, or their job had become so untenable, that they could no longer bear it. Or they felt they had to have all their ducks in a row before taking the plunge. Or both.

What fears fuel your resistance to change?

Write down any fears you think of as you answer the questions below. Consider how they may have limited your success and fulfilment up to now and how, by overcoming them, you can make changes to enjoy greater success and fulfilment in the future.

- *Fear of the unknown.* What is it I'm afraid might happen in the future?

- *Fear of failure.* What is it I'm afraid I won't be able to do or learn or become successfully? What mistakes am I scared I'll make? What am I afraid others might think if I do make those mistakes?

- *Fear of success.* If I change, what other demands will be made of me? What is it that I'm afraid will change if I achieve what I want? What extra pressures or stressors do I fear will accompany success?

- *Fear of loss.* What am I afraid of losing? Am I assessing the potential losses disproportionately from the potential gains?

Ask yourself, if I didn't have any of the fears that I just listed, what would I do differently? What actions would I stop taking? What actions would I start? Who would I speak to? What new skills would I endeavour to learn?

Getting ahead in an accelerating world

While there are many things you need to do in order to succeed in a fast-changing world, I think there are three core skills you must commit to in order to adapt to change.

Together, these core skills will set you up to succeed in a future that you're unable to predict but can be certain will be different from where you are now (as illustrated in figure 5.1).

- *Learn to unlearn: be open-minded.* Be ready to unlearn and let go of old rules and assumptions about how things work and what's possible.

- *Think: be flexible.* Stretch yourself to adapt to change and be ready to yield to the wind and try new approaches.

- *Act: be proactive.* Change before you have to, by preparing for future changes, and be open to embracing the new.

Figure 5.1: the three core skills needed for adapting to change

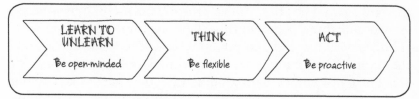

Learn to unlearn: be open-minded

Early in 2012, after more than 10 years of living in the United States, my family and I returned to live in Melbourne, a city that I'd lived in for only one year over the previous 17 (and that was the year my first child was born, so my memories are encased in a sleep-deprived fog). As I soon discovered, my mental maps of Melbourne's road system, good cafés, restaurants and shopping centres were in dire need of an update. While I'd kept my old *Melway* street directory from the 1990s I quickly realised I needn't have bothered. Not only was my *Melway* woefully out of date for many parts of the city—which had transformed from industrial wastelands into vibrant urban centres—but several new, big toll roads, complete with tunnels and bridges, had been built, totally changing the routes around the city.

Thank God for the satellite navigation system in my new car! Needless to say, from driving on the other side of the road to enrolling my kids in new school systems and sports, since arriving back in Melbourne I've had to do a lot of learning, but I've had to do even more 'unlearning' in order to undergo the required 'relearning'. I could never have learned how to navigate around the city had I kept relying on my mental maps or my old street directory. I had to donate the latter to the recycling bin and declare myself a novice navigator before I could once again become a competent one. I'm pleased to say that I can now make my way to the airport without any wrong turns (on a good day!).

We're all born with an intense desire to learn. Babies stretch and grow their skills daily. Not just ordinary skills, but the most complex tasks possible: learning to walk and talk! Sure, their nimble brains are wired for it, but their egos have yet to develop and decide that the mistakes required to attain mastery are all too embarrassing for the effort. They walk, they fall, they get up. They just barge forward, bang their head, have a cry, then barge forward again. Likewise, you've probably seen children as young as two and three manoeuvring their way around their parents' iPhones with a speed and precision that leaves you feeling like the digital immigrant, born in a previous millennium, that you are. They just tinker with things until they've worked it out. For children, free of pride and a need to preserve their public persona, the learning curve isn't something to be avoided or hastened, but rather to be travelled along until they have attained the mastery they want.

> *The most important lessons lay not in what I*
> *needed to learn, but in what I first needed to unlearn.*
> **Jim Collins**

Somewhere along the line though, many of us lose our love of learning. The pressure to excel in school with its ever-pressing emphasis on test scores can rob the enjoyment from the process of learning itself. Whatever the reasons, once they have the basics covered, many people tend to stick with what they know and avoid situations or challenges where they may mess up or be forced to learn something new. So they create a safe, secure and comfortable (and confining) world for themselves. In it, they do their best to mould the changes going on around them—in people, events and the general environment—to fit with their current 'mental maps'. They may say they're open to change, but do their best to avoid it. For a while, that strategy can work fairly well. What it doesn't do is set them up well for adapting to a future that may well require an entirely new set of maps.

As any ex–typewriter repairperson will tell you, refusing to acknowledge that the world is changing will eventually land you in a difficult place with few options and a lot of forced learning, such as how to get a new job with a skillset or knowledge that's lost its value. Or how to live on a minimum wage. When you resist learning, unlearning and relearning the options available to you, from a career standpoint at least, can narrow greatly. Sometimes they can disappear altogether. When it comes to adapting to change, delay is increasingly expensive.

Develop learning agility

If you're not learning, you're not advancing. If you're not learning, you quickly lose your place in a world that's forever marching steadily forwards.

Success in today's world isn't just about how well, how much or how fast you can learn. The rate of change today is so fast that your ability to unlearn and relearn is more important than any other aspect of learning.

We can all acquire bucketloads of knowledge just by sitting on Wikipedia all day. But acquiring new knowledge isn't sufficient for succeeding in a wired-up world that uploads more information to the web each day than existed in all the world's books 100 years ago. With your computer, or even your smartphone, you have more information at your fingertips than you can process in your lifetime, much less retain or put to any practical use.

In 1992 Bill Clinton declared that if you just 'work hard and play by the rules' you'll get ahead, have a good life and pave the way for your kids to have an even better one. It's a nice thought and one that resonates with most people. Unfortunately, it's no longer true. When Clinton made this declaration the internet was only beginning to emerge, few people used email and students were still relying on encyclopedias to research their school projects. It was a world in which technology had yet to revolutionise traditional ways of doing business, a world where working remotely was still a rarity and many people stayed in jobs for life.

Much has changed since then, including the idea that playing by the rules is what gets you ahead. Getting ahead today requires lifelong learning, and that includes unlearning the old rules and relearning new ones. It requires emptying the melting pot of assumptions about how things work, 'unlearning' what you already know and making space to 'relearn' whatever is truly relevant in your job, your industry, your career and your life.

Learning agility is the name of the game. And in the game of life, where the rules are changing fast, your ability to be agile in letting go of old rules and learning new ones is increasingly important. Learning agility is the key to unlocking your change proficiency and succeeding in an uncertain, unpredictable and constantly evolving environment, personally and professionally. There are countless things you may have to unlearn in your job, business and career, even in the course of the next 12 months.

- Unlearn the designs you use.

- Unlearn the methodology you use.

- Unlearn the technology you use.

- Unlearn the way you approach your brand.

- Unlearn the way you communicate your unique value.

- Unlearn who your target market is, what they want and why.

- Unlearn how to get the most from your colleagues or employees.

Unlearning is about moving away from something—letting go—rather than acquiring. Jiddu Krishnamurti, a well-known Indian philosopher, believed that 'truth is a pathless land' and devoted much of his life to freeing his followers from their conditioned responses. Likewise, the process of unlearning is about liberation or freedom from what we think we know. It's a bit like scraping the old paint off a wall before you apply a fresh colour. If you haven't stripped back the old paint, the new layer can't stick. Unlearning is like stripping old paint. It lays the foundation for the new layer of fresh learning to be acquired and to stick. But as any painter will tell you, stripping the paint is 70 per cent of the work, while repainting is only 30 per cent.

Accordingly, the key to learning, unlearning and relearning doesn't lie with the teacher. It lies with the student, with you: in your openness to learning, to being challenged and to letting go of knowledge that the passage of time has rendered obsolete (however hard you studied or worked to acquire it!). Likewise, as you read this book there will be ideas and concepts that resonate with you and that you'll find useful. There will also be ones that won't. That's okay. You don't have to agree with, much less retain, everything you read in this book or anywhere else. Nor should you. Whatever you get from it will be exactly what you need for where you are in your working life right now. While some things will resonate, also pay attention to the concepts you find yourself most resistant to. Sometimes the ideas we react to with the greatest resistance are those that hold the most valuable lessons.

While it may go without saying, you don't need to unlearn everything you know. I may have needed to unlearn many of my old street maps for getting around Melbourne, but I didn't have to unlearn them all. Nor would it have served me to unlearn how to drive my car. By the same token, you don't want to learn everything either. Nor could you. What's important is to be willing to unlearn only what isn't serving you so you can relearn what will. Likewise, if you try to anticipate every change going on around you, you'll become so overwhelmed that you may miss the one that's right in front of you.

Flip your assumptions

Take a moment to amuse yourself with these statements and think about the lens through which those who made them viewed the world:

- *Everything that can be invented already has been invented.*
  Charles H. Duell, Director of US Patents Office, 1899

- *Sensible and responsible women do not want to vote.*
  President Grover Cleveland, 1905

- *There is no likelihood man can ever tap the power of the atom.*
  Robert Milken, Nobel Laureate (Physics), 1923

- *Heavier-than-air flying machines are impossible.*
  Lord Kelvin, President of the England Royal Society, 1885.

Needless to say, time has proven all of these statements wrong—laughably wrong in fact (that's why I included them!). But had you lived at the same time, or even been an expert yourself in the same field as these people, it's probable you would have viewed the world through a similar lens and agreed with them. Many did. Their statements were, after all, the consensus opinion of many of the most brilliant minds of their time—minds likely no less brilliant than yours and very likely more brilliant than mine. And yet we know now that the things they held as 'the truth' were invalid assumptions based on limited and inaccurate information.

According to the *Cambridge Advanced Learner's Dictionary* an assumption is 'something you accept as true without question or proof'. As you're reading this now you have countless assumptions running in your life. Many of them serve you, and most likely at least a few of them don't. Unchallenged assumptions can limit you because where you're coming from often predetermines where you end up. That is, the assumptions that are guiding your choices today will impact where you find yourself in the future. It's possible one day you'll look back and wish you'd challenged some of them more vigorously. Common assumptions that I've heard people make which impair their willingness to change aspects of their career and work, and create a more meaningful career are:

- 'I'm too old to ... (change careers, go back to study)'

- 'I'm too young to ...'

- 'I can't just go and ask my boss to take on this challenge'

I remember when my husband and I were considering having a fourth child. With three young children I was very aware of just how demanding parenting babies and young children can be. I recall a conversation with my sister where I shared how, as much as I'd like to have a fourth child, it just wouldn't be possible to do that and start down a new career path in coaching.

'I just can't see how I can do both,' I remember saying. Fortunately, I have a supportive husband and some wonderful female friends brave enough to challenge my thinking. My friend Janet said, 'Sure you can. I have a girlfriend who has four kids and runs a car dealership. You're every bit as capable as she is'. Another friend told me about her obstetrician who also had four children while working in a demanding profession. Hearing about these women helped me realise that what I'd been assuming to be true simply wasn't. Not only did I need to let go of the assumption that I couldn't do it, but I needed to let go of my ideas on *how* I would do it — by getting more help, doing much of my shopping online, getting up earlier, stocking up on kids' birthday gifts and generally running my home more efficiently as well as accepting that 'good enough is often good enough'.

Like the queen in *Alice's Adventures in Wonderland* who thought of impossible things for half an hour each day, you want to train your mind to be more open to ideas that, at first, seem impractical, impossible or outright absurd. Practise letting your mind wander and come up with as many ideas as you can, however absurd they may seem. Relaxing your standards and letting your imagination off its leash while you generate ideas increases your openness and enhances creativity. If you think of a hundred stupid, impossible ideas but one of them works, then consider it time well spent! When nothing is sure, everything becomes possible.

Creativity requires the courage to let go of certainties.
Erich Fromm

Whenever Thomas Edison interviewed a job applicant, he would take them to lunch, where he would order them a bowl of soup. Then, as he asked them questions about why they would be the best candidate for the job, he would pay careful attention to whether they would season their soup before tasting it. If they did, he would not hire them. He believed that if they had to season their soup before even tasting it, they were operating from so many built-in assumptions about everyday life that it would take far too long to train ('untrain' and 'retrain') them to approach their job with the level of creativity he felt they needed to be successful.

Edison's invention of a practical way of lighting, involving wiring circuits in parallel and then using high-resistance filaments in light bulbs, had never been considered by anyone else. It wasn't that others had assumed it wouldn't work; they just hadn't ever thought of it. But because Edison refused to work with any assumptions, he wasn't constrained in anything he did. The result is that you have light bulbs throughout your home right now as you read this!

Adapt or die: Kodak's cautionary tale against complacency

Kodak was a pioneer in digital imaging technology, introducing the first digital camera in 1975. Rather than capitalise on the opportunity of being first to market, Kodak chose to keep its business focused on its lucrative film business. It was to become a costly choice, along with a textbook case study of change resistance.

Wind forward 15 years to the early 2000s when digital cameras were sweeping the market, Kodak's corporate literature still stated, 'The keys to Eastman's success in making photography a popular leisure-time activity for the masses were his development of roll film and the inexpensive box camera. Although film and cameras are far more sophisticated and versatile today, the fundamental principles behind Eastman's inventions have not changed'. It was another way of saying, 'We still aren't willing to change how we view photography—film photography is still king'.

By 2003, Kodak was forced to lay off 6000 employees globally after earnings plummeted. It was a catalyst to accept the new reality of digital photography, and Kodak set to work to become a leader in that market. By 2005, they'd succeeded in becoming the top seller of digital cameras in the US but continued to lag behind Sony and Canon in the global market and were never able to gain a foothold in the high-end digital camera market.

The demise of film photography and Kodak's sluggish response to the bourgeoning digital photography market, combined with the rise and rise of the market-shrinking camera phone, permanently changed the playing field for Kodak. In 2011, with sales flagging and losses ballooning, Kodak's shares fell by over 80 per cent. Staff cutbacks ensued, reducing their global headcount to 19000 from a high of 145000. For industry analysts, it came as little surprise when, in early 2012, Kodak filed for Chapter 11 bankruptcy. In the months that followed they went on to exit not only the consumer photography market they'd pioneered, but the inkjet printer and document imaging business. (Yes, your old rolls of Kodak film will soon be collectors' items!)

Kodak CEO Antonio Perez stated that the 'reorganisation' was to 'to focus our business on the commercial markets and enable Kodak to accelerate its momentum toward emergence'. Let's hope. At least for those employees still working for Kodak today. Whatever the future holds for Kodak, their experience tells a cautionary tale, for individuals and the organisations alike, against complacency, operating from outdated assumptions and resisting change in a continuously evolving marketplace.

Kodak is one of many examples of organisations that were too myopic in their focus, too rigid in their approach and too complacent in their attitude. It brings to mind other organisations whose failure to adapt—to learn, unlearn and relearn—has led to their demise. Think Borders bookstores, Blockbuster Video, Hollywood Video or my favourite Australian chocolate store, Darrell Lea.

Whatever your business, industry or profession, staying ahead of the game requires remaining vigilant about the changing rules of the game. You must be open-minded and flexible to adapt to changing forces and proactive in capitalising on their inherent opportunity. As W. Edward Deming once said, 'It is not necessary to change. Survival is not mandatory'.

We human beings are assumption-making machines. We make assumptions on a daily basis. Doing so actually helps us to function effectively. However, the problem arises when we delude ourselves into thinking our assumptions are 'the truth'. When you reverse your assumptions you're forced to look for ways to explain just the opposite of what you've perceived to be true. Even if you ultimately can't agree that the opposite of your assumption is valid, it can still shift how you were seeing things.

Management guru Peter Drucker says managers should recognise the value of ignorance: 'You must frequently approach problems with your ignorance; not what you think you know from past experience, because not infrequently, what you think you know is wrong'. When I work with teams to help them build collaboration and effectiveness I often have them list and then reverse their assumptions, just to generate creative thinking. Being forced to approach something from a totally different angle often generates a level of creative thinking that ultimately leads to other ideas. These ideas can often be applied to solve problems and maximise opportunities in different parts of a business.

Vu déjà: see the familiar for the first time

You know that weird feeling? You find yourself in a situation and you could swear you've been there before, except you know you haven't. It's just not possible. That's *déjà vu:* looking at an unfamiliar situation and feeling you've seen it before. 'Vu déjà', a clever term originally coined by author Josh Linker, is just the opposite: looking at a familiar situation as if you've never seen it before.

Which isn't easy to do. That's because your brain is hardwired to play tricks on you. As any neurologist would tell you, your brain been uploaded with special 'pattern recognition' software that has it constantly scanning your environment and matching any patterns it sees with ones that are stored away in your memory bank. For the most part, this is a good thing because it enables you to function efficiently: every time you see a stop sign you don't even have to read it to know that you have to stop your car before proceeding further. When you see something, your first instinct is therefore to conclude that a pattern is the same as one you've seen before, which leads you to react the same way as you have before. The problem is that often this isn't the case, particularly when the environment you're operating in is changing rapidly.

For example, trying to sell a product or service to a customer the same way you did in the past may not produce the outcome you want in the future. Even when things are still managing to produce a satisfactory outcome, it still pays to look at a situation or problem with a fresh set of eyes. Philosopher Bertrand Russell wrote, 'It's a healthy thing now and then to hang a question mark on things you have long taken for granted'.

Assumptions confine possibilities

In the 1980s, NASA challenged aerospace and defence company Lockheed Martin to cut, by several thousand kilograms, the weight of the huge fuel tank that formed the structural backbone of the space shuttle. The effort stalled at the last 360 kilograms. As the blue-ribbon engineering team turned its attention to increasingly exotic lightweight materials, one of the junior and less qualified line-workers suggested not painting the tank as a way to remove the extra weight. It seemed a bit too simple, and one can only assume there were a few PhD engineers whose initial response was to dismiss such a simple solution outright. But as it turned out, the 760 litres of white paint that was to be used to cover the tank would have added close to 360 kilograms to a device whose lifespan in flight was about eight minutes and whose fate was to end up at the bottom of the Indian Ocean. Such is the power of looking at a problem with new eyes and without old assumptions.

Indeed, sometimes the best way to think outside the box is to listen to someone who lives outside the box. People often discuss important ideas with the same inner circle of colleagues, but in doing that you can miss obvious answers. Someone with less expertise and 'inside knowledge' than you may see beyond others' unquestioned assumptions right away. (If you have noticed any typos in this book it's due to the same reason. Writers, and sometimes even highly experienced editors, can get so close to the work that they miss what is blaringly obvious to someone reading it for the first time. Not that I'm making an excuse for my typos—just providing a reason!)

Practise vu déjà

Think of a situation, problem or opportunity you're facing. Now imagine you were approaching it as each of the following people might and see what different perspective, insights and solutions occur to you.

- You're someone you have always admired as being really wise, strategically brilliant or insightful about the things you care about (for example, Steve Jobs, Richard Branson, George Washington, Warren Buffett, your favourite writer). How do you see it now?

- You're Doc from *Back to the Future* and you're 30 years in the future looking at this situation as it is today. How do you see it?

- You're [choose a profession different from your own: builder, pilot, sales representative, designer, teacher]. What do you notice differently?

- You're a brand-new employee, eager to learn, explore and experiment. What ideas come to mind?

It will always serve you to find intelligent people with little knowledge of your business, industry, profession or situation and talk through whatever you're working on now. You may be surprised by the solutions they help you discover.

Think: be flexible

When it comes to adapting to change and finding the opportunity it holds 'blessed are the flexible for they shalt not get bent out of shape'. The ancient Chinese text of the *Tao Te Ching* says, 'Whatever is flexible and flowing will tend to grow'.

If you always respond the same way, you won't always respond the best way.

When you choose to go with the flow of change, you free yourself from being whirled around like leaves on a blustery autumn day. It enables you to choose the actions you'll take, or not take, the conversations you'll have, the requests you'll make and where you'll focus your energy from moment to moment. It also enables you to be that much more flexible in how you respond. Because you're not stuck in any fixed pattern of behaviour, you're not glued to any particular plan of action. You're a free agent, untethered and ready to adjust your sails to optimise your situation and to make the most of the prevailing tide and winds.

While having a plan can help you be more successful in achieving a goal, sticking to it rigidly can work against you. The better approach is to create what I call a 'flexi-plan' that you're open to changing as you get new information and circumstances change.

Be flexible amid changing circumstances

Professor E. J. Masicampo at Florida State University did a study that demonstrated the importance of flexibility in achieving goals amid changing circumstances. He essentially broke his subjects—a group of 98 students—into two groups. One group was given a firm plan to achieve a specific goal of researching information online. The other group had the same goal but wasn't given any plan to follow.

Within the 'plan' and 'no-plan' groups, half of the individuals were given ample time to complete the task, while the other half had their time cut short. The 'plan' group with ample time was 95.5 per cent successful in finding the information they needed, well ahead of the 'no-plan' group (68 per cent). However, the 'no-plan' group's success rate (71.4 per cent) far outrated the 'plan' group's (36.7 per cent) when they were both given a warning that they would have to complete the task early. When the 'no-plan' group was informed their time was to be cut short, they very quickly adjusted what they were doing to find the information they needed, whereas those in the 'plan' group resisted deviating from their plan and were consequently far less successful.

So go ahead: make your plans, set your strategies, get into action, but be flexible and adaptable as you go along. Rigidity can be lethal.

Expand your repertoire

Try crossing your arms right now. Go on, put down this book and do it. Then try crossing them the opposite way. Harder than you thought, isn't it? We're all wired with automatic reflexes, responses and decision-making strategies when faced with seemingly familiar information or stimuli. This enables us to be more efficient. However, you can become too reliant on the same default ways of responding. In any area of life, the greater the number of ways you can respond to a situation, challenge, problem, person or opportunity, the more successful you will inevitably be.

Responding with flexibility and agility in our rapidly changing world requires an ongoing trade-off between your naturally preferred way of responding to a challenge and a way that isn't as natural and easy for you. For every strength you possess, there's an opposite strength or trait that balances it out. If you always respond in one way, and never the other, sometimes you'll respond ineffectively. Mental and emotional flexibility are crucial to changeability.

We all have our default style and approach of getting things done, solving problems and adapting to new circumstances. However, if you always approach your problems and challenges in the same way, you won't always approach them in the best way. The greater the range of approaches you can draw from, the better the outcomes you'll be able to achieve.

Widen your spectrum of responses

As you read through the list below, take note of the way you tend to respond to the changes and challenges in your life. What is your default preference? Consider how responding with its opposite may, on occasion, be more helpful to you, enabling you to be far more effective in achieving the result you want. Just because one way of approaching things has generally worked for you in the past, doesn't mean it will work for you now. Responding well to change requires pulling from the full spectrum of emotional and mental alternatives.

- self-starting—self-stopping
- critical—accepting
- sensitive—tough
- initiating—following
- forceful—gentle
- cautious—bold
- task oriented—relationship oriented

- structured—unstructured
- outgoing—introspective
- planned—spontaneous
- impulsive—thorough
- compliant—noncompliant
- serious—playful
- creative—analytical

The world's top tennis players have developed mastery across the various tennis strokes. Not only must they serve brilliantly, but they must also slice, smash, lob and volley masterfully. Sure, they each still have their favourite shots, those they can execute better than any other player—Serena Williams's power serve or Federer's one-handed backhand, for instance—but they know that a brilliant backhand or a killer serve isn't enough. To be competitive against their top-ranked opponents, they have to be strong across the board. The same applies for other competitive sports. After winning the 1997 Masters Gold Tournament by an unprecedented 12 strokes, Tiger Woods set out to further finetune his golf swing so that he could achieve even greater success. As good as he was, he knew he could be better if he strengthened his golf swing.

> *Only in growth, reform and change, paradoxically enough,*
> *is true security to be found.*
> **Anne Morrow Lindbergh**

According to Malcolm Gladwell, author of *The Tipping Point*, it takes 10000 hours to achieve a level of true mastery. For athletes, this means mastery not just of those shots they are naturally strong at, but those that don't come as naturally to them. They have to be able to pull from a repertoire of different responses in responding to their competitors. So too it is in every domain of life. In reality there's never only one way of responding to a challenge — there are many. It's just that some responses will generate a better outcome than others. And so it's a matter of simple logic that the greater number of options you can draw from — the more alternative ways of responding to a challenge, problem or even to an opportunity — the higher the probability that your response will produce an optimal outcome versus an ordinary one.

Look at the most successful people you know and you'll notice that when it comes to change, they have the greatest number of different options available to them for responding. They know that to successfully navigate the twists and turns of life they must be agile and willing to approach things in different ways, depending on the circumstances; responding in the same way to something again and again will eventually cause grief and fail to produce the desired result. So, if you're feeling some grief right now, while it's comfortable to approach your challenges in the same way you have done so many times in the past, if you're finding yourself with a recurring challenge, consider how approaching it in a different (albeit less comfortable and familiar) way may produce a better outcome.

Unlearning organisational change

For reasons that have never been clear, 60 million years ago dinosaurs suddenly disappeared after more than 100 million years on the planet. Palaeontologists have hotly debated the cause of the dinosaur's extinction, but high on the list of hypotheses is their failure to adapt to rapidly changing climatic conditions—particularly temperature. If a failure to adapt was the dinosaur's Achilles heel, then the dinosaur is not alone in the history of evolution.

In his book *The Living Company*, Arie de Geus wrote, 'In the future, an organisation's ability to learn faster than its competitors may be its only sustainable competitive advantage'. Today's pace of change in business conditions may or may not be unprecedented, but it is surely spectacular and likely to accelerate from here. Like most things in business, rapid change is a two-edged sword: a threat but also an opportunity. Adapt to rapid change better than your competitors and you can make great strides; ignore rapidly changing circumstances and expect to go the way of the slide rule, horse and buggy, wind-up watch or dinosaur. Adapting may be difficult, but it's not impossible.

Organisations, large and small, that are most likely to be successful in leveraging change—internal and external—to their advantage are the ones that no longer view change as a discrete event to be managed but as a constant opportunity to evolve their business or enterprise. Whether it's an external change such as a new technology or tightening economy, or an internal one such as a restructuring or process overhaul, change readiness has replaced change management. It's the ability to continually initiate and respond to change in ways that generate an advantage, minimise risk and not only sustain, but elevate, performance. Adapting isn't therefore something to be done every few years, but something to be done every day.

Keeping up with, and adapting to, the ever-changing environment—whether in your direct workplace, across larger organisations or in the marketplace—requires a fundamental shift in how you approach learning, and a willingness to sometimes be okay with 'not knowing'. Learning, unlearning and relearning must not be regarded as a means to an end but as an end in itself—one that's fundamental to your ability as an individual, and collectively in your team or organisation—if you're to remain relevant to all stakeholders.

Author Spencer Johnson states, 'A change imposed is a change opposed'. Guiding your team or organisation through change requires thoughtful planning and an acute awareness of the underlying concerns and fear that those you're shepherding through change will feel. It's important to do the following:

- *Explain the why.* One of the biggest reasons why people resist change initiatives is because they don't understand what it's trying to achieve. Leaders need to explain the purpose of change and help people understand why the change will ultimately serve them through improving the organisation's long-term profitability. Until employees are sure why the change is even necessary they'll have a tough time embracing it and getting on board with the transition.

- *Clarify the vision.* As people try to come to terms with an unknown and uncertain future, it's important to provide them with as much information as possible on what the organisation will look like when it comes through the other end of the change process. Where are the new roles? What will the new structure look like? What's the time frame for the change to take place? Is training necessary? How much? Why type? What's expected now? The clearer the strategy and plan, the better employees will respond, and the less resistance you will get.

- *Acknowledge concern.* Classic psychological reactions to change move from denial to anger to bargaining to depression and then to acceptance. All sources of resistance to change need to be acknowledged and people's emotions validated. Sometimes people question the motives of would-be reformers, so far better to anticipate resistance and objections than to spend your time putting out fires.

- *Enlist involvement.* When confronted with a change in their organisation, the first thought of most employees is 'How will this impact me?' The second: 'How can I benefit from it?' So if you're leading a group, the best way to get people engaged in the change is to get them involved in it! Assemble a 'transition team' of influencers to see the whole process through. They in turn can get others onboard so that you or they can demonstrate how the new way can work. Pilot programs that model a change and work out any kinks before launching can be valuable. Ultimately people can be cynical if all they get is rhetoric, and so more demonstration can counter resistance, overcome anxiety and move people from 'It can't be done' to 'How do we do it?'

Act: be proactive

While it's important to be flexible and 'go with the flow', it's just as important not to be complacent. Assuming the skills and knowledge that got you to where you are today will get you to where you want to be five years from now could be a career limiting mistake. What got you here will not get you there—not with the pace of change that's going on around you. Rather, you have to actively engage in ensuring that the skills and knowledge that will be valued most highly in the future align with those you have to offer. My message here: don't rest on your laurels—be proactive!

Upgrade your skillset

Being highly skilled at what you do is always a good thing. It's likely what enabled you to get to where you are today. Sometimes, though, you can get so good at operating in a particular skill area that you don't adapt that knowledge to apply it to different kinds of problems and situations. It's not that you're intentionally lazy or arrogant, but you've just never seen the need to spend time on developing other skills or knowledge in areas besides that which was immediately relevant to the job you were doing. Besides, why bother having to go through the learning curve in a new domain of expertise, and risk looking foolish or failing, unless you have to? In 'the good old days' people could afford to take this approach far more than they can today. Banking your career on brilliance in one particular area can be very limiting and highly risky in a world where having skills and knowledge across a broad range of areas is becoming more and more standard and expected.

> *In a time of drastic change, it is the unlearners who inherit the future. The learned find themselves equipped to live in a world that no longer exists.*
> **Eric Hoffer**

As more people spend less time with any one company, HR managers are looking more for growth on a CV than a linear progression within the one organisation. While lifelong learning is not a new concept, if you have more breadth on your CV, rather than just depth, it may stand you in good stead. As Rosemary Howard, from the Australian Graduate School of Management, said 'Knowing what's going on in a different discipline is very important'.

While you may well feel the skills you possess today have you set up to succeed in the future, I encourage you to stay open to expanding your existing skills and knowledge. It seems there's a reverse correlation with age and tolerance for the time and practice required to become proficient in any skillset. Be realistic about learning something new.

The four stages of learning outlined in figure 5.2 show the process we all have to go through to become adept at any new skill or area of expertise. We often start out not even being aware of what we don't know ('unconscious incompetence'). Once we commit to learning we become conscious of our incompetence (like I did the day I switched from PC to Mac). Over time we become consciously competent until we arrive at a point where we're unconsciously competent (as I am now on my computer). Too often we exit the learning cycle at the stage of conscious incompetence, unwilling to go through the awkward and uncomfortable process of learning. But as Thomas Fuller wrote back in the 16th century, 'All things are difficult before they are easy'. Growth and comfort rarely ride the same horse: commit to staying on whatever horse you're learning to ride, keep practising, and eventually you'll do with ease what was once difficult.

Figure 5.2: the four stages of learning

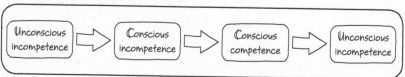

As the global economy evolves and market forces drive competition for jobs to new levels, it's the people who have proactively worked to expand and diversify their skillsets who will be most well placed. When you synthesise your knowledge and skills well, it turns you from a knowledge expert into a knowledge entrepreneur. *New York Times* columnist Tom Friedman wrote, 'Everyone has to bring something extra; being average is no longer enough. Everyone is looking for employees who can do critical thinking and problem solving...just to get an interview. What they are really looking for are people who can invent, re-invent and re-engineer their jobs while doing them'.

Companies today aren't managing their employees' careers as they once were. You have to be CEO of your own career, carve out your own place, keep yourself engaged and decide when to change course throughout your working life. The better you are at reinventing your role and adapting to ever-changing working environments and job challenges, the more highly you'll be valued and the more opportunities you'll create for yourself to advance.

My friend Nicolle Geller, who is CEO of Government Contract Solutions (GCS), makes it a practice to regularly read a diverse variety of books and blogs. She enjoys listening to people who work in different industries and have different areas of expertise. She often attends conferences where speakers who speak on various trends share their insights. While not everything relates directly to her business, which provides acquisition and program management and contracts management solutions to the US federal government, it all helps to broaden her thinking and stimulate different ways of building her business and preparing to make the most of the opportunities that the ever-changing market, the economy and technology provide.

Today, more than ever, people need to be both a CEO of their own career and an entrepreneur within their organisation. Don't leave your career in the care of HR, your boss or anyone else.

This leads to yet another change in the job market—requiring even more skills of tomorrow's knowledge workers—which is that companies will increasingly rely on part-time, contract and freelance employees as an alternative to hiring full-time employees.

This means more and more of tomorrow's knowledge workers will, whether they want to or not, have to run their own companies or partner with others to create small business-services companies. Not only will they need the skills required to manage a business, they must also have the skills required to work independently. Most importantly, they'll need the skills to continually market and sell themselves, their ideas and their unique skillsets. Indeed, in your career you have to step through your reservations about self-promotion, advocate for what it is you want to do and let those you're working for know how you can add even more value than you currently are.

You can be an entrepreneur within an organisation, or you can be an entrepreneur outside of it. Just don't expect anyone else to be taking care of your career path, advocating for your success and giving you a step-by-step template for how to do your job well so that you can advance to the next one. That's totally up to you. Own your success. Own your career. Own your job. Don't let any 'job description' prevent you from doing more than you're currently being paid to do. Nothing will differentiate you more from those around you than showing that you're a person ahead of your time who can be counted on to spot emerging opportunities, see potential problems and find innovative ways of solving them.

While your parents may have had jobs for life, it's estimated that most workers today change jobs every seven years. Many far more often than that. Needless to say, fewer and fewer people stay with the same company their entire working lives. But whether you never change your career path or you change it a dozen times, being open to working in different types of roles, in different types of industries and acquiring new skills and knowledge as you go can only be a good thing.

Complacency is more dangerous today than ever before. So even if you don't feel threatened in any way by the changes around you, you'll still find that investing in your own skills and knowledge is a smart move. Make it a habit to attend conferences, participate in professional groups or enrol in a course that introduces you to information and skills you may otherwise never know about. Not only are these experiences career enhancing, but they can revitalise your approach.

Look for cracks: act or be acted upon

Lamplighters, switchboard operators, typesetters, icemen, buggy builders, copy boys, elevator operators, carriage drivers, telegraph operators…these are all jobs that became obsolete. The reality is that jobs and careers evolve over time, requiring you to adapt your ideas about 'career'. Certainly in many companies today, traditional career paths have gone the way of the dodo, especially those in newly created technology and online jobs. Expecting a step-by-step map for the next year, much less 25 years, is simply unrealistic. You have to take more ownership for mapping out a path of your own that may well veer off the traditional 'career path' but which may be far more interesting than any traditional (and predictable) path ever could be.

People who find opportunities in a changing environment are those who are actively looking for them. They don't wait to be told what they have to do — they're out looking at how they can change what they do in order to add more value and be more effective. The point I'm trying to make is: *act or be acted upon*. Waiting for your boss to tell you what they need from you doesn't set you up for success or differentiate you from anyone else. Employers want people with the initiative to expand their role and identify needs that they may not yet be able to see. They need to know that they're hiring someone dependable who can deal with a variety of different challenges and succeed in a fluid environment. As you advance in your career, you need to be willing to take on a diversity of different roles. If you can't adapt to being in a particular position, you're going to limit the variety of positions available to you in the future.

When asked about his success, ice hockey star Wayne Gretzky explained, 'I skate to where the puck is going to be, not where it has been'. Of course the challenge is to know where the hockey puck is going to be! There are opportunities in the future that we can't yet quite imagine, but by looking around our immediate environment and taking note of the problems people are dealing with and the changes in the way we do things, we can start to anticipate where there will be needs and problems in the future that are yet to fully emerge. Similarly, the jobs of the future have not yet been imagined, much less created or had job descriptions written for them. Look for cracks in the infrastructure of your company and industry. What are they doing that they could be doing better? What problems are there that need fixing? Given the way things are changing, what problems are likely to arise in the future? How can you find solutions to the problems?

Be cognisant of changes in your industry and career field. Notice the market trends and shifts in buyer behaviour. Keep abreast of the latest thinking and future predicted trends that may impact not just on your current role, but the roles you may move into in the future. The opportunity in today's job market is that you have more ability to write your own job description and create roles for yourself simply by being proactive, spotting problems that need to be fixed, anticipating future needs and taking the initiative to come up with innovative ways of filling them. Tenacity is an attribute that will set you apart when it comes to solving problems and bring unique value to your job, your boss, your team and your organisation.

Set realistic expectations

Change, wanted or not, is the only constant you can truly rely upon. And change, wanted or not, is something you must learn to navigate, adapt to and embrace if you're to not just survive but thrive in your career and life. But set realistic expectations: if you find yourself dealing with change, whether it be change you initiated (moving into a new career), change you were hoping for (landing yourself a promotion) or change that was thrust upon you (being told you no longer have your job or being assigned to a role you would never have chosen), don't be hard on yourself when you find yourself feeling less than robust. As I've learnt myself over the years, most recently moving my family to the opposite side of the world, when your world tilts on its axis it usually throws you off balance. At least for a while.

As my friend Elizabeth Keeler said to me as I packed up my home in Virginia, 'Be kind to yourself'. Beating yourself up doesn't help your cause. Rather, take a few big, deep breaths, reconnect with what matters most and then focus on the next step. Whether you're adapting to huge changes in your career and life, or just making some small tweaks as you continue on your current path, what matters most isn't how fast you're moving but that you're moving in the right direction.

Key points

5

> Those who can unlearn old paradigms and relearn relevant skills and expertise will reap the rewards and seize the opportunities inherent in change.

> History has shown that unless you are constantly questioning the assumptions you have about how the world works, you can miss out on opportunities and quickly get left behind.

> As technology and globalisation continue to reshape the world, what's required to succeed will continue to evolve. The skills and knowledge that got you to where you are today will be insufficient to take you where you want to go in the future.

> You have to be your own CEO, carve out your own place, keep yourself engaged and decide when to change course throughout your working life.

> Complacency at both an organisational and individual level can be very costly.

> Fear of the unknown, of loss, of failure and even of success drives our resistance to change.

> Learning to be comfortable with the inherent discomfort of change enables you to handle it and emerge from it better.

> When confronted with change—whether its change you've chosen or change that has been imposed—be patient with yourself as you adjust to the new reality it brings.

> The three core skills for adapting to change are:

> > – *Learn to unlearn: be open-minded.* Be ready to unlearn and let go of old rules and assumptions about how things work and what's possible.

> > – *Think: be flexible.* Stretch yourself to adapt to change and be ready to yield to the wind and try new approaches.

> > – *Act: be proactive.* Change before you have to by preparing for future changes, and be open to embracing the new.

Chapter 6

Seize opportunity from your adversity

Disappointment and adversity can be catalysts for greatness.
Catherine Freeman

We recently bought a powerboat so we could teach our kids to water ski and for them to enjoy tubing behind the boat on the picturesque Gippsland Lakes where I grew up. In the spirit of fun, we created a competition to come up with the best name for our new boat. My oldest son, Lachlan, won the prize. His suggestion: *Usain Boat*, inspired by Usain Bolt's Olympic gold medal haul. As we launched *Usain Boat* into the water for the first time it made me think how the biggest obstacle a powerboat has to overcome is the water against its propeller. Yet if it weren't for the water, the boat wouldn't move at all. The same law, that obstacles are a condition of success, is true for us all.

Mastery of life is not the absence of problems, but the mastery of problems. If you want to achieve greater success in your life, you have to be willing to take on bigger obstacles. The people who live the most rewarding lives are not those with the smallest problems but those who dare to face the most difficult. Just think about the problems that people such as Gandhi, Mandela, Mother Teresa, Aung San Suu Kyi, Bill Gates and Bono chose to take on. Often you can judge the size of a person by the size of their challenges.

People who achieve greatly do so not because they know they'll always succeed, but because they know that however things turn out, they'll be able to deal with it. Their faith in their innate resilience and self-worth fuels their confidence and courage to pursue what many might see as risky or lofty goals. You unlock new reservoirs of courage when you trust that whatever happens, you can handle it.

Think about that for a moment: if you knew that whatever happened, however things turned out, you could handle it, how would it change how you approach your career and life? What goals would you take on that you've shied away from? Where might it fuel new ambition and embolden you to make changes and take chances you've steered timidly away from until now?

The ancient Greek mathematician Archimedes said, 'Give me a lever long enough and I shall move the world'. Likewise, when you build resilience you effectively extend the length of your psychological lever, exponentially expanding your ability to turn the setbacks that can weigh you down into stepping stones that advance you further forward. Building resilience is the name of the game when it comes to leveraging your obstacles into opportunities in a pressure laden world. In today's competitive workplace, how well you manage stress and cope in tough times will make the crucial difference. While avoiding risk and playing safe won't negate your need for resilience, if you're pursuing goals worthy of you then you need even more of it. Resilient people not only take on bigger challenges and handle them better, but when things don't work out they find opportunity in their adversities and use it to their future advantage. The way the founder of Lorna Jane seized the opportunity in the wake of the global financial crisis that rocked the world in 2008 is an example.

Creating opportunity in a turbulent time

Lorna Jane Clarkson is the founder and chief creative officer of Australia's leading activewear label, Lorna Jane. An icon of the Australian fashion industry, Lorna revolutionised the concept of fit-fashion when she started making her own activewear as a fitness instructor. Twenty years later, Lorna's passion to inspire the world to be active has driven her to build over 135 stores internationally, generating over $100 million in annual revenue. But like most businesses, it hasn't always been all smooth sailing. Lorna Jane stores were only just beginning to build momentum when the global financial crisis hit in 2008. As unwanted and unpredicted as it was, Lorna was able to create opportunity in a turbulent time.

'We could have just battened down the hatches and held off opening stores till the economy started to lift, as so many retail businesses were doing at the time. But the economic crisis actually created huge opportunity for us. We were being offered leases in high-profile positions that we wouldn't have been offered in a stronger economy. So we continued to expand when everyone else was closing stores or downsizing. To some it may have looked courageous, maybe even reckless, but for us it just made good business sense: to make the most of the opportunity.'

It turned out to be not just a bold move, but a smart one which led to the biggest growth period in her business. 'To achieve great things, you have to take great risks and have the courage to stick to your vision, while adapting strategy as the environment changes, even when those around you are telling you otherwise.'

Entrepreneurs like Lorna demonstrate a unique brand of courage, trading the security of a regular wage to go out on their own. But as Lorna shared with me, 'Even when the going gets tough, if you work hard enough and believe in what you are doing you can find opportunity regardless of what is happening in the world around you'.

The reality is that no amount of playing safe can ever safeguard you from disappointment or protect you from hardships far out of your control. Even if it could—even if everything you touched turned straight to gold—you'd be deprived of the sense of accomplishment that can only come from jumping the hurdles between where you are now and where you want to go. Aspiring to a life free of adversity is asking for a life low on fulfilment. It's through overcoming your struggles that you come to forge your sense of self and experience life at its richest. The good news is that you can do exactly that.

Resilience psychology: build your inner toughness

Research into brain plasticity has proven that human beings have an innate ability to build 'emotional toughness' right up to the end of their lives. This means no matter how well (or abysmally) you may have responded to your past challenges, you can learn to respond better in the future. What's even better is that unlike most things that atrophy with age, your ability to build resilience only strengthens with every extra candle on your cake.

Which is what this chapter is all about: expanding your capacity for courageous action by bolstering your ability to bounce back faster when you've taken a knock; acknowledge your failures, but not let them define you; and soar above the myriad problems that are par for the course when you refuse to play safe. As illustrated in figure 6.1, the plans, expectations and hopes you have for your future will often fail to conform with reality. It's when life fails to unfold as you want, when people let you down and plans fall apart, that your resilience will enable you to regain your footing and get back on the track of making the best of the new reality you find yourself in.

Figure 6.1: life's reality

A modern understanding of resilience has its roots in the research of Salvatore Maddi. In the mid-70s, Maddi began a 12-year project to evaluate the psychological wellbeing of managers in a telephone company. The study took an unexpected turn six years later when the government deregulated the telephone industry. Half of the employees were laid off. For two-thirds of this group, the transition was traumatic. Many were unable to cope and died of heart attacks or strokes, engaged in violence, got divorced or suffered from poor mental health. But the other third didn't fall apart, despite having been dealt the same hand of cards. Their lives actually improved. Their careers took off on new paths, their health improved and their relationships blossomed. 'At the time the general idea was that you should stay away from stress,' Maddi recalled, 'but it turned out that some people thrive on it'. Maddi found that what distinguished the one-third who emerged from their job loss better off than everyone else was a shared characteristic he called 'hardiness'.

In essence, hardy people have learned how to respond to their challenges with greater resilience. They make a conscious choice to treat their crises (aka problems, pressures, challenges, failures, disappointments, mistakes and setbacks) as opportunities. Maddi believed that hardiness is the key to finding the courage and motivation to do the hard work of growing and developing rather than denying and avoiding. Numerous other clinical studies since have supported Maddi's belief that, with conscious effort, we can improve our ability to cope with stress and handle adversity.

Like pipsqueaks who exercise themselves into hunk-dom, you can buff up your inner 'muscles for life', strengthening your innate ability to take on the challenges that living a full life present. In other words, regardless of the personality you were born with (or even your age!), you can get better at coping with your life when it doesn't go to plan.

> *The human spirit is stronger than anything that can happen to it.*
> **C. C. Scott**

However safe people play it, we all arrive at points throughout our lives where our aspirations and expectations collide head-on with reality, often in ways that we never predicted, much less planned for. Right now there are millions of people out of work around the world—and not by choice. Of those who do have a job, 70 per cent report that their work causes them to feel stressed or anxious on a daily basis. Potentially destructive emotions such as rejection, failure, shame, embarrassment, disappointment, anxiety, resentment, anger and hurt rise to the fore as they struggle to cope with competing commitments, make plans based on a very uncertain future, manage unrealistic expectations, try to adapt to constantly evolving market forces, and deal with a myriad of challenging people and circumstances on a daily, often hourly, basis. Little wonder stress is the number one cause for visits to the doctor's office.

By expanding your capacity to cope with the pressures and problems in your life, you'll be able to find opportunity in your adversity, which you can leverage into more success in your career and life. I have developed The SOAR^2 Approach to help you do exactly that: approach your challenges, from the mundane to the mammoth, so you can 'soar' above them to new heights of fulfilment, confidence and success.

The SOAR^2 Approach

Thomas Edison failed approximately 10 000 times while he was working on the light bulb. J. K. Rowling was nearly penniless, on welfare, severely depressed, divorced and trying to raise a child on her own while attending school and writing a novel before Harry Potter came along. Lee Iacocca was fired by Henry Ford II—grandson of Henry Ford—at the age of 54 before he became CEO of Chrysler. Harrison Ford was told he would never make it as an actor and Julia Roberts was unsuccessful in her audition for the daytime soap *All My Children*.

Henry Ford, who was broke at 40, once said that when everything seems to be going against you, remember that the aeroplane takes off against the wind, not with it. Just as smooth seas don't make skilful sailors, neither does a boom economy or challenge-free environment make for a high-performing employee or, for that matter, an innovative, leading-edge organisation. It's through the process of rising up to meet your challenges and bouncing back from your setbacks (aka 'stuff-ups') that you acquire insights, ingenuity and resourcefulness to succeed in the future.

Study history and you'll find that all stories of success are also stories of great failure.

The SOAR^2 Approach illustrated in figure 6.2 is a simple and easy-to-remember model to help you short-circuit your stress response and rise above your challenges rather than head into an emotional nosedive that diminishes your capacity to respond well and may only worsen your situation. Drawing from a combination of neuroscientific research, age-old spiritual wisdom, positive psychology and emotional intelligence, the SOARR acronym—which I've shortened to SOAR^2—encapsulates the ultimate goal of the approach: to 'soar' above the stressors, setbacks and adversities that might otherwise pull you down and sabotage both your happiness and success. It comprises the following five steps:

1 **S**top and step back

2 **O**bserve

3 **A**sk bigger questions

4 **R**eframe

5 **R**espond.

Figure 6.2: The SOAR^2 Approach

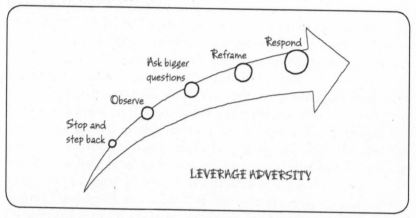

Committing each of the five steps of The SOAR^2 Approach to memory will enable you to intervene in your instinctive response to threats, ward off 'neural hijack' and respond to your situation more confidently, calmly and constructively.

Step 1: Stop and step back

Calm, focused people are far more effective than stressed-out people whose focus is scattered and patience is short. So the first step of The SOAR^2 Approach helps to restore you to calm and clarity by stopping what you're doing and taking a moment to step back from all your busy, anxious, over-wired, pressure-laden busyness.

In the 1997 world heavyweight boxing title match Mike Tyson became so enraged that he bit off a chunk of Evander Holyfield's ear. His momentary lapse in sanity cost him $3 million—the maximum penalty that could be taken from his $30 million winning purse—and a year's suspension from boxing. Psychologists would describe Tyson's highly stupid, and extremely aggressive behaviour as being the result of a 'neural hijack'.

While you may never have felt the desire to bite off a chunk of someone's ear (not my cup of tea!), you've likely experienced your own version of a neural hijacking. Think of the emails you've sent off in a moment of anger. How did they work out for you? Or the way you've snapped something unkind in a moment of anger? Didn't go down too well, right? Road rage is another example—when a driver literally tries to kill their fellow motorist for cutting into the lane in front of them. An extreme example, perhaps, but I'm sure you've had plenty of up-close and personal encounters with neural hijacking that have caused you to react, or *over*react, disproportionately to a situation, producing a less-than-optimal result, if not an outright dreadful one.

The reason Tyson did such an idiotic thing—and why so many of us have done things in the heat of the moment that we've later regretted—can be explained by the primitive emotional region of our brain called the autonomic nervous system (ANS). You might call the ANS the 'kneejerk' part of the brain. About the size of a walnut, it constantly scans your environment for threats and danger. When it perceives a potential threat (generally triggered by a past traumatic experience), it signals to release the hormone cortisol, which is the body-brain's response to stress. Cortisol floods in, mobilising you into action, to escape, protect, defend or change the situation—in other words, to cope. In the process, it overrides the cerebral cortex: the more logical, rational and 'thinking' part of your brain. It's when the 'kneejerk' part of your brain overrides the 'thinking' part, driving you to react in a primitive, instinctive way, that you undergo a 'neural hijack'. When your emotions hijack reason, the results are rarely helpful and often harmful; that is, your emotions hijack reason and logic as you react in an instinctive way to a perceived threat.

Of course, the instinctive fight-or-flight alarm reaction that enabled our cave-dwelling ancestors to fight off predators on the African plains millennia ago can still help preserve our own lives when we're faced with a genuine life-or-death situation. But therein lies the problem: we rarely are. Interestingly, research has found that the same parts of our brain where we process threats to our life are triggered when we perceive the threat of financial loss or even loss of pride (social status). So reacting with alarm is a very helpful thing—once in a life-and-death while—but the rest of the time it can cloud your thinking, and drive you to over-assess a risk and overreact in unconstructive ways.

While you can't just turn off the turbo-charged, 'kneejerk' reactive part of your brain, you can learn to manage it. It takes three to five seconds to re-engage the 'thinking' part of your brain. So stopping and taking a step back can be very beneficial when you find yourself facing a situation that triggers your 'feel alarm' response. It gives your rational brain time to come online and infuse some logical thought into responding to your situation.

Think first, act second

So the first step in The SOAR^2 Approach is to override your stress response. As soon as you notice that you're feeling uptight, anxious or even mildly stressed about a situation, problem or person, press the pause button on all your activity. The simple act of stopping what you're doing and taking at least a few seconds to take a few deep breaths can make all the difference in the world to your life. Mindful breathing has been clinically shown to help people stay calm in a crisis when the fight-or-flight mechanism is triggered.

Of course, this sounds ridiculously simple. But consciously deciding to stop what you're doing when you're mid-flight spinning plates can be the most productive exercise you'll do in your entire day (and week and life!). As you press the pause button, amid your busyness, bring attention to your breath. One of your body's natural responses to feelings of stress is to take shallower breaths. But shallow breaths leave your bloodstream (and your brain's central command centre) deprived of the full quota of oxygen it needs to keep performing at its peak. So as you pause what you're doing and step back from the fray, notice how much oxygen you're breathing down into your lungs and then proceed to take at least five long, slow, deep breaths. Just try it right now and observe the difference it makes even while you're in a relaxed state.

Restore calm and courage — breathe in, breathe out. (Repeat as necessary!)

The stress response occurs when we assess that we don't have the resources to handle the situation we're facing. While you can intellectually know you are capable at doing something, emotionally you may still find yourself feeling anxious, stressed and fearful.

There is no more potent or accessible way to short-circuit your stress response and restore a sense of calm and confidence than through your breath. Research has found that deep, conscious breathing not only helps your brain to override the urge to automatically react to external stimuli, but improves your ability to respond in an optimal way—taking smart actions, not just safe ones.

Breathing is such a natural function that we often underestimate its power to transform our mental, emotional, physical and spiritual states. So be careful not to dismiss this exercise because of its simplicity. Learning how to breathe from your diaphragm, not just when you're under pressure but all the time, will not only help you keep multiple balls in the air with greater ease, but will also help you respond more calmly and clearly to other potentially stressful situations.

You can help to ease nervousness, anxiety and stress simply by taking 10 deep breaths. Start by putting your hand on your belly so you can actually feel it going up and down with your breaths. Then, on each inhalation visualise oxygen spreading throughout your body—making you feel focused, calm and confident in your ability to do whatever needs to be done to get the outcome you want. Then, on each exhalation, visualise yourself breathing out whatever fears, anxieties and thoughts are causing you to feel anxious or upset. Picture them leaving your body and being replaced by strong, positive and calming energy. Do this for 10 full breaths (though you can do more if you like!), counting each on your fingers as you work your way back to the state you need to be in to move forward calmly.

You can enjoy the benefits of deep conscious breathing in as little as two minutes, if not less. If you don't think you have two minutes to spare, that's exactly when you need to take time out to breathe deeply the most.

Step 2: Observe

Neuroimaging studies have found that when people consider problems from the position of a detached observer, they use brain circuits additional to those that involve simply problem solving. Curiosity is an extremely valuable attribute when it comes to finding better ways of approaching problems, engaging with people around you and deciding the best path forward. Indeed, curiosity is one of the most common attributes found in healthy and happy people and one that's most often missing from those who are particularly anxious and depressed. People who suffer from depression are often very absorbed in their own problems and show a marked absence of curiosity about the world around them. Looking outwards on your situation interrupts the stream of negative thoughts.

On returning to earth after his first journey into space, astronaut Neil Armstrong said, 'It suddenly struck me (in the space capsule) that that tiny pea, pretty and blue, was the Earth. I put up my thumb and shut one eye and my thumb blotted out the planet Earth. I didn't feel like a giant. I felt very, very small'. Nothing shifts our experience of life more profoundly than shifting the perspective from which we're viewing it.

When you change the way you look at things, the things you look at change.
Wayne Dyer

Orville and Wilbur Wright didn't invent flight by focusing on the laws of gravitational pull. Nor did they succumb to the pressure to agree with the consensus opinion of the time—that it was a mathematical and physical impossibility to build a vehicle that could defy the laws of gravity, elevate into the air and stay there for more than a moment. With little formal education but a lot of mechanical know-how gained from working in their bicycle repair shop, the Wright brothers kept their focus firmly on building a vehicle that could defy the laws of gravity. Thank goodness they did!

You don't see the world as it is, but as you are. Of the six billion plus people on this planet, not one observes the world the same way as you do. Oh sure, there may be quite a few who see many things similarly to you. There may be many who have the same political views or religious beliefs or who follow the same parenting principles. But no-one sees everything exactly the same way as you do.

So after you've paused, taken a step back and breathed some precious oxygen back into your brain, don the hat of 'curious observer'. Visualise yourself soaring up to skyscraper level (lower if you're afraid of heights!) and look down on the situation you're currently struggling with. When you actively try to see things from a bird's-eye perspective, it expands the choices available to you for responding. What do you see? As you look down, ask yourself what it is about the way you've been observing things until now that's caused you to feel anxious or upset. From your new, heightened perspective, consider how else you could be observing the situation. Where have you been overly focused on one aspect of it and failed to notice others? Consider how someone else—particularly someone whose opinion you really respect—might observe it differently.

How you see the problem, is the problem.

Try now to observe what you're thinking while being asked to observe what you're thinking. Do you think it sounds like an interesting idea, or are you cynical and writing it off as foolish nonsense...or something else? What are you observing about yourself as you do that? William James once said, 'The art of being wise is the art of knowing what to overlook'. For most of our lives we focus too much on the petty and mundane and too often overlook what matters so much more. So try to observe how you've been observing things. Observe the critical judgements that you make. Step back and notice the type of lens through which you view your life. Is it tinted with optimism or pessimism, excitement or anxiety, anticipation or dread, confidence or self-doubt? Notice how that lens shades your interpretation—of people, situations and yourself—and consider how those interpretations may be serving you and how they may be failing to serve you. Simply observing your critical thoughts without judging them can open you up to taming the thoughts that no longer serve you—if they ever did.

Turning setbacks into stepping stones

I once heard a story about a guy from a Fortune 500 company who made a $10-million error. Ashamed, he was readying himself to be marched out of the building when he was hauled up before the division president, who was known for his intolerance of those who failed to deliver. Pre-empting his dismissal, he apologised, then promptly offered his resignation. Refusing the resignation, the president said, 'Goodness, man, we can't lose you now! We've just spent $10 million on your education!'

> *The only real mistake is the one from which we learn nothing.*
> *Failure is an opportunity to begin again more intelligently.*
> **Henry Ford**

You are not determined by your experiences but you are self-determined by the meaning you give to them. That is, no experience is in itself a cause of success or failure. It's what you make of it that determines which it will be. As pioneering psychiatrist Alfred Adler, who founded individual psychology, writes in his book *What Life Should Mean to You,* 'We determine ourselves by the meanings we ascribe to situations'.

When people attribute their failures to factors that can't be changed, adjusted or accommodated—whether internal or external—failure becomes a destructive and debilitating event. It leaves them feeling hopeless about the future, unworthy of success and unwilling to try again. In other words, people who interpret their failures and setbacks as being due to inadequate intelligence, as an ultra-magnet-like ability to attract bad luck, or as evidence that they were born losers, are unlikely to go on to achieve much success in the same, or any, arena.

On the other hand, people who attribute their failures to a lack of knowledge that can be gained, poor systems that can be re-engineered, resources that can be acquired, strategies that can be reworked, timing that can be improved or even a shortfall in prudent judgement (which can be strengthened) are able to transform their failures into invaluable stepping stones. Indeed, the lessons their failures provide can be leveraged into priceless (and hard-earned) knowledge that truly can be the making, rather than the breaking, of their career, business, marriage or life.

Failure is an event, not a person

You can never be a failure, though if you stop playing safe, you will sometimes fail to achieve what you want. Failure is not a person; it's an event. Psychological research has found that it's how you explain your failures to yourself and others that determines your ultimate success.

Walt Disney spent his early years trying to make it as a cartoonist. He was rejected again and again while trying to get an entry-level job with newspapers. Several times he was told he lacked talent and should consider another career. But, fuelled by his passion, he didn't waver from his ambition to become a professional cartoonist. Nor did he listen to those who didn't believe he had what it would take to make a living creating storybook characters. He pressed on long after many would have given up.

Eventually he achieved his first 'lucky break', which came in the form of a minister from a local church agreeing to hire him to draw some cartoons. So Disney went to work in a small shed near the church, which was infested with mice. After seeing a small mouse, he was inspired. And on that day the much-loved Mickey Mouse was born. Walt Disney later said, 'All my troubles and failures have strengthened me. You may not realise it when it happens, but a kick in the teeth may be the best thing in the world for you'.

While Walt Disney's story is unique, it's also universal. The most successful people are also the most resilient; they are those who have had to scale career hurdles and bounce back from setbacks before achieving the success they've become known for.

Steve Jobs was sacked from Apple and went on to start the relatively unsuccessful Next software company. In the mid 1990s, many in the industry regarded both Apple and Steve as has-beens. But only a decade later Steve became CEO of Apple and Pixar and was one of the most celebrated businessmen in the world. Despite his very public failures and setbacks, he never gave up and always kept working towards creating something bigger and better than anything he'd done in the past—right up to the very end of his extraordinary life. By the time he passed away in 2011, his persistence, vision and tenacity had left the world forever changed.

Bouncing back from job loss

My friend's husband, whom I shall call Barry, fell into a year-long depression after he was laid off from his finance job during the global economic meltdown in late 2008. Barry had worked his tail off most of his life, thriving on the pressures and challenges of his work, and had enjoyed the great salary he earned for his efforts. Becoming unemployed for the first time in his mid 40s was a huge kick in the gut, and one he didn't cope with very well.

There's no two ways about it: losing your job is hard. Whether it has everything to do with your performance, or nothing at all, it's still hard. However, if you observe job loss, like any setback, from an enlarged perspective, you realise that success in life is measured far less by your opportunities than by how you respond to life's setbacks and challenges.

In recent years, millions of people have found themselves out of work through no fault of their own. The challenge people in that situation face is how they handle not only the loss of their job, but the many emotions that can arise. These range from a sense of humiliation, failure and vulnerability to anxiety, resentment and self-pity. Sure, losing your job can be a blow to your back pocket, but it's often an even bigger blow to your ego and self-worth.

Whatever the reason you may have found yourself in the ranks of the unemployed, it's how you respond in the wake of it that will set you apart from others when it comes to finding a new job. Too often we take job loss far too personally and make negative interpretations that don't serve us or set us up to succeed in finding another job. It's important not to let your job status define you. Sure your job is *important to you*, but it isn't *you*. Who you are is not what you do. Never was. Never will be.

Research by psychologist Marty Seligman found that the biggest determinant among those who succeed after setbacks of any kind is how they interpret them. People who interpret losing their job as a sign of personal inadequacy or failure are less likely to get back on the horse in their job hunt than those who interpret it as an unfortunate circumstance that provided a valuable opportunity to grow in self-awareness, re-evaluate priorities and build resilience. *You* define who you are—not your job or a company's decision about whether or not to employ you. Don't take it as a personal rejection. It may well be due to economic forces far beyond your control that you found yourself out of work. Potential employers are more attracted to people who have proven their ability to stay positive and confident despite a setback or job loss.

When it comes to job hunting successfully, tenacious attitude is everything—particularly in a tough job market. Responding to your situation with a proactive and positive mindset will differentiate you from the masses, making all the difference in how 'lucky' you get in an unlucky economy. Treat finding a job as a job. Tap into your network and never underestimate the power of your network to open up opportunities and land you that 'lucky break' you were hoping for. The vast majority of jobs are never advertised, so the old adage 'your network is your net work' is particularly relevant when it comes to landing jobs via word of mouth. Get out and exercise, knowing that physical resilience promotes psychological resilience. Spend time with positive people and avoid those who aren't positive. If you're one of many who've been laid off at the same time, don't get sucked into a marathon pity party. It will suck you dry. And finally, as I shared previously, don't take your situation as a personal rejection or reflection of your value.

Looking through the optimist's glass-half-full lens

Life inflicts the same setbacks and tragedies on the optimist as it does on the pessimist. But, as Marty Seligman wrote in his book *Learned Optimism*, 'the optimist weathers them better and emerges from them better off'. Better off in terms of health, better off in terms of relationships, better off in terms of career prospects and better off financially. Psychologist Susan Segerstrom found that 10 years after graduating, law students who were optimistic earned an average of $32 667 more than their glass-half-empty peers.

Stop worrying. Nobody gets out of this world alive.
Clive James

Numerous studies have found that people who choose to view life through the glass-half-empty lens miss out on opportunities that their optimistic colleagues don't. Pessimism breeds the emotions that gridlock hope—resignation, anxiety, helplessness and despair—actively disengaging people from taking constructive actions. Optimism, on the other hand, breeds opportunity. Psychologists call this 'predictive encoding': priming yourself to expect a good outcome actually encodes your brain to recognise the outcome when it arises. So when you believe good things await you, you'll be better able to spot and seize opportunities that can benefit your career. A study by Harvard University found that those who choose to view their problems through an optimistic lens experience better health, including a lower rate of heart disease. So not only is it good for your career, but it's also good for your health!

Optimism enables you to succeed against the odds, not because you beat the odds, but because the odds didn't beat you. I once heard it said that life challenges always have a way of working out in the end. If yours hasn't worked out yet, then you're not yet at the end.

Step 3: Ask bigger questions

Often when things don't go as we want, we spend a lot of time focused on what interrupted our plans, and too little time asking questions to discover the opportunity our challenges always contain. The story of the boll weevil is a wonderful example.

Transforming calamity into prosperity

For much of the 1800s cotton was king in the American south, with millions dependant on it for their livelihood. Then, in the late 19th century, the boll weevil—a beetle about half a centimetre long that feeds on cotton buds and flowers—migrated across the border from Mexico and infested the cotton-growing areas. By the 1920s the cotton plants were gone, devastating the industry and the people working in the southern states.

(continued)

Transforming calamity into prosperity (*cont'd*)

But rather than dwell on the crop they could no longer grow, people went to work finding out what they could grow, and began to plant alternative crops such as soybean and peanut. They also learned how to use their land to raise cattle, hogs and chickens. What they discovered was that, expanded from a single-crop to diversified farming, their farms grew more prosperous. In fact, the people of Enterprise, Alabama, were ultimately so grateful for the boll weevil that they built a monument to it. The inscription read, 'In profound appreciation of the boll weevil and what it has done to herald prosperity'.

In this case, the farmers discovered that their assumed answers to the question, 'What is the best use of my land?' were wrong. It was the boll weevil that drove them to consider the alternatives which ultimately made them wealthier people.

Growing up on a dairy farm I came to realise that the biggest problem about milking cows was that they never stayed milked. The fact is, you will never solve all your problems. And those you do solve will very quickly be replaced by others eager to take their turn in the line. When we rail against our problems we rail against the fabric of life. It's only by choosing to view them from a different perspective that we can elevate ourselves above them, distinguish those we can solve from those we must accept and then go about finding better solutions than those we've tried before.

When you don't like the results you're getting in life, it's probably because you're not asking the right questions. Nobel laureate Naguib Mahfouz once said, 'You can tell a man is clever by his answers. You can tell he is wise by his questions'. Wise people don't assume they have all the answers. Rather, they ask questions to try to deepen their understanding of a situation or problem. Of course, you may not be able to find all the answers you're looking for, but by being willing to simply ask the questions, you will shift your perspective and you may find yourself coming up with answers you wouldn't have otherwise.

Our society places a lot of value on cleverness. Having spent a lot of time over the years with many clever people, I've come to learn that cleverness — as measured by IQ scores or even bank balances — has very little to do with wisdom and even less to do with genuine happiness. As I wrote in the chapter 5, we live with access to more knowledge than ever before, which is why we have to ask ourselves, 'knowledge for the sake of what?' Too many outwardly smart people have a marked absence of inner serenity. They live in a semipermanent state of anxiety, anger, resentment and sadness, or quiet, desperate resignation. They're often full of answers to all but one question, 'So if I'm so bloody smart, how come I have this problem?'

As you ponder your current list of challenges and 'problems', consider that your problems aren't 'out there', but that they're actually within you. Your problems are not the problem; it's how you view them that creates the problem. When you give up arguing against your problems and using your smartest answers to work them out, you can begin to ask better questions that can fundamentally shift how you see the problem itself. Your smartest answers landed you the problems you have today. Asking smarter questions confronts the reality you've constructed for yourself. Needless to say, that can be challenging. But what matters most is your willingness to sit with the questions. Who knows what gems of wisdom you might stumble upon along the way? Here are a few questions that could shift your perspective, the emotions you're feeling and the actions you'll ultimately take.

Elevate your questions

Albert Einstein once said, 'Problems cannot be solved at the same level of thinking at which they were created'. When you ask bigger questions, you get better answers. Bigger questions serve to elevate and expand your level of thinking, which in turn enables you to take more effective actions to address your challenges, achieve your goals and make the most of your opportunities.

(continued)

Elevate your questions (*cont'd*)

Think of a challenging situation or person you're dealing with right now. Then ask yourself the following questions and see what new insights and ideas you get from doing so. Not all questions will be relevant to your situation, but write down your answers to those that are. Remember, it's okay not to have all the answers. What matters most is that you're willing look at all the questions.

- How has my aversion to avoiding risk or emotional discomfort perpetuated this problem?

- Why have previous attempts to resolve this problem failed?

- What is my ideal outcome for this situation? What would need to occur to achieve it?

- What is it about this situation that I'm resisting? What would happen if I gave up that resistance?

- What is the fundamental underlying challenge for me here?

- How would someone I really respect and admire approach this?

- What emotions—fear, anger, jealousy, sadness, guilt—am I failing to acknowledge fully that could be undermining my ability to respond well?

- Where am I focusing too much on some aspects of this situation and too little on others?

- What valuable lessons does this problem hold that I need to learn?

- What untested assumptions am I making that could be limiting my response?

- Where am I letting other people's opinions limit how I'm viewing this problem?

- Is there a pattern to this challenge or problem? If so, what is it?

- What is the single best thing I can do (or stop doing) right now?

- How can I apply the lessons I've learned from similar situations to deal better with this one?

- If I were to be really courageous right now, what would I do?

Step 4: Reframe

We can't always change the world around us, but we can always change the world within us. We can do that by reframing how we're viewing our situation, and thus how we're experiencing it. When you change your core thoughts it leads you directly to a new paradigm, generating new perceptions of yourself and the world around you. So when confronted with a challenge always remember, you need to reframe your perspective, not your problem. There's a world of difference between a person who has big problems and a person who makes their problems big.

When your car breaks down, your car doesn't have a problem. You do. The problem is yours because suddenly you find yourself stuck on the side of the road, or somewhere equally inconvenient, and unable to get to your intended destination. The same applies to whatever problems you're dealing with right now. What you're viewing as the problem is really not the problem. The problem is the way it's impacting on you and your life. By seeing that your problems reside in you, you can step back and observe them from a fresh and heightened perspective and reframe them in a new way.

Stress is not your enemy; stressful thinking is

We experience stress to the extent to which we feel our resources are being threatened or depleted and will become insufficient to meet a threat, real or perceived. In other words, it's not that any particular person, event or circumstance is in itself 'stressful', but rather it is the assessment you make as to your ability to cope with that event. It's how you process or interpret that event (the 'stressor') that gives rise to feelings of anxiety or fear, which in turn produces a physiological change in your body (your heart beats faster, your palms sweat, and your breathing grows faster and more shallow) and this in turn is what you label as stress. For example:

- 'I had a stressful day.'
- 'You're stressing me out.'
- 'I had a really stressful meeting.'
- 'I'm feeling stressed out.'
- 'They really stress me out.'

- 'My boss gives me too much stress.'
- 'This colleague is such a stress-head.'
- 'My job is so stressful.'
- 'It was a stressful drive home today.'

The irony is that by talking about how much stress you feel you actually create more stress. As your internal stress barometer goes up, your ability to cope with other events that may trigger a stress response goes down, and the toll stress has on your body mounts. That's because we think of stress as a 'bad' thing we want to be rid of, akin to a virus or medical condition such as arthritis. Reframing stress through a new lens can help you avoid the downward spiral that stressful thinking can trigger.

Research shows that a certain amount of stress is actually good for you. It helps people achieve peak performance, whether in a sales presentation to a new client or preparing for an interview. Stress serves to focus you on what you're about to do. Stress sharpens your focus. Harnessed well, stress helps you perform better and be more competitive, particularly when the stakes are high, the pressure acute and even the smallest competitive edge can make a difference.

Don't wish away all your stress. It's your stress that compels you to stretch, to grow and to perform at your best. You just have to keep it in check.

Dr Hans Seyle, who first coined the term 'stress' in the 1930s, once warned an audience at a conference where he was asked how people could eliminate stress, 'If anyone tells you they can eliminate your stress, run. What they are really saying is that they want to kill you. The absence of stress is not health, it's death'. The reality is that stress is not a medical condition, but a psychological one that triggers physiological responses in the body.

When horticulturalists are preparing their plants for life outside the hothouse, they gradually expose them to greater variations of temperature in order to toughen them up for the variability they will be exposed to in the natural environment. While we're more complex creatures than plants, the same principle applies to us.

That is, only by being exposed to situations that put some strain on you and take you outside your comfort zone can you build up your internal fortitude and build your inner muscles for life. Conversely, without a period of strain you actually lose strength, endurance and natural resilience. A certain amount of stress is good for you. Scientists have proven that exposure to stress is the most important stimulus for growth. Without it, you wither on the vine of life.

It's therefore important not to buy into the notion that stress is your enemy and something to be avoided. Rather, think of stress as a valuable force of life that can be very constructive or destructive, depending on how you manage it. Managed well, stress can be leveraged so that it will improve, rather than impair, your ability to live a full and productive life.

Yale psychologist Charles A. Morgan III studied naval personnel who undergo an intensive 12-day course that realistically simulates the experience of being captured and interrogated by an enemy force. Morgan found that people who embrace adversity as a natural part of living are less likely to exhibit symptoms that could grow into post-traumatic stress disorder (PTSD) and are more likely to experience what has been called post-traumatic growth. Expecting that you'll sometimes have to confront new situations and deal with challenges that make you feel uncomfortable will enable you to respond to them more constructively and get more from the experiences. This applies as much to those circumstances you may choose to put yourself in as to those thrust upon you.

Focus on what you can do, not what you can't

In April 2008 my brother Frank was in an accident while riding his motorbike across the large sand dunes outside Doha, Qatar, where he was working as an engineer. Having grown up riding motorbikes on our parents' farm, Frank was an experienced rider who always wore the best protective safety gear. On this particular ride, accompanied by two riding buddies, Frank went up a large sand dune that looked no different to any other. Unbeknown to him, over the peak of this particular sand dune there was a sheer drop of about 10 metres onto a layer of solid rock. As Frank sailed through the air he wondered if he would be alive after hitting the rock beneath him. Fortunately he survived, but the impact of the crash shattered one of his vertebrae, T12, and left him paralysed from the waist down.

I arrived at the Doha Rehabilitation Hospital 10 days after the accident. In the days that followed I spent a lot of time sitting beside Frank's hospital bed, where he was to stabilise for a few weeks before being flown back to Australia for his full rehabilitation.

On the third day a specialist spinal injury surgeon visiting from Sweden made his way through the spinal unit to visit the patients. When he arrived at Frank's bed he asked him how he was doing. Frank gave his usual cheerful reply, saying something about looking forward to walking into the ward one day to say hello to the nurses who had taken such great care of him. The elderly doctor looked at him kindly yet solemnly and said, 'Frank, I know this is very difficult for you to hear, but it is important for me to be honest with you. You will not be able to walk again. There is no cure for your injury. And so it is important for you to focus on your rehabilitation and on learning to live without the use of your legs. Your rehabilitation will not be able to help you walk again. But it will teach you how to live well within the limits of your injury'. It was a brutal moment. I still get a lump in my throat just recalling it.

The next day I arrived at the hospital and talked to Frank about how he'd slept and what the latest estimate was on when he would be able to fly to Australia for rehab. He looked over at me and said, 'Margie, can't say I much liked what that doctor said yesterday'.

'Nup. I get it Frank. Who would, right?' I replied, tears welling in my eyes and as my throat tightened.

'But you know,' he said reflectively, 'I'm not going to give this injury the power to keep me from living my life. There may be a thousand things I can no longer do, but there are still five thousand I can'.

It was life at its most poignant, raw, brutal and beautiful all at once, yet in that moment I was a witness to courage I had never before known my brother to have.

Talk about a reframe. I had never been so proud of Frank. And there have been countless times since then when I have felt the same pride overwhelm me as Frank has reframed his circumstances and focused his attention not on the many things he can no longer do, but on the many things he still can. Last time we caught up at my home for our weekly Sunday night roast Frank had just returned from a scuba-diving holiday in Bali. The holiday before that was to the snowfields to learn how to ski without the use of his legs. Next month he will be travelling overseas on business.

As I've witnessed Frank respond with courage, resilience and humour time and time again, I've pondered how many people who have legs that work perfectly well, live their lives confined to 'mental wheelchairs' of their own making. Feeling resentful of their circumstances and powerless to change them, their perspective on life prevents them from accepting what they cannot change and trying to change what they can. Reframing your problems through the lens of possibility can make a powerful difference to your life.

Step 5: Respond

Things don't necessarily happen for the best, but that shouldn't stop you from making the best out of what happens. Psychologists have actually coined the term 'adversarial growth'—or 'post-traumatic growth'—to describe the benefit many people experience from situations they would never have chosen.

If you can't do something about a problem it's not a problem: it's a fact of life.

The previous four steps of The SOAR[2] Approach have been designed to expand your mental map, setting you up to respond as effectively as possible to whatever challenge or setback you're facing—to emerge from your adversity better off, not worse off. There's a very distinct and important difference between reacting to a situation and responding to it. Responding well requires a clear head and calm hand, rather than lurching reactively from one defensive position to another like an outmatched sword bearer—all parry and no thrust. Reacting is driven by the innate flight-or-fight instinct, which drives us to lash out, shoot from the hip, retaliate or run for cover. In our conversations it compels us towards 'silence of violence'. Responding is more thoughtful, reasoned and constructive. It's easy to react, whereas to respond takes more thoughtfulness, maturity and self-discipline. So whether it be a significant life crisis or a mid-level work challenge, taking time to respond rather than react to your situation will make all the difference to your success in the long run. Following each of the steps of The SOAR[2] Approach will put you in a position to respond far more effectively to the challenges you're faced with throughout the course of each day and over your life.

The power of choice

Your failures (whether in the form of job loss, career derailment, relationship breakdown or a business investment that tanked) only define you if you choose to let them. It all boils down to the power of choice. Of course, sometimes the choices you have available to deal with a situation aren't ones you feel are viable. For instance, a part of you may like nothing more than to tell your over-controlling, upwardly focused boss where to stick his job, but your family depends on your income and the impact of being out of work makes quitting your job, for now at least, not a viable option.

So when I refer to choice, I don't mean that all your choices are equal or even viable, but rather that you have the power to make them if you wish. Acknowledging that you do have options available to you, and consciously choosing which option you will take, will move you from a place of weakness and victimhood to one of power and ownership. As illustrated in figure 6.3, by actively choosing your response to a less than optimal situation—a stimulus—you'll shift the way you approach it and the spirit you bring to it.

Figure 6.3: the power of choice

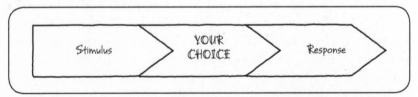

For instance, if you're in a job you really don't enjoy, or working for a boss you can't stand, or in a company you think is toxic—but for various other reasons you don't feel you can choose to leave—then you're still in a position to choose the attitude and spirit you'll bring to doing your role each day. Because you have the power to choose, you're only ever a victim of your environment if you choose to be. As the great philosopher Seneca once wrote, 'Most powerful is he who has himself in his power'.

Fail gloriously

Cate Blanchett once said, 'If you know you are going to fail, then fail gloriously'. At first the idea of failing gloriously might seem like an odd ambition. Yet, it speaks to the importance of being willing to risk failure if you're ever to achieve the success you truly want. I believe we all fail far more from failing to 'fail enough' than by failing too much.

The greater danger we face in life is not overreaching for goals that are too mighty for us to accomplish and falling far short of the mark, but setting the bar too low and achieving everything we set out to do. If you're succeeding at everything you set out to do, you're surely not aiming high enough. Failure is not something to be feared or avoided. It's the lack of it you need to be careful about because one day, as you look back on your life, you'll see that it was from your failures that you grew the most, and gained the most wisdom, and that they provided the stepping stones to your success (even if it didn't feel that way at the time) and to all the other challenges that came along after them. Defeat is not the worst of failures. The worse failure is not to have tried. So if you want to succeed more, double your failure rate.

Failure is an event, not a person, providing more valuable lessons than success ever can. People fail far more from timidity than over daring.

In life you'll fail more from timidity than you ever will from over daring. To paraphrase Abraham Lincoln's words, it's not about whether or not you've failed in life, it's about whether or not you can look back and be content with your failure. When you look back on life, you'll regret far more the things you didn't do than the things you failed in trying to do.

So as you step forward into your life, think of failure as evidence that you're living your life fully—that you're putting yourself at risk and daring to do more and be more than you have until now. To me that's not failure; that's success. And while it's only human to want each of the risks you take to pay off a hundred fold, appreciate that if you're taking risks, you're also going to have to miss the mark now and again.

If you're not missing a few shots here and there on a regular basis then consider that it's not because you're playing smart, but because you're playing safe. One day when you look back on your life you'll see that it's how you coped with your failures, not the failures themselves, that determined the shape of your life and the state of your heart.

Responding: commitment vs attachment

Having an exciting goal that you're working towards achieving, or an inspiring vision you want to turn into reality, is a glorious thing: it propels you into action with a greater sense of purpose. But as the saying goes, life is what happens when you are making other plans. The reality of life is that sometimes the best laid plans can go to pot, and the noblest of aspirations can fall to the ground with a mighty thud. As Australian's legendary outlaw Ned Kelly was once quoted as saying, 'Such is life'.

It's at times like this that the distinction between being 'committed' and being 'attached' is invaluable. Attachment to a goal is characterised by an external motivator and expectation about how things 'should' be. You want to get the promotion, win the business or gain the recognition. You can measure your progress and success—or lack thereof—through external measures. When you get the promotion, pay rise or corner office you assess yourself as being a success. When you fail to do so, you assess yourself as a failure and insufficient in some way. When things work out as they should, it strokes your ego and reinforces the image you like to have of yourself: successful, smart, accomplished. The downside is that when things don't work out as they should, it can be crushing and send you into an emotional tailspin.

Commitment, on the other hand, comes from a different place, an inner place. Commitment to a goal or vision is characterised by an internal motivator: desire to fulfil a larger purpose, to serve a bigger goal. It's intrinsically connected to your *why*. So while external measures can help to validate what you're doing, you're not dependent on them for validation nor as a means of assessing whether you're a success or a failure.

Sure, we all like to have our ego stroked, be told we're amazing and get the equivalent of a standing ovation for our efforts. But we're not doing it for the ovation. We're doing it for the difference we want to make. Sometimes we make the difference; other times we fall short. But our commitment to making it doesn't waver. Our key source of validation is therefore from ourselves, and knowing that what we're doing, and who we're being, is aligned with a purpose that is bigger than ourselves and more worthy than our ego.

You shouldn't prevent yourself from remaining committed to who you want to be and to the change you want to create around you just because life doesn't always bend to your aspirations and expectations. Mother Teresa was committed to eradicating poverty and having every person die with dignity. Did she achieve that outcome? No. Did Martin Luther King Jr achieve equality for all people, regardless of the colour of their skin, in his lifetime? No. But did they still live extraordinary lives because of their commitment to affecting profound change? Of course. When you operate from a place of commitment to the positive change you want to create, rather than attachment to how the end result should look, then no matter what unfolds or how things turn out—in the short or long term—you don't have to adjust your direction, only the path you want to take to get there. When Plan A fails, you still have 25 other letters to try.

Whether to respond to your setbacks from a place of indignant attachment or committed acceptance will impact whether or not you experience post-traumatic growth or its counter opposite. Ultimately, it all boils down to your power to choose. When you respond to life's setbacks and struggles, hardships and hurdles from a place of commitment, it infuses a deeper sense of purpose and meaning into your day-to-day life. Operating from commitment shifts the context of your life from being focused on the results you're *producing* each day, to the person you're *being*. It's not about what you achieve or do, but about who you become by doing it. Ultimately, it all boils down to your power to choose.

Five steps to SOAR² above adversity

Bring to mind a challenge (aka problem) you're dealing with right now that triggers a strong emotional response, whether it be fear, resentment, anxiety or frustration. Then go through each of the five SOAR² steps in relation to your problem and, as you do, notice how doing so shifts your emotional state and opens up new ways of dealing with the challenges at hand.

1 *Stop and step back.* Breathe 10 times, long enough to override your stress response and restore the sense of clarity, calm and confidence you need to focus on the task at hand.

2 *Observe.* Imagine yourself 30 metres up, looking down on your challenge and ask yourself these questions:

   – How has the way I've observed this challenge limited how effectively I've addressed it?

   – How can I re-interpret past failures to rewrite my story in a more powerful way that moves me into action?

   – What are the most precious lessons I have learned from my mistakes and failures in life? How can I apply them to live a better life and make wiser choices in the future?

   – Where might guilt, shame or fear be clouding how I'm observing my circumstances, and limiting opportunities?

3 *Ask bigger questions.* Read through the questions in the previous 'Elevate your questions' Courage Challenge on p. 169. Here are a few: Why might this challenge be perfect for my growth as a human being? How might others view this situation? What are the opportunities?

4 *Reframe.* Given your enhanced vantage point, how can you reframe this 'problem' so that you focus on what you can do, versus what you can't; on what you do want, versus what you don't; and on how this problem might really be an opportunity in disguise.

5 *Respond.* What would be the most constructive way for you to respond to the situation at hand? What can you start doing? What can you stop doing? What will you let go of? What larger purpose will you work towards in resolving this issue (if it still is one)?

(Step 6: Repeat steps 1 to 5 as often as necessary)

Taking yourself through the five steps of The SOAR² Approach isn't a one-off exercise in building resilience, managing emotions and responding better to life's myriad problems and problem people! It's something you'll find helpful again and again — sometimes for the very same problem or person! That's not because you're a slow learner (as if?!) but because you need to strengthen your brain's well-practised default way of responding to your environment. Just as a once-off walk along a new path through a forest doesn't create a new track, so too will you have to practise thinking, feeling and acting in ways again and again before they become your default way of responding.

Trust yourself: you can handle more than you think

Daniel Gilbert, a Harvard University psychologist, said people are generally not good at forecasting their feelings when they're in the middle of an adversity, challenge or crisis. When they're in bad emotional shape they tend to think they'll feel similarly in the future. He speculates that this negative forecasting bias developed because it's useful, serving to overestimate risks and steer people away from dangers. But, he argues, this also means they tend to underestimate their capacity to recover: 'It's not that things don't hurt. It's that they don't hurt quite as long or as much as we think they're going to'. Needless to say, career crises — job loss, corporate restructure or otherwise — drive people to play safer than serves them, undermining their response, their recovery and their actions going forward.

It's not your adversities that shape who you are, but who you are in the face of your adversities.

Truly successful people are those who have succeeded in mastering the game of life. They're fully engaged in living a life that matters, but they can also respond to their setbacks, struggles and sorrows from an enlarged perspective. They still feel the pain associated with everyday living, but they don't judge it as good or bad, rather as an invitation to feel more deeply and live more wholeheartedly. And while they may never have heard of the five steps I have shared with you in this chapter, they most certainly live them.

Avoiding risk, playing safe and keeping your guard cautiously up is no way to live and certainly isn't a recipe for achieving outstanding success in your career or fulfilment in any area of life. As scary and uncomfortable as it can be to put yourself at risk of failure or looking foolish, achieving anything truly worthwhile will demand no less. Your life is far too short and way too precious to cautiously tiptoe your way through it and veer wide around any potential dangers. You become more resilient every time you take a step outside your comfort zone and realise that whatever happens, you can handle it. Courageous action is therefore crucial for building self-confidence in your ability to not just survive, but to thrive, even when things don't go your way.

You're capable of more than you think

Phillip and Caren Merrick started a business called webMethods in the basement of their townhouse. After a year of working in the basement developing business-integration software they finally managed to sell their first contract for $5000. While Phillip—a self-confessed tech geek who grew up in the western suburbs of Melbourne and studied IT at university—had a natural affinity and strength for writing code, having to step out and sell the software he developed didn't come so naturally. But his commitment to getting software he knew would benefit businesses around the world into the marketplace overrode his aversion to selling. The fact that he was turned down at his first 70-odd meetings with venture capitalists wasn't an encouraging start. Again and again potential investors didn't think the business he and Caren were trying to build had solid market potential. But their persistence paid off, as persistence so often does.

Eventually they found a venture capital firm that was willing to provide much needed capital for webMethods to expand. Phillip shared with me what he learned from the experience. 'No matter who you are, or what you do, you can do a whole lot more than what you think you are capable of doing. That's what holds people back: thinking they can't when in fact they can.'

In the years that followed, Phillip and Caren invested everything they had to grow their business, constantly having to step outside their comfort zone as they pursued their vision to build a world-class business from the basement up. Their effort paid off: webMethods went on to be the most successful software IPO to date, with the fourth most successful debut on the NASDAQ. While they are no longer involved in the webMethods business, their success was as much a result of their tenacity and timing as it was of their willingness to trust themselves that they could do far more than others—sometimes even more than they thought possible.

Choosing to trust yourself more deeply and approach life with a belief that 'no matter what happens, I can handle it' moves you to an infinitely more powerful place emotionally, mentally, spiritually and physically.

Adversity has a way of introducing you to yourself on a whole new level. It invites you to explore new dimensions of your humanity. It challenges you to take another look at how you've been looking at your work, your relationships and your life. All the while, it expands your ability to turn your greatest adversities into your most valuable assets. So as you dare to *do* more and *be* more than you have until now, take a moment to trust more deeply that whatever happens, within you lie all the resources you need to handle it.

And that begs this question: If you knew that you could handle anything, what changes and challenges would you step into in your career and life?

Key points

> The most successful people are those who are willing to take on challenges that increase their risk of failure. Mastery of life is not the absence of problems, but the mastery of problems.

> In today's competitive workplace, your ability to handle pressure, manage stress and take setbacks in your stride will set you apart from the pack and elevate your success.

> Stress isn't the enemy; stressful thinking is. You create unnecessary stress through the way you talk and think about your daily challenges. Without stress, you can't perform at your best level.

> The more resilient you are, the greater your ability is to find opportunity in your adversity and to turn your setbacks into stepping stones.

> Neuroplasticity has proven you have the ability to become more resilient, to build emotional hardiness right up to the end of your life.

> Studies of people who have experienced significant trauma have found that people can emerge from adversity with 'post-traumatic growth', depending on how they choose to process their experience.

> The five steps of The SOAR[2] Approach can help you avoid a neural hijack and respond more calmly and constructively to the pressures and problems you face:

  – **S**top and step back

  – **O**bserve

  – **A**sk bigger questions

  – **R**eframe

  – **R**espond (repeat steps 1–4 as necessary!)

Chapter 7

Lead authentically, cultivate courage

Nothing so conclusively proves a man's ability to lead others as what he does from day to day to lead himself.
Thomas J. Watson

Anita Roddick, founder of the Body Shop, once said, 'If you think you're too small to have an impact, try going to bed with a mosquito'.

Too often we abscond responsibility to effect change and fail to own the power we have to influence those around us. People refer to 'management' as though they are beings from another planet with an exclusive access to power. Nothing could be further from the truth. Regardless of your current position, *what* you do every day, and *how* you do it, affects everyone around you. People who act powerless only perpetuate the problems they complain about. Those who own their power, which I define as one's ability to effect change, can make a profound difference. However limited their power may seem relative to others, by refusing to think small or deny their influence, people at all levels of seniority can become highly effective catalysts for change.

Leadership is not the domain of a few; it is the domain of anyone with the courage to act with it. So put aside your old paradigms that confine leadership to a plushed-up corner office, removed from the daily grind of the minions in the trenches below. Leadership is far larger than any corner office ever could be. In an era where organisations are growing flatter, fewer and fewer leaders of the future will direct action from an ivory tower (and those who try will fail). More and more will emerge from within the ranks. It will be the people whose actions are driven by a clear sense of purpose and intrinsic power—rather than by fear of losing power—who will command the respect and grow the influence needed to shape the future: in business, in government and in society; locally, nationally and globally.

The most successful leaders today are men and women who have refused to settle for mediocrity, play safe or cling to security. They speak candidly, embrace change and seize opportunity from adversity. They're willing to lay their career and executive bonus on the line for their beliefs. In doing so, they embody the Courage Mindset. Sometimes their actions produce extraordinary results. Other times they fall short. But their ascent to the highest levels of power and influence isn't purely for the results they've produced. Rather, it's for their courage to challenge tradition, to hone their judgement through deep listening, embark on ambitious endeavours, execute them with tenacity and persevere amid adversity—all things that you can also do.

All leadership begins with self-leadership

'Leaders are made, not born. And they are made more by themselves than by any external means. Everyone, at any age, is capable of self-transformation.' These words by renowned leadership expert Warren Bennis echo a timeless truth. While there are people who possess natural traits we tend to associate with leadership, the truth is that *any* person, at *any* age, at *any* level, in *any*-sized organisation can be a leader. And in today's increasingly fearful business environment, there has never been a greater need, nor more opportunity, for *all* people at *all* ages and at *all* levels in *all* organisations to step up to the plate of leadership, grow their sphere of influence, and own their power to make an impact.

While writing this book I was asked numerous times whether I was writing a leadership book or a personal-development book. Is there any meaningful difference?

Most of the 75 000-odd books on leadership are focused on the specific challenges and strategic choices of those in positions of formal 'leadership' authority. All well and good. But unless that person has first done the hard work of leading themselves, all the brilliant leadership advice in the world won't transform them into a great leader. It likely also explains why so many people who have been anointed as 'leaders' fall short when it comes to inspiring the best in those around them. They simply haven't done the hard 'inner' work to address the core fears and beliefs that mire the best in themselves. Leadership is *all* about personal development; it extends from the inside out.

Leadership is not the domain of a few; it is the domain of anyone with the courage to act with it. You can't lead by playing safe.

A leader with unchallenged assumptions, unacknowledged insecurities, ungrounded stories, unbridled ego and unwillingness to listen will be limited in how they engage with those around them. This in turn will profoundly undermine their efforts to build trust, get 'buy in' and harness the full potential of those they lead.

You exert influence by virtue of the trust you build in your relationships. Where trust is limited, so too are the results you produce. Which begs the question, 'How can you build a solid network of trusting relationships in your organisation that enables you to wield influence regardless of your authority?' While there are many different ways to answer that question, at the core of each lies your ability to create meaningful connections, to become a person others can count on to say and do what's right—even when it costs you—and to be a person of true vision, character and courage others can look to for much-needed inspiration.

So, when you commit to playing a bigger game in your work, you also, by default, commit to being a leader. Leadership demands courage, and courage creates leaders. From Oprah to Aun San Suu Kyi—their commitment to courageously pursuing the work of their life's calling paved their path to power.

By building your own brand of courage,
you help others build theirs.

So whatever your current position or level of authority, you have the ability to demonstrate leadership, make an impact and positively influence those around you. You do it every time you refuse to play safe. You do it every time you speak up about what's important to you. You do it every time you hold someone accountable. You do it every time you refuse to let your failures define you. And you do it every time you ask yourself, 'If I was running this company, what would I want the person in my situation to do?' That question alone can provide the clarity of purpose and compel you into leadership.

As organisations grow flatter in structure, and traditional career paths become a thing of the past, opportunities for leadership will emerge more and more from the ground up, rather than by decree from the top down. By finding and building your own unique brand of courage, you help others build theirs. Starting with self-leadership, you can amplify your efforts through others, harnessing their talents, passion and expertise so that, together, your team and organisation can develop synergies that enable it to achieve more than any sum of the individual parts ever could.

While there are countless models and theories on leadership, my experience working with people and groups across different cultures, industries and hemispheres is that the most powerful paradigms are also the most practical.

I have broken the core challenges of growing your impact and influence as a leader into the three core domains of Engage, Inspire and Embolden, as illustrated in figure 7.1:

- Engage and connect authentically to build trust and grow influence.

- Inspire greatness and connect to purpose.

- Embolden people to take action, cultivating a Culture of Courage.

Figure 7.1: the three elements of courageous leadership

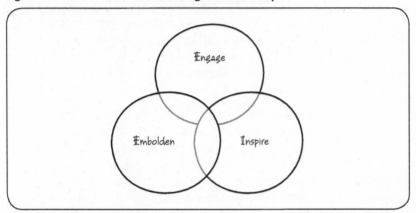

Engage authentically

Engaging authentically with people around you is the first task of genuine leadership. Relationships are the currency of the workplace, and so the stronger your connections, the more influence you wield and the bigger impact you can make. Everything else hinges from that. Daniel Goleman's research into emotional intelligence found that human beings are wired for connection. We not only *want* to belong and connect with others, we *need* to connect! We are at our best when we enjoy meaningful connections with people around us that go deeper than surface-level exchanges. But meaningful engagement can't occur unless we're connecting from a place of authenticity. Yet interacting and leading authentically is often an act of courage in itself. As James Strong, whose case study follows, shared with me, 'One of the most important elements of authentic leadership is the ability to confront and overcome fear'.

Authenticity demands vulnerability

James Strong is one of Australia's most respected and successful business leaders, with a career spanning from mining and retail, to insurance and law. Former CEO of Qantas, James has been chair of some of Australia's leading organisations including Woolworths, Insurance Australia Group (IAG), the Australia Council for the Arts and the International Air Transport Association (IATA). He currently serves as chairman of the Australian Institute of Company Directors and Kathmandu Holdings as well as serving on the board of other prominent organisations.

An Officer of the Order of Australia (AO), one of the hallmarks of James' leadership has been his ability to communicate, engage and lead positive change. So as I researched this book I was curious about his insights into the role of courage in engaging employees, building trust and creating a culture that provided a competitive edge in an increasingly competitive and fast-changing global marketplace.

'As a leader you have to be willing to put yourself at risk in the way you communicate and interact with employees,' he shared with me. 'It's essential to be willing to expose yourself as a CEO, a leader, and as an individual. Many people in positions of leadership shy away from engaging in unstructured and unprepared dialogue, easily justifying their failure to do so by the many demands on their time.' Yet James believes that truly effective leaders don't let their fear of uncertainty or awkward confrontation get in the way of having real conversations about the often contentious issues on people's minds.

James shared with me that it is essential for leaders to overcome any natural shyness and their own personal fears for the sake of something more important. 'Being willing to engage in open dialogue is much more challenging than making a speech or issuing a statement. It puts you on your mettle without support.'

'Being willing to talk to people at every level, especially at the front line, in unstructured ways can be daunting for many leaders. It takes courage to expose yourself in an unstructured session of discussion where you risk direct criticism, difficult questions, hostility and even unsuccessful outcomes because you are leaving the safety of a scripted message delivered in a controlled environment.'

Finding the courage to step out of your comfort zone in how you engage with others sets a powerful example that helps to cultivate a culture of courage throughout the organisation. As James said, 'Engaging in open dialogue is one of the most powerful interactions a leader can have. It makes a dramatic statement of respect and has an equally dramatic effect on leadership credibility. People notice when a leader puts themselves at risk and shows a genuine interest in people, their tasks, their contribution, their concerns and their problems. They also respect them more for doing so'.

At the heart of leadership is the impact you can make on your fellow human beings by virtue of who you are. If you think about the people who've influenced you the most over the course of your career and life, it's got less to do with *what* they ever did, and far more to do with *who* they were. Your power, therefore, doesn't reside in being right, but in being real. In our culture today, which places so much focus on the superficial, people crave authenticity and are hungry for unaffected, down-to-earth, what-you-see-is-what-you-get realness. I know myself there's little I enjoy more than the company of people who live their lives on purpose but are without a need to impress others with their accomplishments. My guess is you do too.

When you're able to interact authentically with people you become imminently more approachable, trusted and influential. We trust people who don't need to protect themselves in how they communicate nor prove their superiority, success or significance in any way; people who can share from a place of being 'human' rather than one of being a little bit better than the rest of us.

Leaders inspire not because of what they do,
but because of who they are.

Leadership is far more about who you are being than about what you are doing. As I wrote in chapter 1: the *being* comes first, the *doing* follows. The five ways you can engage authentically with those around you are to:

- *listen authentically*—the power of presence
- *share authentically*—the power of vulnerability
- *express authentically*—the power of individuality
- *acknowledge authentically*—the power of appreciation
- *serve authentically*—the power of other-centredness.

Listen authentically: the power of presence

Most of us struggle to listen to people around us with the level of authenticity that makes them feel truly heard. That's because while we're pretending to listen, we're really just 'reloading', waiting for our turn to fire back our opinion to help them 'see the light'. But genuine listening is done not with the intention of being understood, but with the intention of understanding. Too few of us do it well.

When was the last time someone asked you how you were doing and then sat and listened to your response, without cutting in or interjecting their own thoughts, opinions or suggestions? Putting aside the time to truly listen to someone is an act of generosity. It validates who they are in ways that nothing else can. It also helps you appreciate the world they're living in, which, while it may have a lot of outward similarities to your own, may be starkly different from yours.

Listening is often highly underrated; yet it's the most powerful tool in any leader's toolkit. Listening authentically impacts the quality of every career and business relationship you have. It breaks down the barriers that keep people from being able to trust, collaborate and work together in the most optimal way. It provides a means to growing truly powerful, collaborative relationships and optimising cooperation with your co-workers, clients, suppliers and employees.

Unlock the power of presence as you listen

Listening is a powerful way of building quality relationships and growing influence. There are many different modes of listening, but they can roughly be broken down into three core levels that are distinguished from each other by where the listener is focusing their attention. Each level is of value in its own right for different situations. However, engaging authentically with those around you requires being able to listen from all three levels. As you read through the descriptions below, think about how often you listen at each of these levels. Then make a commitment to upgrading the quality of how you listen, focusing your attention first and foremost on deepening your understanding of what *they* think and feel, rather than on what *you* think and feel.

- *Level 1: informational listening* is listening for how things affect you. It is typical of information gathering: you call the accounts department to find out whether they've processed your expense claim, or call a vendor to see if a supply item is back in stock. You listen for answers to your questions and pay attention to how those answers affect you and your plans.

- *Level 2: focused listening* is when your attention is focused on the person you're listening to. This is the attention you may bring to a co-worker who seems unhappy about a recent decision. You ask questions and listen to what's going on for them. You listen beyond their words to their tone and body language and pay attention to their emotions. Listening from level 2 can be aided by practising listening techniques such as reflecting back in your own words what someone has said to clarify understanding and asking questions to encourage sharing—all of which can be very useful.

(continued)

Unlock the power of presence as you listen (cont'd)

- *Level 3: authentic listening* is centred in presence and transcends technique. It requires pressing 'pause' on your own agenda and concerns and being fully present, in the moment, for someone else (in other words, no multitasking!). It's listening through their frame of reference, not your own. It demands your full and undistracted presence as you listen from a place of generosity and compassion, trying to put yourself into the other person's shoes, see the world as they see it and feel the world as they feel it.

At level 3 you're listening beyond just what you're seeing or hearing to what your intuition is telling you about this person (and which often goes unsaid.) Silence has a special place when you are listening at this level. If you speak while listening from level 3 it's only to deepen your understanding further, to affirm and acknowledge their emotions. Knowing that you're giving them your full attention—that you're truly present to them—serves to deepen trust and pave the way for genuine change, making others more receptive, and less defensive, to your opinion, however different it may be. Authentic listening creates a platform for building stronger teams, growing collaboration and enhancing synergies in ways that transcend all others.

When you lecture, explain or prescribe without first listening, you alienate people and raise their defences. But when you genuinely try to understand their perspective, and listen in a way that resonates with respect and sincerity, you can enrol others in your aspirations and vision and influence change in ways that those who fail to listen well never can.

Share authentically: the power of vulnerability

Sharing yourself authentically—revealing your humanity—is a bit like investing in the stock market: you can't benefit from the upside (open, caring and trust-filled relationships) without also having the downside (vulnerability.) Leaders to whom others can relate as fellow human beings—rather than simply as people with the power to cut their budget or outsource their job—have the ability to engage employees and raise performance beyond anything leaders without authenticity can. As Harvard researcher Shawn Anchor wrote in his book *The Happiness Advantage*, 'The more genuinely expressive someone is, the more their mindset and feelings spread'.

Mother Teresa, a woman respected the world over for her raw courage and total lack of pretension, once said, 'Honesty and transparency make you vulnerable. Be honest and transparent anyway'. The word 'vulnerable' carries a negative connotation but it's through becoming vulnerable that we can connect most deeply with others. That said, I want to be clear that vulnerability does not equate to weakness or limitation. No leader in their right mind would advocate a weak position on the market battlefield or want those around them to look weak in any way. Quite the opposite: strength of character and position are critical in balancing vulnerability.

Sharing yourself authentically can run against your protective instincts. This explains why when you anticipate finding yourself in a vulnerable predicament your automatic reaction is to put up your guard and protect yourself: to pull out of the launch, cancel the meeting, step back from the relationship or retreat from centre stage.

While allowing yourself to be vulnerable goes against your instincts, it's also how you connect most deeply to other people. Yet, as Brene Brown wrote in *The Gift of Imperfection*, 'Heroics are often about putting our life on the line. Ordinary courage is about putting our vulnerability on the line.' Indeed, genuine leadership calls for each of us to embrace our own vulnerability, not only so that we can connect more authentically with the people around us, but so that we can inspire them to embrace their own vulnerability. By revealing your humanity. By revealing your humanity you can create trusting relationships in the team around you in a way that showing only your strengths never can.

Express authentically: the power of individuality ('Brand You Inc.')

Your brand is the unique promise you make to your organisation, clients and colleagues. You build your brand in every interaction, conversation and action—from the most mundane to the most significant.

Priscilla Bryans, a partner at Freehills law firm, shared with me her journey of coming to realise the power of simply owning what made her different. An extrovert by nature, early in her career she felt she needed to be more like the many introverts she worked with in order to be successful. For years she was concerned that if she just acted herself others wouldn't take her seriously and that it could impede her career. But over time Priscilla came to realise that by daring to express herself authentically, as vulnerable as that initially made her feel, she was able to forge more meaningful relationships. When all you do is conform, all you have to offer is conformity; when all you do is try to fit in, you negate the difference your difference makes. All the while you deprive your co-workers, your clients and your organisation from the full quota of unique value that you, and only you, can bring. When you're preoccupied with a need to impress people, the impression you usually make is a far cry from the one you want.

If I were to go into your workplace and ask everyone you interact with what words come to mind when they think of you, what common attributes do you think would come up again and again? If I were to do the same for everyone else in your organisation, what would stand out about you that would differentiate you from others?

 ## You can't lead from the crowd

To achieve outstanding success you have to be willing to stand out. Authentic self-expression is about embracing what makes you unique and refusing to succumb to conformity for the sake of fitting in and avoiding criticism.

Owning what makes you different enables you to differentiate yourself and build a strong personal brand in your work and organisational 'marketplace'. While it's important to be mindful of how others are perceiving you, when you allow their perceptions of you to determine who you will be, you sell out to conformity and deprive yourself and the world of what makes you unique.

Britain's indomitable Margaret Thatcher once said, 'You cannot lead from the crowd'. While sometimes leadership entails taking on powerful forces of opposition in the organisational, business or political environment, as Thatcher did with the unions in the UK during the 1970s, more often it requires standing firm against the powerful inner forces that drive us to conform, fit in and vanilla down what makes us different.

Coco Chanel said, 'In order to be irreplaceable, one must always be different.' Expressing yourself authentically, therefore, means having the courage to stand out from those around you. Not for the sake of being different or seeking attention, but because you are committed to expressing yourself in a way that's truly congruent with who you are, even if who you are isn't everyone's cup of tea. Margaret Thatcher most certainly wasn't, but she will go down in history not only as one of Britain's most formidable prime ministers, but as one of the strongest leaders of the 20th century. When it comes to having Tall Poppy courage (which I wrote about earlier in this book), Margaret Thatcher had it in spades.

Therein lies the distinction between sharing authentically and expressing authentically. Where sharing is about revealing your humanity, expressing is about owning your individuality. Expressing yourself authentically is about owning what makes you different and refusing to conform to an expectation of how you 'should' be. Authentic self-expression is what enables you to build your own unique brand in your organisation and differentiate yourself from everyone else around you.

Your personal brand creates the identity you have in your organisation, industry or profession. It's how you 'show up' for people around you and is shaped by the attributes that first come to mind when they think of you. Just as you may associate Mercedes Benz with quality high-end cars or McDonald's with universally consistent fast-food burger chains, so too do people associate qualities with you when they think of you. While the concept of a 'personal brand' may be a relatively newly coined term (just Google it to see how many hits you get), the impact of it on your career and professional success is not. You have always had a brand; you just may not have realised it.

Every interaction and conversation you have — from the most mundane (passing someone in the hallway on your way to the copy machine) to the most significant (presenting to the board) — shapes and builds Brand You Inc. Every time someone deals with you, or hears someone speak of you, it generates an impression. First impressions matter a lot, but so too do the countless other impressions people make of you over time. Each one reinforces those that have gone before, shaping a general perception of you, which, over time, can set like cement and become increasingly difficult to reshape. It matters little whether the perception others have of you is fair or aligned with how you see yourself. Given the cardinal rule that 'perception is reality', the way others perceive you and the qualities you possess (or don't possess) combine to create Brand You Inc. That brand will either open doors or close them, grow your influence or erode it, for richer for poorer, for better for worse, until work do you part.

When all you do is conform, all you have to offer is conformity; when all you do is try to fit in, you negate the difference your difference makes.

Looking at this through the lens of a marketer, you might also define Brand You Inc. as the unique promise that you implicitly make to your organisation, your clients and those you know and work with: your 'unique value proposition', if you will. It's what differentiates you from your peers. Too often the strength of your brand — as a leader and as an employee — is undermined by your insecurity, anxiety and concern about 'what people will think'. That doesn't mean you shouldn't be mindful of the corporate norms and standards of dress and behaviour that enable you to perform your job effectively and be taken seriously by those you work with. It does mean that you don't give up those elements of yourself that reflect who you are.

Social psychologists have found that two out of three people are dramatically out of touch with how they see themselves compared to how others see them, the irony being that people who strive the hardest to be liked or to impress others often have just the opposite effect on those around them. Most people have an inbuilt 'realness' detector that starts flashing red when they find themselves in the company of someone who seems to lack it. We can sniff out insincerity, inauthenticity and practised charm a mile away. We sense incongruence even if we can't put our finger on what's missing. Expressing yourself authentically requires not letting others' opinions matter more than your own, particularly given that your assumptions about what other people are thinking are so often off the mark. As Dr Seuss so wisely said, 'Be who you are and say what you feel because those who mind don't matter and those who matter don't mind'.

Acknowledge authentically: the power of appreciation

It's easy to criticise others. Many people are exceptionally talented at it. But while constructive criticism—delivered in the right way at the right time—has its place, to be effective it must be balanced with hearty doses of praise, appreciation and acknowledgement.

A few years ago I was a speaker at an event with Jim Clifton, CEO and chairman of Gallup Organization. I happened to be speaking right after him, so I was able to hear what he had to say. As he shared the lessons he had learned over the course of his career, he emphasised that people should focus more on their strengths, on what they're naturally good at—and less on their weaknesses—because it's through leveraging your natural strengths that you make your biggest mark, not by offsetting your weaknesses. Given that a recent Gallup survey found that only 11 per cent of employees worldwide are engaged in their jobs, it would seem that one of the most significant and tangible ways leaders can boost engagement is to help employees know their strengths—and that starts by acknowledging them.

Leaders—from team supervisors to C-Suite executives—are constantly on the alert for behaviours that might jeopardise team results. But keeping people focused on strengthening their weaknesses can come at the cost of not gaining the full benefit of their strengths. As attention and effort is invested in bolstering weakness, natural strengths atrophy. Finding the right balance is an ongoing challenge, but there is no better place to start than by acknowledging and celebrating what they do well.

In *Why Marriages Succeed and Why Marriages Fail,* John Gottmann found that relationships that had a 5-to-1 ratio of appreciation to criticism were the most healthy, happy and productive. Relationships that were at or below a 1-to-1 ratio of appreciation to criticism were headed towards failure. His ability to predict divorce based on his observations of how couples communicated was alarmingly accurate (better than 90 per cent!). Work relationships are not dissimilar.

Many people go to work each day not feeling that their strengths, efforts and accomplishments are valued fully by those around them. Too few are encouraged to focus on them. Acknowledging authentically means taking time out from your busyness to focus on what people are doing well and acknowledging them for it. Don't be limited to a result that someone has achieved. Focus on the virtues they've brought to the task at hand: perseverance, collaboration, a sense of humour, tenacity, resilience, initiative, creativity, assertiveness, flexibility, strong organisation or a great work ethic. Often we assume that others don't need our affirmation in order to know they've done a good job, yet I have yet to see a pat on the back go unappreciated.

> *Everyone likes to feel part of a tribe, nurtured and celebrated.*
> **Megan Quinn**

Likewise, if you'd like to see others demonstrate more of a particular virtue, you can do what I call 'acknowledge into the future'. I often do this with my children, encouraging them to continue working on a specific skill, problem or task (such as tidying their room) in a more positive way. My nine-year-old son Matthew isn't particularly fond of homework, having declared it to be the worst idea any teacher ever came up with. So when I find him sitting quietly in the afternoon doing his homework on his own initiative, I say, 'Matthew, it's wonderful to see how responsible you are about getting on with your homework. I think your idea to get it done and out of the way when you get home is really smart'. Of course, he doesn't always arrive home and pull out his homework straight away, but catching him doing something right reinforces the positive behaviours moving forward.

This isn't child psychology; it's performance psychology. You can do the same for those you work with to encourage and reinforce the behaviours you know will help people be more successful in their work and contribute more to the outcomes of your team. Take time to 'catch people doing something right'. Acknowledging someone not just for what they do, but the way they do it, can make someone's day. If you were raised with the 'people shouldn't need a pat on the back to do their job' school of thought, it may feel awkward and uncomfortable at first. Get over yourself! Step out of your comfort zone and show by example what it means to see the best in people, even those who drive you crazy. Most people are starved for acknowledgement (those who drive you nuts are likely the most starved of all!), so you have no idea what a huge impact your few words may have. Just imagine what your team or organisation would be like if everyone took more time to acknowledge and appreciate the great work done by those around them. Amplify your ability to influence those around you by taking a few more moments out of your day to acknowledge them.

Serve authentically: the power of other-centredness

Studies have found that how we support and celebrate people when things are going well and they're enjoying success makes an even bigger impact on our relationships with them than how we support them in times of crisis. Transferring this finding to leadership means that actively supporting people to be more successful—even when there isn't any imminent crisis—places big deposits into the relationship's bank account that can make the crucial difference when a crisis does arrive. If others feel you've been good to them when you haven't needed to, they'll go the extra mile when you need them. Indeed, a Gallup study found that employees who feel genuinely cared for are more productive, more profitable and less likely to jump ship when another offer comes along. So when you engage with others from a place of service, making them feel genuinely cared for, it's not only a nice thing to do; it's smart for business.

> *Life's most persistent and urgent question is:*
> *What are you doing for others?*
> **Martin Luther King Jr**

In *Leadership from the Inside Out* Kevin Cashman wrote, 'Ultimately a leader is not judged so much by how well he or she leads, but by how well he or she serves. All value and contribution are achieved through service'. In other words, it's not about being self-centred, but being other-centred. Of course, while it's a noble goal to approach leadership from a place of service, in our desire to achieve more success we're often drawn away from serving others, to serving ourselves. We are, after all, human beings. The more you remember that it's about them, not you, the more effective you'll be as a leader.

Regardless of its size, no carrot or stick will ever trump the effect you have on those around you when you engage with them from a place of genuine service.

 ## Amplify your leadership brand

Leaders inspire by virtue of who they are. For you to be the kind of person that others think of as a leader—and to build your leadership brand—you'll need to reflect deeply on who it is that you're being. That is:

- What experience do people have of working and interacting with me?

- How do others feel when they're in my presence?

- In what ways could I share more openly?

- Where do I sometimes fail to be fully present to people because I'm preoccupied with what I want them to understand from me?

- How well do I own what makes me different, or am I trying to 'vanilla myself down' to fit in?

- Where do I sometimes hold back sharing authentically for fear of criticism, vulnerability or rejection?

- How can I engage with others by helping them through what I can give rather than what I can get?

Inspire greatness

An IBM Global CEO study found that the best leaders never settle for the status quo, even if that state is positive. However well their business is doing, the best leaders don't rest on their laurels but continually work at doing better. Their example infiltrates down through their senior managers and into the rest of their organisation. Accordingly, the best leaders ultimately create organisations that are best placed to respond to the challenges of an increasingly competitive, uncertain and complex business environment. Regardless of how many layers there are between you and the C-Suite, there's no more powerful way to inspire and influence those around you than by role-modelling the behaviour and mindset you'd like to foster in them.

As leadership expert Lance Secretan wrote in his book *Inspire: What Great Leaders Do*, 'A leader who does not inspire is like a river without water'. Inspiration is something that engages us in every aspect of our lives, not just in certain parts. When you inspire someone to trust themselves more fully, to share their talents more boldly or to use their skills more purposefully, it flows over into every area of life and out to others around them.

Inspiration sets the ripple effect in motion.
At the heart of leadership is inspiring others to dream
more, learn more and become more.

The most valuable gift you can ever give anyone is to reveal to them their own. If you're a parent, it's part and parcel of the role: nurturing your children to grow in confidence, believing in their ability to exceed their expectations, helping them discover where their gifts lie, teaching them the value of hard work combined with courageous action, and setting them on a path to creating a more rewarding and meaningful life.

As a leader within your organisation, your role is not dissimilar. Naturally you may feel very differently about the people you work with than you do about your own children, but don't forget that everyone you work with was once a child and they may not have had the encouragement, role models and mentors they needed...until now (that's where you come in!). Just because it's hard to see potential in some people doesn't mean they don't have it.

One of the deepest needs of the human spirit is to be inspired. In a climate of fear that has so many people playing safe with their skills and talents, the need for inspiration is greater than ever. You inspire greatness by reminding people of what's at stake, connecting them to the purpose underlying what they're doing and elevating your expectations of them.

Leaders remind people what's at stake

In her keynote MacTaggart lecture at the Edinburgh Television Festival in 2012, Elisabeth Murdoch's comments made international headlines. In the wake of the phone hacking scandal that rocked the News Corporation empire her father, Rupert Murdoch, built up from an Adelaide newspaper, what Elisabeth said in her lecture was regarded by many as a rebuke of her brother James's comments at the same lecture three years earlier. Ms Murdoch said that her brother's speech, which asserted that profit is the 'only reliable, durable and perpetual guarantor of independence', told only part of the story.

'Profit must be our servant, not our master,' she said. 'After the past year of scrutiny into our media standards and the sometimes self-serving relationships between the great institutional pillars of our society—be they police, politics, media or banking—we would all do well to remember Voltaire's (or even Spiderman's) caution that, "With great power comes great responsibility".'

Ms Murdoch asserted that profit without purpose is a sure-fire recipe for disaster, as her family had witnessed: 'Sadly, the greatest threats to our free society are too often from enemies within'.

> *There's nothing more demoralising than a leader who can't clearly articulate why we're doing what we're doing.*
> **James Kouzes and Barry Posner**

Profit without purpose is costly on so many levels. Helping to connect people to a greater sense of purpose in what they do and how they do it—a purpose that, hopefully, can be fulfilled and aligned with the larger purpose of your organisation—will inspire them to engage on a level that no carrot-and-stick motivational techniques can ever do. Keep in mind, as we explored in chapter 1, that you can connect to purpose not only through *what* you're doing, but through *how* you're doing it. So even if people don't feel passionate about the widgets that your company produces or the service you deliver, they can still be passionate about doing their job with excellence.

While there's no arguing that traditional carrot-and-stick motivational approaches to leadership can produce results, they're limited by the size of the carrot and the length of the stick. The most powerful motivation for anyone to work hard, engage fully and persevere in the face of challenges can only come from within them, through their intrinsic desire to achieve something worthy of their effort through inspiration. We see this style of leadership being adopted more and more, particularly in industries that are not shackled by traditional approaches to human resource management. Whatever the approach of your organisation, just imagine the difference it would make if instead of people being treated as units to be moulded and motivated to meet target results, they were regarded as human beings to be nurtured to fulfil their own highest purpose through your organisation.

> *Profit is like oxygen, essential for our survival*
> *but not the reason for our existence.*
> **Lance Secretan**

While spirituality and business may seem an oxymoron, organisations that can connect their employees to a bigger purpose—to a *why* that transcends their pay cheque—are those that can retain and inspire employees to continually go the extra mile, not for the prize of recognition or a promotion, but for the personal fulfilment they get from achieving something worthwhile and personally meaningful to them. Leaders help remind people what's at stake, not just in terms of the bottom-line profitability, but in terms of their own success and fulfilment in their careers. They help them understand why they're doing something beyond just the obvious. When people can find meaning in what they're doing, however mundane it may be, it elevates how they do it and the outcome they achieve. It grows engagement and helps them to think beyond compliance to how they can improve systems, processes and products. It not only improves performance and builds confidence, but sets them up to go on to doing bigger things in the future.

Martin Luther King Jr's 'I Have a Dream' speech connected millions of people with a bigger vision, a bigger purpose, a bigger *why*. While King's speech was one that rallied people behind a cause, if you listen to the background noise you can hear the muffled sounds of the many hundreds of thousands at the Lincoln Memorial on that humid August day clapping, hollering and shouting, 'Amen', 'Oh, yes', and 'Alleluia brother'. King connected them to a vision they had not dared to dream for themselves. He tapped into their sadness, their anger and their fear. Most of all he tapped into their desperate hope that the future could be brighter than the past. Through their shouts, nods, claps and responses they were letting him know, 'You're telling me what I know is true. You're feeling what I'm feeling. You're seeing what I want to see, but have dared not imagine. Your dream is now mine'.

Leaders see not just what is, they see what can be.
They don't permit what's probable to limit achieving
what's possible.

When you help others to learn more, to grow more, to dream more and to become more, you fulfil the greatest call of leadership: to cultivate the leader in others.

Elevate expectations

Being a leader goes beyond any 'tricks of the trade' or 'techniques' you may pick up in any of the thousands of books written on leadership. Transcending anything you may do or say, truly inspiring leadership comes back to how you see the world that so profoundly shapes who you are in the world. For this you will need to be able to see the world, your work and those you work with, from three levels, as shown in figure 7.2:

- *Level 1:* Seeing what is now through the eyes of reality. This is the level of perception. A leader listens from this level.

- *Level 2:* Seeing what will be through the eyes of discernment. This is the level of probability. A leader manages from this level.

- *Level 3:* Seeing what can be through the eyes of vision. This is the level of possibility. A leader lives and inspires from this level.

Figure 7.2: leaders see what can be

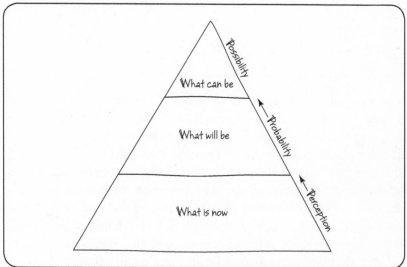

You inspire greatness when you help people move up from 'what is now'—often a place that's lacking in ambition, where decisions are driven by fear rather than by inspiration or ambition—to 'what could be'—a place of possibility, purpose and courage.

In ancient Greek mythology, Pygmalion was a Cypriot goldsmith who carved the sculpture of a woman out of ivory. On the day of the Venus festival Pygmalion made an offering at the altar of Venus, where he quietly wished that his ivory sculpture would be changed to a real woman. Returning home he kissed his statue on the lips only to find they felt warm. He kissed it again, then proceeded to caress her body which had lost its hardness. His wish had come true! Venus had granted Pygmalion his heart's desire, and so, at least according to legend (and Wikipedia!) Pygmalion went on to marry his creation and they lived happily ever after.

Psychologists have borrowed from Greek mythology to describe the impact of positive expectation, which they've called The Pygmalion Effect. It has been well documented as a simple and effective way to boost performance in the classroom, in the workplace, in the military and elsewhere. In the realm of leadership, when you believe in the potential of those around you to make a meaningful contribution and ascend to greatness in their own right, the stage is set for them to do just that.

The more you expect from others, the more they will deliver.

The Pygmalion Effect was first studied in the famous experiment by psychologist Robert Rosenthal on elementary school students. In his study, Rosenthal led teachers to believe that certain students in their classrooms had been identified as 'intellectual bloomers', children who would show an intellectual growth spurt during the school year. In actuality, the students were randomly given the designation of intellectual bloomers, but at the end of the term these students did indeed show higher academic achievement. Why? Because the teachers believed in them. How? Later studies showed that teachers unconsciously gave more positive attention, feedback and learning opportunities to these students. In short, teachers were able to nonverbally communicate their positive expectations for academic success to these students.

Professor Dov Eden from Tel Aviv University went on to demonstrate the Pygmalion Effect in all sorts of work groups, across all sectors and industries. If supervisors or managers hold positive expectations about the performance of those they lead—for example, by believing they could solve a very challenging problem—performance improves. A recent meta-analysis (a statistical analysis that combines the results of numerous studies) found Pygmalion leadership training to be the most effective leadership development intervention.

On the other hand, if the leader holds negative expectations—expectations that their team or group will fail—performance weakens. This has been called the Golem effect. It's where lowering the expectations of people (including ourselves!) leads to poorer performance. Both the Pygmalion and Golem effects are forms of 'self-fulfilling prophesy'. To summarise both: *Expect much, get more. Expect little, get less.*

Of course, expecting that everyone in every situation will meet or exceed your expectations is naive. Just as you don't always act with the level of courage, commitment and character that you aspire to, so too will others sometimes falter and fall short. Don't be blind to obvious inconsistencies in behaviour. Blind trust is foolish. Rather, trust that people, by and large, are good, mean well and have within them the resources to solve their own problems. Likewise, trust your intuition when something feels amiss.

Whether you're a leader of two or a leader of 2000, when you expect more from those you work with, you can do more yourself.

As you move up into roles with greater demands and responsibilities you'll become more discerning about how you spend your time. The challenge for many people who rise up from the ranks of a solo-contributor into a managerial role is to 'get out of the weeds' and delegate more to others. While delegating may not seem like a particularly brave thing to do, it can be for people who fear that the potentially substandard work of others will impact their reputation and success. There's no getting away from it: delegating and outsourcing involves risk. However, in failing to delegate you can run the greater risk of failing to deliver what's expected of you.

David Ogilvy, founder of the giant advertising agency Ogilvy and Mather, used to give each new manager a Russian doll which contains five progressively smaller dolls. He put a message inside the smallest one that read, 'If each of us hires people we consider smaller than ourselves, we shall become a company of dwarves. But if each of us hires people who are bigger than we are, we will become a company of giants'. Beyond the need to hire people who have skills and talents that complement and exceed our own is the need to inspire those we already work with to use their skills and talents in ways that complement and exceed our own, by inspiring them to greatness.

The focus of a leader should be to build big people, because big people take bigger actions and handle problems in bigger ways. When you trust others to get on with their job, it elevates their performance. When you micromanage and fail to trust them to perform within their ability, it undermines it. While giving people extra responsibility and involvement in decision making increases the risk, it also increases their engagement. Delegation is therefore one of the most powerful managerial tools for increasing productivity and helping others to tap the power of courage in their own working lives. The bottom line: hold high expectations that they will rise to the challenges they face, and more often than not they'll exceed your expectations.

Embolden to action

Engagement. Inspiration. Action!
The most effective leaders in today's fearful environment foster a Culture of Courage where people feel safe and inspired to take risks, to innovate and to experiment. To do that effectively leaders have to take into account the two ecosystems that impact how the people around them think, feel and act:

- *Internal ecosystem*—what's going on inside us
- *External ecosystem*—what's going on around us.

Cultivate a Culture of Courage

Once upon a time there was a leader who was afraid. He had convinced himself that everything that could go wrong, would. He was frightened about industry changes, global competitors, disruptive technologies and frightened that his company, in which his success was staked, would lose its competitive edge. His fear overshadowed every decision and infiltrated every conversation. He worked in fear, spoke with fear and led from fear. Gradually but surely, his fear seeped through his management team, then filtered down into every department until it weighed down the spirit of everyone in his organisation. Everyone was afraid. No-one felt secure.

As his anxiety grew his judgement weakened. He cut spending, and random staff reductions were little more than self-fulfilling prophecies of doom. He kept his cards to his chest and his plans even closer. He watched every move his subordinates made. After a while, their initiative ceased. Those bold enough to challenge him were soon shown the door. Distrust spread through the ranks as fear had before it. When he tried to hire new staff he soon found word had passed around: this was not a company for trailblazers, innovators and fast movers. The organisation lived on the fumes of past success. Eventually it was gutted by an investment firm and sold for whatever they could get.

Once upon a time ... *ahhh* ... don't we wish. While the story is *largely* fictitious (and any resemblance to people in your workplace is purely coincidental) the reality is that it's a tale far too common in many organisations today.

People play safe when they don't feel it's safe to do otherwise. Leaders make it safe for people to take risks and make mistakes.

Often the biggest threat to an organisation isn't the most visible one; it's the fear that resides within its walls. As headlines blaze with news of cutbacks and jobs going offshore, fear can spread like a virus, driving potentially courageous people to take the path most travelled, play safe and hunker down to protect what security they think they have. Many workplaces *are* unsafe and dysfunctional, perpetuating fear and driving creativity and innovation into a ditch. To do well people have to feel that it's safe to explore, to try new things and to take risks. If they don't feel safe, they won't take them. Stagnation will ensue.

Needless to say, the need for leaders to embolden others to rethink risk and act more boldly is greater than ever. Those who accept the invitation will stand out, and because they stand out they'll find themselves in a unique position to see opportunity where others see none, to grow influence where others grow anxiety and to plant seeds of courage in those around them where others plant only seeds of doubt. In an emotionally safe environment, mistakes are not career-enders, and failure becomes a valuable teacher, teaching us things we wouldn't otherwise learn. So when you make others feel respected and cared for, you encourage (en+courage) them to go forward and take risks.

In many ways, a leader acts as the emotional guide for those around them. Like a barometer, they help to set the emotional temperature: people take their cues from them on how to respond and react to situations. By tuning in and acknowledging the fears and anxieties of those around them, leaders can help people navigate their way through change and uncertainty more confidently. Even in the presence of fear, uncertainty and risk-averseness, they can help to cultivate a Culture of Courage.

Online retailer Zappos has become famous for doing just that. In their 2011 *Culture Book*, which all employees are invited to contribute to, Courtney B. wrote that at Zappos, 'You are empowered to excel at your position in the manner that you see fit. You are given freedom to prioritize. You are given freedom to take initiatives. You are given freedom to go outside to the temporary carnival and get your face painted if you need an afternoon break. Excellence is expected—even demanded—but mistakes are also understood. Most importantly, it's about being part of something bigger than yourself and bigger than the bottom line, and that breeds fulfilment'.

Who wouldn't enjoy working in an environment like that? Too often managers fixate on what will happen if people fail. How often have you heard others warn, 'If you screw up, you're a goner' or said to yourself, 'I'll die if I mess this up'? The problem is that the more attention we put on what may go wrong, the less we have left for what could go right. As Bill Treasurer wrote in *Courage Goes to Work*, 'By focusing solely on the consequences of failure, such managers are, in effect, widening the holes in the safety nets'.

Creating a 'have a go' culture

In the late 1990s I worked as a consultant with Darrell Wade and his team at Intrepid Travel in Melbourne. While a move overseas ended my work with Darrell, I enjoyed keeping tabs on the company he founded with his mate Geoff Manchester.

Darrell and Geoff came up with the idea for Intrepid Travel on an epic journey across Africa in 1988 with a group of friends. They felt they could offer travellers a new way to travel: small group adventures that would have all the benefits of independent travel with none of the hassles. They weren't focused on the money but, Darrell said, 'We never set out to build a big business. We just wanted to travel, share our passion and have some fun doing it. And—oh, yes—hopefully pay the bills! As time went on we employed people who were as passionate as we were and so the energy in the business just kept growing'.

And grow it has! Darrell is now CEO of PEAK Adventures, a joint venture between Intrepid Travel and the world's largest leisure travel group, TUI Travel, which consists of more than 20 businesses, has an annual revenue in excess of $400 million and takes 340 000 passengers on adventures to all seven continents each year.

Darrell's passion for authentic and 'off the beaten path' travel experiences has made him a trailblazer in the adventure travel industry and a recognised leader in adventure travel, business and environmental sustainability. When I asked him about the importance of taking risks and challenging assumptions he said, 'I love challenging the status quo. Some might see this as taking a risk. I just see it as progress. If we've always done something a certain way, then it is probably time to challenge the assumption behind that and see if there is a better way. I also like pushing the business in new directions—be that into new markets, new products or new destinations. Sure, sometimes this doesn't work and we lose a few dollars and maybe a bit of pride, but ultimately I think even failure is positive. It creates a culture of "having a go" and "we can do anything". If we fear failure from taking a step into the unknown our business is doomed'.

(continued)

Creating a 'have a go' culture (*cont'd*)

In 1992 Intrepid Travel was still very small and had just started operating its first trips in Vietnam. 'This was quite a thing in those days. Back then many still thought of it as a war zone!' Darrell recalls. Around the same time there was a significant article on Vietnam in a large-circulation magazine. As soon as the article came out Darrell booked a full-page advertisement in the next edition of the magazine, hoping to capitalise on the article and get some tour bookings. The cost of the advertisement was roughly equal to Intrepid's annual marketing budget at the time. 'Everyone thought I was crazy. But it felt right to me and sometimes you just have to back yourself,' recalls Darrell. As it turned out, the advertisement was transformative and doubled Intrepid's business overnight!

Darrell believes too many people invest too much time and energy worrying about what might go wrong and encourages those in his company to embrace the Nike tagline, 'Just do it'.

'Sure, things go wrong and good planning and risk analysis is important,' he says, 'but ultimately you have to step forward, put one foot in front of the other and just do it!'

To create a Culture of Courage in your team or organisation you need to ensure people feel safe to push the envelope of what's possible, to think outside the box and to challenge status-quo thinking. Naturally, sometimes decisions will be made that, with hindsight, are viewed as less than optimal. But unless people feel they're able to make the odd bad decision, will they be able to take the risks to make truly good ones? Smart risks lead to smart mistakes, and smart mistakes are always an incredibly valuable part of the learning process.

People feel safe when they know that if what they try doesn't work out, they won't have to walk out the door. Reassuring people that their risks won't be punished—assuming they're doing their homework and not being reckless or foolhardy—helps to offset their fear and promote their willingness to try new things.

In his book *Emotional Intelligence*, Daniel Goleman wrote, 'Like second-hand smoke, the leakage of emotions can make a bystander an innocent casualty of someone else's toxic state'. As a leader, you have the responsibility to ensure that whatever emotions you're spreading around your team or organisation, they're setting others up to be more successful, not less; more confident, not less; more calm, not less; more adaptable, not less; and more willing to do whatever it takes to find opportunity in adversity and to go the extra mile when the extra mile truly counts.

Build courage in increments

If you start with 40-kilogram weights on the first day of a workout program, you'll either not be able to lift them or become so sore you won't go back. But if you start with 15 kilograms and give yourself a day of rest in between workouts, you can gradually add more weights onto your bar. It's the same for building 'courage muscles' in both yourself and those in your team.

Nicole Geller, CEO of GCS, shared with me that, 'Just because I see something in a person doesn't mean they see it in themselves. Sometimes as a leader we have to push people a little to get them out of their comfort zone because we know that they have what it takes to do more but they just don't know it themselves. Most of the time they are far more successful than they think they will be. But whether they are or they aren't, it's important to help them to see and celebrate what they've accomplished'.

The term 'comfort zone' is widely used to describe the place where most people tend to live unless they've made the decision to step out of it towards something they want to achieve, or they've been forced out of it by virtue of a challenge that's been thrust upon them. Either way, being out of your comfort zone is ... drum roll please ... uncomfortable. The more you step outside your comfort zone, the more courageous you become, gradually expanding the perimeter of your courage zone, as illustrated in figure 7.3 (overleaf).

However, while it's important to step outside your comfort zone to discover new skills and develop confidence, if you find yourself on the outer periphery of terror you won't learn anything and it can do you far more harm than good. The same applies to those around you. Sometimes people need to be gently coaxed out of their comfort zone in small, but increasingly braver, steps in between periods of regeneration.

Figure 7.3: expand your courage zone

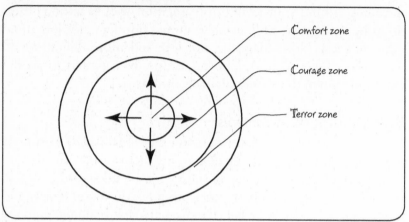

The more often people are exposed to situations that are out of their comfort zone, the more comfortable they become with those situations. The psychological term for this is the 'mere exposure effect' and it explains that the more someone is 'merely exposed' to a situation that's making them uncomfortable, the more they become desensitised to it, until they reach the point where they're comfortable with it.

Bomb disposal experts, when given both the right training to disarm highly explosive bombs and sufficient practice at doing it, are able to handle situations that would frighten the socks off most people—with extraordinary calm. Helping people build competence through developing new skills and increasing their exposure to new situations reduces their fear of failure. In doing so, you create a scaffolding that builds their confidence to take bolder actions in the future.

Asking someone to do something they haven't prepared for and that's too far outside their comfort zone—such as leading a presentation in front of a large group of people—can produce the exact opposite of the outcome you want. But asking them to assist in preparing and co-presenting a few times before they take on the lead role (thereby building their competence and confidence) will set them up for success when they take the lead.

Reward courageous behaviour

From small businesses to large corporations, only by continually trying new things can organisations hope to prevail over the longer term through the inevitable economic oscillations. Ongoing experimentation enables a team or organisation to maximise its chances of developing better ways of doing things that put it at an advantage over others that don't. Of course, experimentation can't take place without mistakes, so organisations must be willing to make them.

A senior executive from one of the world's largest corporations shared with me that when he sees people who never make mistakes, it's a sign that they have become too comfortable. 'If people are going to be ready for bigger jobs, they have to be put into roles that have some element of risk. Even if managed carefully, there is always some risk. We all have to be willing to stretch ourselves, or we will never know how much we can do, and neither will anyone else,' he said, adding that 'of course it's also important to have safeguards so any mistakes do not put at risk the safety, security and financial viability of the operation'.

Many big corporations only recruit highly skilled people who have demonstrated performance potential. Those who rise up the ranks into leadership are those who are willing to stretch themselves, add value beyond what's asked of them and show their ability to influence without authority. In organisations where the operational risks are very real (as with any manufacturing organisation), being able to assess and mitigate against operational risk while taking on the political risks involved in growing influence is crucial to success.

While courage doesn't guarantee success, it always precedes it. Reward it accordingly.

In *How Winning Leaders Make Great Calls*, Noel Tichy and Warren Bennis wrote, 'Courageous leaders often get their courage from their fear about what will happen if they *don't* step up and boldly step out'. Sometimes people are afraid but they're not even sure what they're afraid of. Sure, they're scared that something will change or that they might fail or that they might lose their job.

But what fears lie beneath the obvious? What is it about change that makes them so fearful? What is it about losing their job or being passed over for promotion that gives rise to their anxiety? As I shared in chapter 2, fear of the consequences of failing to take action can be a great motivator in getting the job done quickly and efficiently. In his book *Peak Performers*, Charles Garfield says that peak performers are able to ask themselves the questions, 'What's the worst that could happen?' and 'What would I do if the worst actually did happen?' Helping those around you explore those two questions significantly lowers the perceived risk and helps to harness the energy of fear to move forward.

Likewise, it's important to acknowledge people when they act courageously, even when their actions don't produce the outcome they want. When you reward courageous behaviours—not just successful ones—you're also demonstrating to everyone the values you want them to adopt, and teaching them the value you place on those who refuse to stick with status-quo thinking and play safe. After all, while courage doesn't guarantee success, it always precedes it.

The reward doesn't have to be a trophy or a bonus; it could be a handwritten note from a manager, a pat on the back or a story shared at a team meeting in front of peers. The type of reward doesn't matter so long as it's meaningful to the person receiving it and is linked to the emboldened behaviour you want to encourage.

Set the ripple effect in motion

Any time you drop an object into water, you witness the ripple effect. However small the object, by piercing the surface of the water it sets off an energy force within the body of water that extends outwards. When you choose to step up to the plate of leadership you do just the same.

The extent to which those around you will be willing to act courageously is determined by how much you are. Never underestimate the power of your example: it speaks far more loudly than your words ever can.

The ripple effect is at play every day in everything you do and everything you say. Organisational psychologists have found that each workplace develops its own group emotion, or 'group affective tone', which over time creates shared 'emotional norms' that are proliferated and reinforced by behaviour, both verbal and nonverbal. But it can also work for the positive. Whatever your position, you can affect the emotional tone of those you work with.

'People the world over have always been more impressed by the power of our example than by the example of our power.' The sentiment of these words by Bill Clinton at the 2008 Democratic National Convention, while set in a political context, hold true across all contexts. People everywhere will always be more swayed by the power of your example than by the example of your power. How you engage in doing your job, the way you handle difficult people and difficult situations, and your willingness to take the riskier path over the path of least resistance, will have a far more potent impact on others, and on your career, than any other single factor.

Daring to make a meaningful difference in your organisation and in the world takes courage—leadership courage. Courage to trust in yourself that you have something of great value to contribute. Courage to stand out and risk the possibility that there will be some who may actively work against you. Courage to become vulnerable to falling short, looking foolish or failing outright. Courage to refuse to side with conformity, take the path of least resistance and succumb to the fears and doubts that bombard you daily. Courage to dare to believe that what you do makes a meaningful difference, and that how you do it matters even more.

If it were easy to be a leader in our own lives, much less in the lives of others, everyone would be. If it were easy to live a life of purpose, the world would be a vastly different place. The organisation you work in would be also. Leadership is not the domain of the timid or idle. It takes a special type of person, but it also takes no more than is within the reach of any single person. It takes no more than is within you.

Be the change you would love to see in others.
Everything else will flow from there.

So, as you look at your future—your career and your life—I invite you to think about the impact you want to make on those you'll encounter along the way. While you can never be guaranteed to achieve all the ambitious goals you set for yourself, what is guaranteed is that if you commit to engaging authentically with those around you, to emboldening others to greater feats of bravery and to inspiring them to fulfill their own unique potential, then the mark you'll leave on the world throughout the course of your working life will be far greater than any single professional accomplishment ever could be.

Key points

> All leadership begins with self-leadership. Influence extends from the inside out.

> Through the brand you create you can grow the perception others have of you as a leader and expand your ability to influence change.

> You can't lead by playing safe. Leadership demands the courage to take risks, to speak up, to interact in open dialogue and create a vision that engages and inspires others.

> Leaders must take into account the two ecosystems that impact how people think, feel and act:

 - *internal ecosystem:* what's going on inside us—building a Risk-Ready Courage Mindset

 - *external ecosystem:* what's going on around us—cultivating a Culture of Courage.

> Leaders set the emotional tone for their team and organisation. People take risks when they know it's safe to do so. Likewise, people play safe when they don't feel it's safe to do otherwise.

> The Pygmalion Effect has shown that when you expect much from people, they deliver more, and when you expect little, they deliver less.

> The three core challenges of leaders are to:

  - *engage authentically* to build trust and grow influence

  - *inspire greatness* to remind people of what's at stake and connect them to a bigger purpose

  - *embolden others* to take courageous action, rewarding those ready to take risks.

> The focus of a leader should always be to build bigger people, because bigger people respond to challenges better and take the bolder actions needed to create more beneficial business outcomes.

Part III

Take Courage

Set yourself up for success!

> *Playing safe is probably the most unsafe thing in the world. You cannot stand still. You must go forward.*
> **Robert Collier**

Chapter 8

Trust yourself—take action!

Until one is committed there is hesitancy, a chance to draw back.
Boldness has genius, power and magic in it. Begin it now.
Goethe

In ancient Rome, a centurion had the power to command those who were not Roman citizens to carry their equipment for a mile. At first the conquered people of Rome's expansive empire were very resentful about being forced to carry the load of a Roman centurion and would go only as far as needed to avoid a brutal beating or even death. But in the first century Christians began the tradition of 'going the extra mile'. Not only would they do what was a forced necessity, but they would do more ... by choice.

Two thousand years later the saying 'go the extra mile' has become a powerful philosophy. The idea of not just exerting the minimal effort required to 'get by' but of intentionally 'going the extra mile' has become the hallmark behaviour of successful people the world over. While the marketplace of mediocrity is a crowded space, it's never crowded on the extra mile. That's because going the extra mile takes extra commitment, hard work and sacrifice above that needed to 'get by'. Which is what this chapter is about: helping you identify the 'extra' actions you can take to set yourself up for success, creating for yourself an environment—internal and external—that continually compels you into the courageous and purposeful actions needed to enjoy the success you want in your work and beyond.

No monkey grip

Albert Einstein once said, 'Nothing happens until something moves'. Unlocking the power of courage to create positive movement and momentum in your life takes more than a one-off decision to rethink risk and take bolder actions. It necessitates a commitment to 'going the extra mile' in how you live your life—not succumbing to the excuses, justifications and pressures that can so easily pull you out of action and back into playing safe and living smaller than serves you or anyone else.

While reading this book you have likely had numerous insights on things you could do differently. Insights are nice. They can even be useful. But unless acted upon, they're utterly useless. Taking a bold leap of faith, through your fears and beyond the familiar, is where the rubber truly hits the road. It's where you put your commitment to the test as you move from thinking about what you *could* do, to actually doing it. This is where you reclaim the power that fear and self-doubt have had in your work, relationships and life as you build your own brand of courage.

Rowena Clift is executive director of a large regional hospital in Ballarat, Australia. Rowena began her career as a general nurse and moved into administration, working her way up to the role she's in today, where she ensures that patient care is coordinated across the various hospital departments. Rowena shared with me that she has always felt called to a vocation to care for people in need of medical help, and does her job with a strong sense of purpose. She also shared the motto that has guided her decisions throughout her career: 'no monkey grip'.

Early in her career Rowena realised that to make the maximum impact she wanted to make, she had to be ready to let go of doing purely clinical patient care. She told me, 'You have to be willing to trust, invest and be true to your vision. Otherwise fear of not having what it takes to "make it" on a new branch can hold you back'.

Just as monkeys can't make their way across a rainforest canopy without continuously letting go of the branch they're holding onto, neither can you reach out towards a future that inspires you with both hands holding tightly onto the security of where you are now. You have to trade the safety and familiarity of your present situation for the possibility of something better, whatever uncertainty that creates.

We all arrive at points in our lives where we have to make decisions about whether to take a giant leap of faith in who we are and who we want to become. We can't know for sure that our situation will be better or brighter, which is why we have to 'lean into risk', as I wrote in chapter 2. To paraphrase Henry Thoreau, we have to trust in ourselves that what lies ahead for us is nothing compared to what lies within us, knowing we can never become who we truly want to be unless we are willing to let go of the safety ropes that keep us where and who we are. In the end, that's what courage is ultimately all about: permitting yourself to become vulnerable to all you fear so that you can bloom into the fullest expression of who you are, more powerful than any fear you ever have. Will that sometimes be scary? You bet. And when it is, just feel your fears, acknowledge it, then loosen its grip on the security of where you are now. Only then can you step towards the future you want and discover just what mettle you are truly made of.

To help you do that, it's vital to create an environment around you to support you in being the person you aspire to be, and taking the bolder and riskier actions you need to take to accomplish what inspires you, and make the mark in the world that only you can make. Never underestimate the power of your environment to help or hinder you in achieving the success you want, and being the person you need to be to achieve it.

Don't go it alone: enlist support

While no-one is responsible for your success but you, you'll go much further and faster with the support of other people than you can ever go alone. Designing an environment that sets you up to succeed means actively building a strong network of caring, confident and encouraging people you can reach out to for support, advice or to give you a kick in the pants when you need it. When you're surrounded by people who believe in you and the value you have to contribute, it creates an environment that makes success easier to achieve.

As Ita Buttrose shared with me when we spoke about what it takes to get ahead and stay focused on where you add the greatest value, 'No person is an island. We all need help to get ahead.

People who try to go it alone will find it much more difficult than those who enlist support.' She said that finding a mentor can be extremely beneficial for many people. 'A mentor is someone who has walked the path ahead of you and who can help you assess in which direction you want to go, determine the best strategy, keep you focused on what's most important and help you overcome barriers. If you're nervous about asking someone to mentor you, don't be. Just ask them. Many young editors have made their way to my door. Most people are flattered to be asked for help.'

So many of the most successful people I've met over the years have shared similar sentiments. My friend Joan Amble, former executive vice president of American Express and co-founder and chair of WOMEN in America, an organisation focused on supporting more women into the senior executive ranks of Fortune 500 corporations, often tells women to build their own personal board of directors. Creating your own board of directors made up of a diversity of people with relevant experience, insight and wisdom who are willing to tell you what you should hear—not just what you want to hear—can make a huge difference as you advance in your career. They can help you stay focused on what matters most, make optimal decisions when you come to a crossroads, better navigate new and uncertain territory in your career and remind you of your value if ever you come to doubt it.

Whatever you do, don't go it alone. To quote an African proverb: 'If you want to go fast, go alone. If you want to go far, go together.' Other people can support and help you do things that you can't do yourself. So engage a coach, find a mentor, join a professional association, enlist a trusted friend to hold you accountable or create your own board of directors or mastermind group. Not only can these people help expand your perspective and focus your actions on what matters most, but many (particularly those who work within your industry or profession) can also provide valuable introductions that can open doors to new relationships and opportunities.

Prune your tree

Psychological research has found that people who watch less TV are emotionally healthier, less fearful and more accurate judges of life's risks and rewards than those who subject themselves to the stories of crime, tragedy and death that fill the airwaves on TV drama and news shows. If watching scary movies and sensationalised news stories can impair your ability to assess risk, inciting irrational anxiety and fear, then the people you interact with can have an even more detrimental impact on how you perceive and engage with the world.

Every interaction you have with people around you involves an exchange of energy, positive or negative. When friends, family or colleagues are constantly responding to you with cynicism, pessimism, resignation, anxiety and outright despair, it makes it near impossible to maintain the positive Courage Mindset you need to achieve what you want. I call these people 'emotional vampires'. They literally suck the life out of you and they most certainly don't help build your confidence to play a bigger game in your work or life. Rather, they dampen your confidence, heighten your caution and dilute your courage. To quote George Washington, 'Better to be alone than in bad company'.

Nick, a colleague of mine who runs a consulting business, keeps a picture on his desk of a huge tree with three words underneath it: Prune Your Tree. The picture helps to remind him to always make sure to prune the clients and business relationships that are no longer ripe with opportunity. He's learned from some less-than-enjoyable experiences of staying in relationships that distracted his focus, weighed him down and on a few occasions set his business back financially. Likewise, when you 'prune your tree' of those people who limit your ability to provide the value you want in your career, or drag you down, it doesn't make your life smaller. Rather, it creates space for more rewarding relationships to grow and more fruitful opportunities to emerge.

If you can't prune emotional vampires out of your life (sometimes you're related to them!) or exit a toxic environment where they abound, at least become more vigilant of them and limit contact as much as possible. Like second-hand smoke, it's easy to become a casualty to the toxic mindsets of other people if you're not paying attention. You may want to tell them, as kindly yet as firmly as you can, that you value yourself too highly to give any more time listening to negativity.

Likewise, be wary of those people in your work or social environment who may feel threatened by your desire for change.

As you go about making changes to how you engage in your work and in the world, you may find an almost magnetic force pulling you back into your habitual default ways of thinking and acting. Prepare yourself. People have grown accustomed to relating to you in a certain way. They expect you to act in certain ways and conform to the expectations they have of you. When you begin to step out and speak out, sometimes friction will ensue. Remember it's generally about them, not you. Give them time to adjust to your new approach to life. Let them know that you'd like their support, not their cynicism. Just never give other people's beliefs and insecurities about what they're doing with their life the power to undermine what you're doing with yours.

Sometimes you need to let go of old relationships in order to grow. Don't let others play you small or pressure you to suppress who you are and who you want to become. As author Marianne Williamson wrote, 'Your playing small does not serve the world. There is nothing enlightened about shrinking so that other people won't feel insecure around you'.

Clear your clutter

While it's important to be mindful of your social and emotional environment, your physical environment can also undermine your ability to be courageous in what you do and productive in how you do it. Disorganised people who work and live in chaos simply can't be as focused, purposeful and productive as organised people are.

The Pentagon Federal Credit Union (PenFed) engaged me to run a leadership development program for their employees. As I often do with clients, we set up a meeting to discuss exactly what they wanted to achieve and how I could add maximum value. The initial meeting was with their HR manager and James Schenck, the senior executive on their management team who had engaged me. On arriving in James's office I noticed how many piles of paper he had around his desk. I couldn't help but smile as we shook hands and he gestured for me to take a seat at the table in his office. Noticing the expression on my face he looked over to his cluttered desk and then back at me. 'It's organised chaos,' he assured me with a grin that told me he knew I wouldn't be convinced. 'That's what everyone with a messy desk says, James,' I chided him. I went on to tell him about a study that found that when people with offices that resembled his own were forced to put everything into a well-organised filing system, their productivity went up by between 40 and 60 per cent. He raised his eyebrows and promised me he'd clean it up before my next visit.

About three months later months later I returned to PenFed's head office to run a workshop. On seeing me, James proudly told me that his office was the picture of organisation. He went on to admit that his productivity had improved so much he even tidied up his closet at home! I told him I'd be doing random office spot checks in the years ahead just to keep him on his game. My sense is there's no need. He's found the light!

Clutter undercuts courage. It's much harder to take bold and focused actions when you're surrounded by chaos.

Your physical environment has a huge impact on your ability to achieve at the level you're capable of. Clutter in any area of your life creates clutter in every area of your life. It doesn't help you be more courageous; it keeps you stuck in head-spinning tail-chasing chaos. While you may be able to function relatively well with piles of 'stuff' located randomly around your office or home, you will function far better without them. So get your base camp in order and make sure that it sets you up to embark on whatever mission you want to take on with the maximum chance of success. If this seems to stink of effort, get over yourself. Effort is as essential to success as bravery. Roll up your sleeves and do the work!

Cultivate rituals to fuel courage

Successful people do things others don't. One of them is incorporating regular rituals and habits into their lives that enable them to maintain physical energy, mental focus and the emotional wellbeing to stay on track towards their goals, 'go the extra mile' as often as needed and take new challenges in their stride. They know that who they are is what they repeatedly do and that small, daily actions, repeated often, can make a profound difference.

Cultivating rituals that bolster resilience and build stamina will therefore expand your capacity for courage.

> *First we make our habits, then our habits make us.*
> **John Dryden**

Research has found that taking time out to 'disengage' from your work to engage in other activities — whether to rest, exercise or pursue a hobby or creative pursuit — actually improves our effectiveness and productivity during the time we are engaged in our work.

As exhilarating and rewarding as it can be to face your fears, stepping out of your comfort zone can also be very taxing of energy. Daring to change the status quo can be as demanding physically as it is mentally and emotionally. Leading a team of people through change and uncertainty is no less demanding. Indeed, the more you want to take on in your work, the more important it is for you to invest in regular rituals that 'top you up' and ensure you're operating with optimal levels of health and wellbeing in body, mind and spirit.

Likewise, if you're feeling run-down, overwhelmed, continually distracted or often upset, you're not going to be blazing a bright trail in your organisation or career. So deciding which rituals and habits you'll incorporate into your busy schedule will ensure you can add the maximum value each hour you're at work and achieve optimal outcomes. The busier you are, the more crucial this becomes. As Jim Loehr and Tony Schwartz wrote in *The Power of Full Engagement*, managing energy, not time, is crucial to success in today's high-pressure and competitive workplace.

While your rituals are personal to you, there are many that people everywhere benefit from incorporating into their life — whether it be quiet time at the start or end of each day to read something uplifting, writing down your day's priorities, a morning run to work off the stress of a pressure-laden job, journaling, a Friday night movie with your kids to reconnect with them, regular prayer time or meditation, a weekend cycle with friends or a lunchtime walk through a nearby park. All of these things can help you sustain the perspective, energy, focus and motivation to stay in consistent action and achieve the success you want.

Cultivate courage-building rituals

Psychologists estimate that 95 per cent of what we do on any given day is habitual and that only 5 per cent is actually done consciously. Expanding your capacity to stay in focused and bold action will require taking more conscious actions and intentionally developing better habits of mind and behaviour on a daily basis.

By cultivating daily and weekly rituals and habits—for body, mind and spirit—you help to set yourself up for success, particularly when the going gets tough and your motivation runs low.

Get out a pen and paper and write down what you will do for yourself on a daily or weekly basis that you're currently not doing but that you know will help you maintain the focus, energy and inspiration you need to stay engaged and in action over the longer haul.

- *Physically.* Physical strength promotes psychological strength and grows stamina. What will you do on a regular basis to stay physically strong, energised and healthy?

- *Mentally.* It's easy to get distracted by urgent, unimportant things if you don't have clear priorities. What will you do to minimise distraction, manage stress and stay focused on key tasks and priorities over the course of each day?

- *Emotionally.* Emotions can quickly hijack your thinking and productivity if you're not intentional about managing them. What can you do for yourself to work through any fears and destructive emotions, enabling you to respond more calmly, confidently and constructively to daily challenges and stress?

- *Spiritually.* When you become disconnected from your deeper purpose, you can quickly lose perspective on what matters most and waste time and energy sweating the small stuff. What can you do to stay connected to your bigger *why*, and live in alignment to what truly matters most to you as a parent, friend, leader or simply as a human being?

Don't wait for courage: just do it!

Action is the most potent antidote to fear: it breeds confidence and nurtures courage in ways nothing else can. As discussed in chapter 7, the more you step out of your comfort zone into your courage zone, the more you build your tolerance for risk and the confidence to handle its consequences. Don't wait for your fears to fade to take action. Don't wait to feel brave to act bravely. Courage begets courage. As Theologian Mary Daly writes, 'Courage is a habit, a virtue. You get it by courageous acts. It's like learning to swim by swimming. You learn courage by couraging'. So trust yourself, holding firm to the knowledge that the more you act with the courage you aspire to have, the more courageous you will become. As Nike put it, in one of the world's most well-known slogans, *Just do it!*

Courage is a sequence of moments

Maria Eitel, CEO of Nike Foundation, shared with me how she learned to become comfortable with the inherent discomfort of fear. When she was young her dad and older brother Nick would take her hiking with them. Self-described as a 'skinny bean-pole and not particularly strong' she said the hikes took her way outside her comfort zone, as they were often long and demanding. At the end of one of their regular hiking paths they would arrive at a cliff overlooking a lake. Maria would be absolutely filled with fear as she stood on the cliff top looking down at the water. As afraid as she was of jumping off the cliff into the lake below, her brother wouldn't let her off the hook by allowing her to take the easier, less intimidating path of clambering down the side of the cliff and entering the lake along the shoreline. So, despite feeling filled with fear, on the urging of her brother and dad she'd take a giant jump into the air and splash into the water below.

Certainly Maria's early childhood experiences taught her how to manage the physical sensation of fear and take bold and focused action in its presence. 'Courage is not one moment; it's a sequence of moments where you have to keep drawing from a reservoir of courage that's surrounded by a pool of fear. You have to keep tapping and tapping it day by day, moment by moment, and not let your fear overtake you,' she said to me. 'Coming from a position of fear, of not succeeding, losing your job or not being admired handicaps the potential of your career. I've never let my fear of losing my job keep me from doing something I knew was the right thing to do.'

Today Maria continues to push through the very human fears and doubts that handicap many people in their careers. She leads the Nike Foundation's efforts to get girls onto the global agenda and drive resources to them with the goal of eradicating global poverty, something which requires her to make a stand for the greatness of women around the world every day.

One of the biggest obstacles you have to overcome as you connect to the vision that inspires you (which was one of the Courage Challenges in chapter 1) is overload. So if you have a goal or vision that inspires the hell out of you but also makes you immediately overwhelmed, break it down into small goals and then into smaller, 'bite sized' steps.

While I didn't climb Mt Everest while travelling around Nepal, I did meet a few hardcore climbers who did. They explained to me about the series of base camps that are set up at increasing altitudes to give aspiring climbers the opportunity to acclimatise to the increasingly rare air before they continue on their upward ascent. Every expedition includes days for resting, recovering and acclimatising to ensure the climbers' maximum chance of success. Likewise, it's smart to break down your big vision into smaller, less daunting goals that are less intimidating and more doable in the short to medium term.

Action is the most potent antidote to fear. It nurtures courage and breeds confidence in ways nothing else can.

As you move forward in building momentum, be mindful that there are times when you may need to take a rest from your risk-taking, restock your reserves and reassess which direction you want to take next time you head out of your comfort zone. Don't make yourself wrong when you make a choice to play safe. Sometimes that's the best choice for you at that moment in time, given everything else going on in your life. Whatever choices you make or actions you take, just own them—along with the benefits and costs of making them.

William James, the father of modern psychology, prescribed that people make 'daily strokes of effort' towards their goals, thereby becoming more comfortable with the discomfort of stepping outside their comfort zone. By breaking down your big goals and aspirations into more doable short-term goals and specific action tasks, it sets you up for success when it comes to staying in action on a daily basis. Some of these things may include more mundane actions (such as signing up for a course or brushing off your CV), but challenge yourself to do at least one thing on a daily basis that pushes you out of your comfort zone. It could be making a phone call you've been putting off; setting up a meeting with your boss to discuss promotion opportunities, or with a client prospect to pitch for new business; addressing a long-standing issue with someone; volunteering to lead a project team; attending a networking event; or introducing yourself to someone in your industry who can help your career. The more you act with courage, the more courageous you'll become. Life rewards action. Always has. Always will.

> *You've always had the power right there in your shoes;*
> *you just had to learn it for yourself.*
> **Frank L. Baum**

Courage is a muscle. Unless you work it, regularly, you won't know how strong you can become. Having done many things over the years that have scared me as much as they've inspired me, I can promise you that it's incredibly empowering.

Harness the power of vision

Scientists have found that the mental process of visualising completing any task in space actually fires the same neurons in the brain as if you were doing the actual task. When a tennis player visualises hitting the ball hurtling towards them at 200 kilometres per hour, they're activating the same sections of the brain as they would if they actually did hit the ball.

Visualisation creates an internal comfort zone so that when you're actually in the real-life situation, the actions you need to take are more familiar. You've essentially taken them already, reducing your anxiety and improving your performance.

The power of visualisation can be applied just as much to a sales presentation, a difficult conversation with a colleague or a job interview or a long-held goal. Imagine yourself succeeding in whatever situation you aspire to do well in, whether giving a knock-out sales presentation, running a business, or managing a large team of people. Picture yourself in a specific situation, feeling confident and able to respond comfortably to whatever happens with the sense of self-assurance, humour and focus needed to achieve whatever it is you want. Imagine yourself in the role you'd really like to have, capable, purposeful and ready to make whatever changes are required to produce the outcome you want. When you imagine this, visualise yourself being the most courageous version of who you are. This sets the stage for you to engage in any conversation, handle any situation and take on any challenge with the confidence needed to make it a success.

Just as we are all inspired by a different vision, everyone has their own path to forge and their own brand of courage to build. Like the lion in *The Wizard of Oz*, too often we undermine our own courage by falling into the trap of thinking we should possess the same courage we see in others. Not so. Don't fail to exercise your own courage because you're preoccupied with making negative and disempowering comparisons with others. The way I see it, if we were all supposed to be like British adventurer Bear Grylls, God would have made us all that way. Thank goodness He didn't!

Make your stand for greatness

It's a well-worn saying that if you don't stand for something, you'll fall for anything. In today's fearful and uncertain world, that usually means succumbing to the temptation to take the path of least resistance and greatest safety. If you picked up this book because the title spoke to you, then it's possible you've already journeyed down that path, at least in some way, and you know that it won't take you towards any destination you're inspired to travel to.

This book began by inviting you to ponder the question, 'For the sake of what?' as it related to how you'll use your time, energy and talents over the course of your working life. Knowing what it is that you want your life to stand for is an irreplaceable prerequisite for courage. So as you get ready to start taking actions you may never have taken before, ones that take you outside your comfort zone in different ways and new directions, it's vital to make a stand for greatness. As you know so well, it's all too easy to find reasons not to take the actions you know would benefit you. Too busy. Too tired. Too uncertain. Too soon. Too late. Too much effort. Too little guarantee. But people who live extraordinary lives don't settle for ordinary excuses.

Making a stand for greatness means giving up living a life that's run by excuses, justifications and insecurity. Of course, in the short term it's often hard to find the motivation to make the extra effort; to go the extra mile. Effort takes work. Work can be ... well, tiresome at least, loathsome at worst — at least for those who don't see any utility in it beyond its immediate, often financial, reward. That's why it's important to look at what you do through the lens of your entire life and to decide that you will make a stand for something, whether it be for your own innate potential or for something far beyond you. For your children or your children's children. Or for people you may never know but who matter to you anyway. So let me ask you a question:

What is so important that it's enough for you to go the extra mile, forgoing the ease and familiar safety of the status quo?

Victor Frankl once wrote, 'Everyone has his own specific vocation or mission in life. Therein he cannot be replaced, nor can his life be repeated. Thus, everyone's task is as unique as is his specific opportunity to implement it'. There are things you can do that no-one else can. You have a unique and unrepeated combination of skill, experience, talent, opportunity and passion that enables you to add value in your community and in your world, and to make a difference in ways that no-one has before and no-one will again. Making a stand for greatness is your declaration to the world; it's what will compel you to step beyond your comfort zone to make that contribution—that difference—more powerfully and more successfully than you ever otherwise could.

Make your life one you will look back on with deep satisfaction for what you made of it and deeper fulfilment from what you gave in it.

As you put this book down you will very quickly be faced with choices that will put your commitment to courage to the test:

- to speak the truth others need to hear, or to stay safe in silence

- to stand out, or to surrender to conformity

- to ask for what you *really* want, or to settle for what you have

- to push back or be pushed about

- to take a leap of faith across the crevasse of uncertainty towards a future that inspires, or to stay where you are

- to go the extra mile inspired by what's possible, or do just enough to get by, resigned to what's probable.

Will you take a risk or will you play it safe? Sometimes the answer will be very clear for you. Other times it won't. You'll have to weigh up the pros and cons, evaluate the risks, assess your ability to handle it before making your choice. No-one can do that for you. You alone have to decide and you alone have to live with the outcome. Forging a courageous path—in the weeks, months and years ahead—that honours the best of who you are requires living each day intentionally and making every choice consciously.

Of course none of us knows what new challenges and opportunities the years ahead will bring. The world is changing so fast, it's hard to imagine what it will look like five years from now, much less 50. But as uncertain as it is, what is certain is that those people who are willing to go the extra mile needed to engage in their work with purpose and courage will be those who can one day look back with the greatest fulfilment that they put their life to good use.

Theodore Roosevelt once said, 'By far and away the greatest prize life offers is the chance to work hard at work worth doing'. People around you may not always appreciate when you go the extra mile. They may not even notice it. You will not always be rewarded for the risks you take or your courage to break ranks and speak up as others forfeit their truth for the safety of silence. At times you may wonder if your hard work is in vain. It's at times like this that you must carve out time in your busy life to reconnect with what called you to step out, speak up and refuse to play safe in the first place, and remind yourself that you get only one precious chance to live your life. Make it a life that you'll look back on with deep satisfaction for what you made of it and deeper fulfilment from what you gave in it.

In the end, whatever success you achieve in your working life will matter so much less than the spirit you bring to the work you do, to the life you live, and the people you share it with. Yes, it's great to have an end to journey towards — but it's the journey that matters in the end. Your journey along the extra mile will call for extra courage but it will also reveal to you new horizons of possibility you have yet to even imagine.

Gandhi said, 'My life is my message'. Yours is no less. And every day you're writing that message through the choices you make, the chances you take and the way you engage with those around you. There are things that you, and only you, can do. Things that will never be done if you don't do them. So don't wait for good things to happen. Go out and make good happen. The world is waiting on you to rethink risk and play a bigger game that honours the best of who you are. After all, playing safe is by far the riskiest thing you can ever do.

Fortune favours the bold. So too does life's deepest fulfilment.

Key points

> Knowing what you want your life to stand for is an irreplaceable prerequisite for courage.

> *Go the extra mile.* Successful people do things others don't. Making the 'extra' effort to create an environment that sets you up to stay in purposeful and courageous action will make the vital difference for you.

> *No monkey grip.* You can't move forward with both hands holding tightly onto the security of where you are now. You have to let go of your grip and enter into the in-between zone where nothing is certain or secure.

> *Don't go it alone: enlist support.* When you surround yourself with people who believe in you, it creates an environment that makes success easier to achieve.

> *Prune your tree.* Sometimes you need to let go of old relationships in order to grow. Don't let others' beliefs, fears and insecurities about what they're doing with their life undermine what you're doing with yours.

> *Clear your clutter.* Clutter in any area of your life creates clutter in every area of your life. It doesn't help you be more courageous—it keeps you stuck in head-spinning chaos.

> *Build courage daily.* The more often you act with courage, the more courageous you become. Break your goals into bite-sized steps and do at least one thing every day that pushes you outside your comfort zone.

> *Cultivate courage-building habits and rituals.* Build habits and rituals into your daily life that bolster your innate resilience and expand your capacity for courageous action.

> *Make your stand for greatness.* Ask yourself: What will be so important to me that I would forgo the familiar safety of the status quo?

> *Life rewards action.* Playing safe is by far the riskiest thing you can ever do. Fortune favours the bold. Reclaim the power fear has had in your life—just do it!

Appendix

The Courage Key

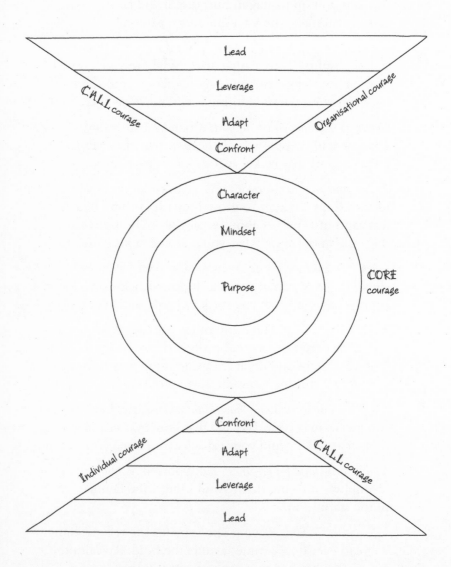

The Courage Key by chapter

Part I—Core Courage

        Chapter 1—Purpose

        Chapter 2—Mindset

        Chapter 3—Character

Part II—Working Courage

        Chapter 4—Confront

        Chapter 5—Adapt

        Chapter 6—Leverage

        Chapter 7—Lead

Index

Additional courage-building resources

A speaker, writer, coach, media contributor and founder of Global Courage, Margie Warrell is committed to providing people and organisations around the world with the resources and tools they need to live and lead with greater courage and become more effective agents for positive and lasting change in their lives and those of others.

If you or your organisation would benefit from more support in applying the concepts and strategies shared in this book please visit **www.stopplayingsafe.com** to:

- download your copy of the *Stop Playing Safe Workbook*

- take the *Courage Quiz* to determine your C.Q. (Courage Quotient) and find out where you can be more courageous

- get your copy of the *Stop Playing Safe* book club discussion guide

- watch an inspiring video of Margie discussing this book.

For other resources, videos, information about Margie's programs, or to sign up for her *Live Boldly!* Newsletter please visit **www.margiewarrell.com.**

Direct enquires for Margie's popular speaking and corporate programs can be made at **courage@margiewarrell.com.**

Media enquiries can be directed to **media@margiewarrell.com.**

WILEY *Learn more with practical advice from our experts*

Outlaw
Trent Leyshan

How to Present
Michelle Bowden

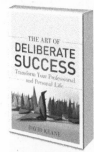

The Art of Deliberate Success
David Keane

Power Stories
Valerie Khoo

First Be Nimble
Graham Winter

Dealing with the Tough Stuff
Darren Hill, Alison Hill and Dr Sean Richardson

Play a Bigger Game
Rowdy McLean

Think Write Grow
Grant Butler

The One Thing
Creel Price

Available in print and e-book formats *e*